Camps and Campsites of the Civilian Conservation Corps (CCC)

in

New Mexico

1933–1942

Camps and Campsites of the Civilian Conservation Corps (CCC)

In

New Mexico

1933–1942

Dirk Van Hart

SUNSTONE PRESS

SANTA FE

Sunstone books may be purchased for educational, business, or sales promotional use.
For information please write: Special Markets Department, Sunstone Press,
P.O. Box 2321, Santa Fe, New Mexico 87504-2321.

Book and cover design › R. Ahl

Library of Congress Cataloging-in-Publication Data

Names: Van Hart, Dirk, 1941- author.
Title: Camps and campsites of the Civilian Conservation Corps (CCC) in New
    Mexico 1933-1942 / Dirk Van Hart.
Description: Santa Fe, NM : Sunstone Press, [2020] | Includes
    bibliographical references and index. | Summary: "A history of the camps
    and campsites and those who participated in the Civilian Conservation
    Corps (CCC) in New Mexico, 1933-1942"-- Provided by publisher.
Identifiers: LCCN 2019044460 | ISBN 9781632933393 (hardcover)
Subjects: LCSH: Civilian Conservation Corps (U.S.)--History. | Civilian
    Conservation Corps (U.S.)--Officials and employees--New Mexico. |
    Camps--New Mexico--History--20th century. | Camp sites, facilities,
    etc.--New Mexico--History--20th century. | Public works--New
    Mexico--20th century.
Classification: LCC GV191.42.N6 V36 2020 | DDC 796.5409789--dc23
LC record available at https://lccn.loc.gov/2019044460

WWW.SUNSTONEPRESS.COM
SUNSTONE PRESS / POST OFFICE BOX 2321 / SANTA FE, NM 87504-2321 / USA
(505) 988-4418

CONTENTS

List of Figures

PREFACE

In 1997, as a newly semi-retired geologist, I became involved in a personal, geologic mapping problem in the so-called Juan Tabó area located along the north-west side of the Sandia Mountains, just north of Albuquerque and within the Sandia Mountain Wilderness. A prominent feature in this area is the ruin of a walled-in stone cabin, sometimes called the "Juan Tabó Cabin." Upon nosing around, a Forest Service employee told me that it had something to do with the "CCC." What's the CCC? I later learned that this moniker stood for the Civilian Conservation Corps. Despite flattering myself at the time as being a somewhat capable amateur historian as well as a geologist, I knew nothing of the CCC. I was embarrassed.

Then on December 22, 1997, I read an Op-Ed letter in the *Albuquerque Journal* entitled, "Time is right for rebirth of CCC," by Charles L. Singletary, President of Albuquerque's Chapter 141 of the CCC Alumni. Excellent timing. I mailed him a letter on January 2, 1998, asking about the CCC, and of course about that Juan Tabó cabin. Three days later I received a phone call from Chuck, inviting me to the chapter's next monthly meeting. In February I informed the attendees of my geologic work around the Juan Tabó cabin area, and of my curiosities. The ambience, camaraderie, and enthusiasm of this vibrant group of "CCC boys" (the "Greatest Generation") was infectious even though I was a generation younger. They asked me to come back.

That began my twenty-year association with the group. I was hooked and both my wife and I joined the chapter as "associate members." After the chapter's wonderful thirty-year run (1988–2018), and my twenty-year rich involvement (I was president for about the latter twelve years or so), the chapter finally disbanded in February 2018 due to the inevitable deaths of members. Today, the "boys" are gone. I deeply miss all of them. This book is my tribute to them.

Scope and style of this book.

I focus here on the physical footprint that the camps left in the state of New Mexico, not the good work the enrollees did. Many of these sites lie off to the side of the highway or tucked away in the woods, crumbling, unmarked, and forgotten. Many consist of merely a wisp such as an isolated chimney, a lonely vehicle grease rack, some kind of incinerator pit, or a cryptic concrete foundation. Others are hidden away on private land, and some are completely built over and obliterated. However, some still persist to tantalize the passer-by. They can be visited and explored. The latter are the main subjects of this book.

We start with a primer on the Civilian Conservation Corps (CCC), plus some background information. I've subdivided New Mexico into 11 areas of interest, which cover 26 of the 33 counties that have campsites. Next comes the main section of the book, which is a virtual tour of 90 CCC campsites. The book ends with eight appendices that provide references for little-reported historical data about the camps and various miscellanea.

As to style, I have elected to present much of the narrative that follows in the first person. This for the simple reason that this is not a technical report, but rather a deeply personal project. It is difficult for me to properly express my deep respect for the "boys" of the CCC and their generation living through the Great Depression. We–of my generation–can simply not appreciate the way it was back then. This book is my attempt to memorialize what is left of their presence that has unfortunately been swept away by larger events, like WWII and that memory destroyer, time.

BASIC RESEARCH TOOLS.

The tools used to identify and locate the campsites include *Google Earth* satellite imagery, contemporary and historic topographic maps, 1935 aerial photographs, vintage photographs, historical documents and reports, oral histories, the Internet, and of course, personal on-the-ground visits.

Google Earth is a boon to geographic researchers. It has been available for free on the Internet since 2004 when *Google* acquired the pioneering company *Keyhole Inc.* Since then it has added *Street View* (2008), *Historical Imagery* (2009), and *3D Imagery* (2012). Its resolution is superb, far superior to conventional aerial photography. I have used these images in the figures when they add useful information about the camps. Also, the ability to tilt the images to oblique angles to see the surrounding terrain and—most importantly—to recognize the distinctive profile of diagnostic land forms, such as mountains and hills, is extremely useful. These profiles can be matched up with those seen on some vintage camp photos and thus become vital in pinning down the exact locations. I can't imagine doing this research without *Google Earth*.

Modern topographic maps of New Mexico were of limited help in locating the camps because on only two occasions are old CCC campsites shown. Historical topo maps, though, can be of help. Some of these are available on the website (active at the time of the publication of this book): *legacy.lib.utexas.edu/maps/topo/newmexico*. I however have used modern topographic maps in the figures to delineate the camps once they have been located by other means. The modern maps are available on DVD via National Geographic Holdings *TOPO!* (2001).

Another good source is the aerial photo collection taken under the auspices of the Soil Conservation Service (SCS) in 1935 by Fairchild Aerial Surveys. Sherman Fairchild (1896–1971) was a pioneer in aerial photography. One of his first contracts was with the SCS to document the status of soil erosion in the state. An extensive collection of these photos is archived at the University of New Mexico's Earth Data Analysis Center (*EDAC*). The photos are available for digitization onto CD. Resolution is not quite up to modem standards, but nevertheless provides useful, if somewhat slightly fuzzy images.

A number of panoramic photos of CCC camps with their enrollees appear in this book. Some of these photos have the little identifier, "A. Newman, Silver City," tucked down in a corner. This signifies Almeron Newman, a well-known photographer at the time. Newman was born in 1875 in Portland, Michigan. After graduating from high school in 1893 he became a student of photography, and somehow wound up taking a famous photo of Apache warrior Geronimo. In 1899 he moved to the small town of Deming, New Mexico, where he worked as a photographer. He was in Tucson, Arizona in 1900, and then in Trinidad, Colorado in 1909 where he apparently was a successful commercial photographer. By 1918 he again lived in Deming, where he registered for the WWI draft. His profession was listed as "military photographer." (Hendricks and Stanford 2010) By then he had learned that by taking photos of large groups of people, i.e., military units, he could sell a lot of copies. He lived in Silver City during the 1930s when he took many wonderful panoramic photos of CCC sites. During WWII he served as Director of Photography for the U.S. Government in Denver. He died in Trinidad in 1964 at the ripe old age of 88, and was buried there. (*Lansing State Journal* 1964)

A few publications and reports are also available. Invaluable are two out-of-print, large-format, soft-cover books, *Official Annual – 1936, Albuquerque District*, and *Official Annual – 1936, Fort Bliss District*. These cover two of the three CCC administrative districts in New Mexico. Strangely and regrettably, the third administrative district, the Silver City District, never put out an annual document. These publications list the camps, names of enrollees, company histories, and camp photographs, but only 1936. Another source is an in-house report for the Bureau of

Indian Affairs (BIA), by Peter McKenna (McKenna 2006) that provides exquisite detail about two camps northwest of Albuquerque.

I recorded and transcribed interviews with eight men who served in New Mexico CCC camps. They were Archie Archuleta (2002), A.B. Barela (1999), Felix Cabrera (1999), Alex Gallegos (2003), James Langley (2004), Max Trujillo (1999), Carl Walker (2006), and George Walker (2006). They are all gone now.

And then there are the old-fashioned personal visits. My wife Rusty and I roamed the state since 2001 in search of the campsites, and have photographed most of the camp remains. There's nothing like first-hand experience.

ACKNOWLEDGMENTS

First of those who helped me with this project is my wife, Rusty, who soldiered along with me on our numerous research trips. Second is fellow geologist, Erich Thomas, who performed the very unenviable job of hard-editing the manuscript. His sharp eyes found glitches and typos that I had become blind to.

Others who graciously offered their time and assistance are listed below, in alphabetic order, definitely not in order of input. I humbly tip my hat to all of them and offer my sincere "thank yous."

Adkins, Lynn: Daughter of CCC-camp commanding officer, Albuquerque, New Mexico.

Alexander, George: Resident, High Rolls, New Mexico.

Alvarez, Steve: Recreation Planner, Boiling Springs National Wildlife Refuge, Roswell, New Mexico.

Arnold, Jake: Resident, El Rito, New Mexico.

Bestelmeyer, Brandon: Supervisory scientist, USDA/ARS Range Management Research Unit, Jornada Experimental Range, New Mexico.

Bolling, Harriette: Elephant Butte, New Mexico.

Bosque del Apache: National Wildlife Refuge Visitor Center staff, San Antonio, New Mexico.

Brown, Linda: Proprietor: Fite Ranch B&B, San Antonio, New Mexico.

Call, Marta: Public Affairs Officer, Gila National Forest, Silver City, New Mexico.

Dixon, Donna: Rancher, Virden, New Mexico.

Dunnahoo Janice: Archivist, Southeast New Mexico Historical Society, Roswell, New Mexico.

Eckles, Jim: Secretary, Doña Ana County Historical Society, Las Cruces, New Mexico.

Eidenbach, Pete: Archeologist/historian, instructor at New Mexico State University, Alamogordo, New Mexico.

Fierro, Julio: Former CCC-boy, El Paso, Texas.

Fletcher, Sherry: Author, Sierra County, New Mexico.

García, Pam: Daughter of former CCC boy, Albuquerque, New Mexico.

Gallegos, Alex: Former CCC-boy, Albuquerque, New Mexico.

Gleasner, Laura: Earth Data Analysis Center (*EDAC*), University of New Mexico, Albuquerque, New Mexico.

Hawley, Dr. John: Retired geologist, Albuquerque, New Mexico.

Hrivnak, Marty: Resident, Edgewood, New Mexico.

Hyde, Anthony: Proprietor, *ClayWorks*, High Rolls, New Mexico.

Hyndman, David: Sole Proprietor, *Sunbelt Geophysics*, Socorro, New Mexico.

Kadas, Steve: State Resource Conservationist, Natural Resources Conservation Service, US Department of Agriculture, Albuquerque, New Mexico.

Keener, Will: Resident, Las Cruces, New Mexico.

Langley, James: Former CCC-boy, Albuquerque, New Mexico.

López, Rupert: Former CCC-boy, Corrales, New Mexico.

Manzanares, Daniel: Chief Operations Officer, Ghost Ranch, New Mexico.

Michanczyk, Max: Superintendent, Bottomless Lake State Park, New Mexico.

Nelson, Brenda: Resident, Sierra County New Mexico.

Román, Arturo: Archivist, Deming-Luna-Mimbres Museum, Deming, New Mexico.

Saucedo, Edmond: President, Hidalgo County Heritage Society, Lordsburg, New Mexico.

Schaller, Diane: President, Historic Albuquerque Inc., Albuquerque, New Mexico.

Schiowitz, Robert: Apache National Forest, New Mexico.

Sutton, Wendy: Archeologist, Gila National Forest, Silver City, New Mexico.

Walton, Margaret: Resident, Virden, New Mexico.

Volf, William: State Cultural Resources Specialist, National Resources Conservation Service, U.S. Department of Agriculture, Albuquerque, New Mexico.

Westmoreland, Jim: Resident, Albuquerque, New Mexico.

Williamson, Don J.: Archivist, Luna County Museum, New Mexico.

Introduction: Civilian Conservation Corps (CCC)

This book is about a piece of New Mexico's "lost history." Specifically, it deals with the footprint left behind by the camps of the Civilian Conservation Corps (henceforth referred to as the CCC) on New Mexico's landscape from spring 1933 through June 1942. An enormous volume of material has been published about the CCC, their work, and how it forged the men of the "Greatest Generation," but very little about the actual camps, i.e., where the "boys" lived and worked, especially in New Mexico. This book is designed to provide this missing information.

The word "camp" as used here does not infer what we normally think of as a camp–something like a campground in the National Forests, or maybe a boy/girl scout camp. We are dealing here with major encampments, housing some 200 souls and their supporting infrastructure. It is also important to realize that these camps were not for recreation, but rather for conservation work on public lands. The work done by the CCC was emphatically not "make-work." Everything that was done was for a purpose: to add value to the land.

The origin and administration of the CCC are massive subjects in their own right, but here this book only touches on the highlights to set the stage. (See Origin of the CCC below.) Interested readers should refer to historian Richard Melzer's wonderful volume, *Coming of Age in the Great Depression: The Civilian Conservation Corps Experience in New Mexico, 1933–1942.* (Melzer 2000) At the time of the publication of this book, Richard is a professor of history at the University of New Mexico's Valencia campus. A second, excellent general source is the book by Stan Cohen (1980), *The Tree Army: A Pictorial History of the Civilian Conservation Corps, 1933–1942.*

Origin of the CCC

A mere two days after the inauguration of Franklin Delano Roosevelt (FDR) on March 4, 1933, while deep in the throes of the Great Depression, the new president proposed the creation of a civilian conservation corps. FDR realized at the time that there was more at stake than the nation's fallen economy. The nation's self-confidence and indeed its very future were at stake. More than five million young men and World War I veterans were out of work. A generation of young men was discouraged, undernourished, undereducated, restless, and whose potential was in danger of being squandered. The CCC was intended to build them up both physically and morally, and at the same time to restore the public lands that were in wretched shape due to years of erosion and neglect. It was clearly a win-win situation.

Congress gave its approval on March 31, 1933 and provided funding for two years. The new agency was called the Emergency Conservation Work (ECW). This was the very first of FDR's New Deal programs. (Only later would the ECW be officially known as the Civilian Conservation Corps, the CCC.) The program was intended to be temporary and not to interfere with normal employment. At its outset FDR stated: "The overwhelming majority of unemployed Americans, who are now walking the streets and receiving private or public relief, would infinitely prefer to work. We can take a vast army of these unemployed out into healthful surroundings. We can eliminate to some extent at least the threat that enforced idleness brings to spiritual and moral stability. It is not a panacea for all the unemployment but an essential step in this emergency."

Existing arms of the federal government were called on to administer the program. The U.S. Army had the task of operating the camps nationwide. Various other agencies within the Departments of Interior and Agriculture, which were responsible for the public domain, were to plan and supervise the specific work projects. The Department of Labor coordinated the enlistment of enrollees. The vast federal government was fully mobilized and operated at "full tilt."

The enrollees came from four sources. About 85% came from the ranks of poor, unmarried, young white men, age 18 to 25 (later expanded to 17 to 28), who were called "juniors" or simply "boys." To be eligible an enrollee had to be a U.S. citizen, male, single, of sound physical health, unemployed, and his family had to be on some sort of relief. Each enrollee was to be paid $30 per month, $25 of which was to be sent home to help support his family. (In today's dollars, $30 and $25 are equivalent to $552 and $460, respectively.) This caused some rancor in the Army, as a private's monthly pay was only $22 ($405 in today's dollars). Young women were not included. There were some black enrollees, but they were generally segregated into a few separate camps. This was not utopia. This was the 1930s.

A second source was of local experienced men (LEM) who served as project leaders in the Junior camps. A third group consisted of World War I veterans, mature men in their 30s and 40s who were assigned their own camps. The fourth source was American Indians and "territorials" (men from Alaska, Hawaii, Puerto Rico, and the Virgin Islands), who lived at home rather than in camps.

Enlistment was for six months, with re-enlistments allowed for up to a total of two years. Each six months constituted a *Period*. These should not be confused with Fiscal Years, which at that time ran from July 1 through the following June 30. Odd-numbered, spring/summer periods ran from April through September, and even-numbered, fall/winter Periods ran from October through the next March. However, despite the Period system being fundamental to the operation of the CCC, they can be difficult to relate to years. Therefore, for each campsite discussed here only months and years are listed. Nineteen periods passed during the lifetime of the CCC. (*Appendix I*)

The U.S. Army was responsible for the administration, supply, shelter, medical needs, essential education, and a degree of moral uplift of the CCC enrollees. The Army's nine U.S. Army Corps regions provided the framework for administration. New Mexico was included in the 8th Corps area which also included Arizona, Texas, Oklahoma, Colorado, and most of Wyoming. Immediately after sign-up the enrollees were sent to training and conditioning camps, usually located at or near an Army post, where they were clothed and vaccinated. The enrollees were then organized into 200-man "companies."

The company was then transported to its assigned camp location by train and/or truck. The physical camps were given a letter designation representing the sponsoring or "technical" agency, such as "F" (Forest Service), "SCS" (Soil Conservation Service), "DG" (Division of Grazing), etc. Each camp had a company commander who was a regular army or reserve officer, a junior officer, education advisor, and camp doctor. A project superintendent represented the technical agency sponsoring the work and he had a number of foremen (LEM) under him. Each camp required a communication and supply link with a main highway or railroad, and a nearby post office.

For the first two years the work of the ECW was restricted to the National Forests, National Parks and Monuments, and the State Parks. (*Appendix II*) The Forest Service took the lead and ran the first camps. This led to the first contingent of enrollees being referred to as the "Tree Army." At the end of the first two years FDR concluded that the ECW program had proved itself beneficial to the nation. It was indeed quite popular–something that Roosevelt, the consummate politician, noticed.

In 1934 Congress passed the infamous *Taylor Grazing Act*, intended to ameliorate the destruction of public grazing lands that had occurred via many years of overgrazing and erosion. The act mandated the regulation of grazing land-use and restoration where possible. This led in 1935 to a surge of ECW activity. Accordingly, in early 1935 FDR requested that Congress provide funding for an additional two years. A surge of camp construction expanded onto the public domain outside of the National Parks and National Forests. (*Appendices II and III*) These new areas included land administered by the Soil Conservation Service (SCS), the Bureau of Reclamation (BR), and the Division of Grazing (DG). By September of that year the project peaked at an enrollment of about 500,000, distributed among 2514 camps in every state and several territories.

By early 1937, as the second two-year funding cycle approached its end, FDR envisioned reducing the size of the ECW but making it a permanent institution. He now formally referred to it as the Civilian Conservation Corps (CCC). Congress provided funding for an additional three years, to 1940, but balked at making it a permanent agency.

By 1940, as rumblings of armed conflict were heard from Europe, the CCC began to have difficulty fulfilling its quota of enrollees as more and more men found employment elsewhere and as the nation braced itself for possible war. The reserve military personnel in charge of the camps were withdrawn to active duty. After the fall of France in June 1940 many companies of enrollees were put to work on military facilities for national defense work. As the number of enrollees continued to decline in 1941 the number of CCC camps was reduced accordingly. After the attack on Pearl Harbor on December 7, 1941, recruitment plummeted and all CCC projects unrelated to the war effort were terminated.

The CCC officially came to an end on June 30, 1942. As the program wound down all camp equipment–vehicles, construction and office equipment, tools, etc.–were inventoried and transferred to the military. The policy concerning camp buildings was that they were to be used or torn down. However, there were a few exceptions. As the war ground on it was unexpectedly realized that something had to be done with prisoners of war (POWs) brought to the U.S. The few CCC camps still left standing suddenly became choice spots to house Italian and German prisoners. Camps in Las Cruces and Fort Stanton, for example, were restructured for this new function.

Most camps though were stripped down to their concrete foundations, which remain today as quiet reminders of past activity. Others were bulldozed down to the grass roots. Today little is physically left of most of the camps, but with a few important exceptions. What did persist was the intangible and enduring effect the program had on its three million enrollees.

NATIONAL SCOPE OF THE CCC

Although this book is about New Mexico's physical campsites, a few words about the national magnitude of this program seem appropriate. Some three million young men passed through the ranks of the CCC during its less-than-a-decade existence. According to the U.S. Census Bureau, the nation's population in 1935 was approximately 128 million (123 and 132 million in 1930 and 1940, respectively). Roughly half of that would have been male, or 64 million. The median age of males in 1935 was about 28 years (26.7 and 29.1 in 1930 and 1940, respectively), so about half of the 64 million were young males, or 32 million. In 1940 the total population younger than 18 years was 30.6%. Assuming about 30% for males younger than 18 in 1935 gives a remaining CCC-age male population of about 22.4 million (70% of 32 million). Therefore, the three million CCC enrollees represented a significant portion, roughly 13%, of the male population of CCC age.

OVERLAPPING ADMINISTRATIONS OF THE CCC

The CCC had a rather complex administration. The Departments of Agriculture and Interior were responsible for the planning and organization of the work to be done. The U.S. Army was tasked with mobilization of the nation's transportation system to move the enrollees to where the camps would be sited, and was charged with the training, housing, feeding, and educating the young male recruits, as well as construction of the camps.

For five eight-hour days per week the Army turned the company loose to the technical agency, which then took charge of them at a work site. At day's end the company returned to the Army's fold. At the individual camp level, the

Army and the technical sponsoring agency came face to face and had to work together. Sometimes there was friction, usually involving conflict between the Army's need for men to do work around the camp, vs. the superintendent needing men for his work in the field. Despite this overlap of departments and day-to-day administration, the CCC functioned amazingly well.

U.S. ARMY'S ROLE

Most of the CCC enrollees lived in the East, but by far most of the camps were in the West. Only the U.S. Army possessed the ability and infrastructure to move them. The Army organized the enrollees into "companies," usually numbering about 200. Despite recruits coming in and out of the companies every enrollment period, and the companies moving from location to location, the company identification number generally stayed the same. Enrollment was for a six-month Period, but re-enrollments were allowed for up to a total of two years. The young CCC enrollees self-identified primarily by their company number rather than by their camp number. Because this book's focus is on the geography of the state's camps, little more will be said about company names and numbers.

The camps were not military camps, but they did have a military aspect. In fact many Americans, leery about what was becoming the Hitler-Youth camps in Germany, wrongly suspected that the camps were places of indoctrination. They were not, but a certain level of Army discipline was imposed. Wake-up time was fixed, barracks were neatened, roll-call was taken, breakfast was eaten on time, and the day's work-orders were obeyed.

The experiences of discipline, hard labor, and team work molded this generation of young men. When America's involvement in WWII began they easily transitioned into the military. That ready reservoir of can-do experience was of incalculable value to the U.S. victory in WWII.

FEDERAL GOVERNMENT SPONSORING AGENCIES AND THEIR CCC CAMPS

The camps of the CCC, not just in New Mexico but throughout the U.S., were identified by an array of abbreviations (shown in the table below), keyed to the technical government agency involved. The New Mexico campsites are shown in *Figure 0-1*.

Department	Agency	Abbreviation	# NM camps
Agriculture	Biological Survey (through 1939)	BS	2
	U.S. Forest Service	F	41
	Park Erosion Service (through 1934)	PE	2
	Soil Erosion Service (through 1934)	SES	1
	Soil Conservation Serv. (from 1935)	SCS	30
Interior	Bureau of Indian Affairs	BIA	no permanent camps
	Bureau of Reclamation	BR	5
	Division of Grazing (through 1938)	DG	10
	Grazing Service (from 1939)	G	11
	Fish & Wildlife Service (from 1940)	FWS	2
	National Park Service	NM, NP	5
	State Park Division	SP	6
War (1942)	Military/Defence	A-SCS, FWS(D), G(D)	4

Nationwide, during the 9 1/3 years of the CCC's existence there were about 4,000 camps established, including "side" camps. The latter were temporary, usually tent camps, each tasked with a project located too far for convenient daily commuting. The Department of Agriculture, via its subsidiaries the Forest Service and the Soil Conservation Service, administered about two-thirds of the main camps while the Department of Interior administered the other third. From the above tally it can be seen that in New Mexico by far the lion's share of the camps were administered by just three agencies: Forest Service (41), Soil Conservation Service (30), and Division of Grazing/Grazing Service (21).

CAMP LAYOUTS AND ORGANIZATION

First it must be understood that a CCC "camp" was more than what the term implies. A CCC camp was a large affair. With about 200 men the camps were in a very real sense "small towns." (*Figure 0-1*) Choice of a site for a camp was a serious undertaking. It required easy access via railroad if available, certainly via an all-weather road, and preferably an area of up to twenty acres on reasonably level terrain if at all possible. And, importantly, a reliable source of fresh water was essential because a typical 200-man camp required at least about 3,000 gallons a day. Politics was normally a contributing factor in location because many communities vied for the local business that the camps generated. This point cannot be ignored. Each camp required construction crews usually drawn from the nearby towns. The camps' food supplies were often drawn from those towns, boosting the health of the local stores.

Once selected, the site was carefully surveyed and laid out. Cost for a typical camp in the 1930s was about $30,000—$350,000 to $400,000 today. (*Albuquerque Journal* 1938) The Army was responsible for designing and physically constructing the camps, and therefore the camps were usually standardized and made as rectangular as possible. (*Figure 0-2*) Barracks (or tents) were often arranged in regimented tiers and rows with administrative, recreational and dining facilities at one end of the camp; enrollee toilet facilities often centrally placed in the barracks area; blacksmith shops and vehicle facilities located to one side of the camp; use of topography and camp-perimeter walls being common." (McKenna 2006)

A typical camp had about 24 buildings, including about four, large, elongated, prefabricated barracks, each of which housed about 50 enrollees. The barracks were one-story wood frame buildings with pitched or hipped roofs that were often set on low exposed piers. (Kammer 1995b; *Figures 0-3B, 0-3C, 0-3D, 0-3E, 0-4A*) Other camp structures included officers' quarters, offices for technical staff (e.g., Forest Service, SCS, etc.), medical dispensary, mess hall, recreation hall, and education building. Most companies had a central courtyard with a flagpole in a rock base. (*Figure 0-4C*) Other structures included sturdy concrete blocks for fuel-oil tanks and an electrical-generator, a rectangular array of four small blocks for a windmill or water tower, sometimes a grease rack (*Figure 0-5A*), an incinerator pit, a latrine and bathhouse/showers (*Figure 0-6C*), tool shop, motor vehicle repair shop and garages. Many if not most companies landscaped their camps using rocks to neatly line walkways to avoid becoming lost at night and to frame company-entry signs and bulletin boards.

It should be remembered that this was only fifteen years after the end of WWI. There was much matériel left over from the war effort and the CCC put it to good use. The early camps and those used for summers only were usually collections of large tents set on wooden platforms, housing four to six men each. (*Figure 03A*) These had to do until more "permanent" barrack structures could be erected, often by the enrollees themselves. The first permanent buildings came later in 1937.

When the camps were dismantled due to completion of its mission or especially after Pearl Harbor in December 1941, they were cannibalized for anything of immediate value to the government, usually the U.S. Army. All useable materials such as transportable buildings, fuel tanks, etc., were stripped away, down to their immobile concrete foundations. Those concrete pads remain. The barracks though had been propped up on wooden supports and were typically the first to go, leaving nothing at all behind except heavily compacted soil around their borders from the feet of many men. Many of the campsites today have been converted to modern campgrounds, obscuring their earlier history.

Today's traveler, though, given the context of the requirements of a working camp of about 200 people, can often identify and piece together the camp's layout by function. It's an intriguing, challenging, and fun exercise.

RANKING OF CCC CAMPSITES

A central purpose of this book is to guide the traveler to the sites of greatest interest. Ranking the 90 sites in New Mexico of course is a very subjective exercise. I have a ranking system of three-categories. The first category, accessibility to the site, is most fundamental and is denoted by Roman numerals. Accessibility ranges from "I" for fully open (i.e., go ahead, walk in). It is unposted but you may have to thread every-so-gently through a barbed-wire fence. "II" is for a campsite that is somewhat available to explore but needs permission to access. "III" sites have posted signs ("Private Property").

The second category, denoted by capital letters, refers to what physically remains of the camp. The range is from "A" meaning a significant amount left; "B" a moderate amount left; and "C" little or nothing left.

The last category denotes how tough or convenient is it to get to the site, by numbers. Remember that all the camps had to be supplied by rail and/or tuck, so none was truly remote. Category "1" extremely convenient (off of a paved highway); "2" moderately convenient (such as off a gravel road); and "3" relatively remote (requiring a bit of effort.)

The ranking or interest-level system then devolves into a three-part designation for each campsite. The ranking is shown in the listing below and is applied to each camp. (*Appendix IV*)

Rank	Number		Characteristics
Rank #1	1a	I-A-I	Accessible, much to see; easy to get to.
	1b	I-A-2	Accessible, much to see; less easy to get to.
Rank #2	2a	I-A-3	Accessible, much to see; somewhat remote
	2b	I-B-l	Less accessible; much to moderate amount to see.
Rank #3	3a	II-B-2 & I-B-3	Less accessible to a bit remote; moderate amount to little left.
	3b	II-A to II-B	Restricted access; much to moderate amount to see.
Rank #4	4a	I-C	Accessible; but little to see.
	4b	II-C	Restricted access; little to see.
Rank #5	5	I-D, II-D, III	Inaccessible; nothing left (forget about it!).

At the discussion of each campsite that follows by geographical area, the ranked interest level is noted below its name. On each of the general maps preceding the state's 11 Areas (*Figure 0-1*), the campsites are shown via symbols denoting their interest rank. When a camp name is shown as a composite, i.e., names divided by a slash (/), it means that the camp carried more than one designation over its lifetime.

LEGACY OF THE CCC

Besides the vast amount of physical improvements to the American landscape, there was the long-lasting effect of the CCC on the young men of the 1930s—the "Greatest Generation." I therefore close this introduction with the following three quotes. The first by Fred Eberhart in 1934 (an Educational Advisor at camp F-17-C in Colorado) is a little long, but is full of meaning and speaks volumes for the value of hard, focused, and meaningful labor:

"Two hundred men from every strata of society moved into a wilderness of scrub oak, piñon, and cedar. Many of them hadn't been employed for months. Many of them were soft in muscle and weakened in morale. Theirs had been a discouraging fight, a disheartening battle to provide the barest necessities of life for their families. Many of them were almost beaten, almost ready to quit.

"Seven months have passed. Gradually the road these men are building has crept up the side of the Mesa. Bronzed and hardened in muscle, these men now have a new confidence in their bearing, a new light in their eyes. Some have quit. Those who have stuck are perhaps not aware of the change, but they will find it when they get back to their places in society. Often they grumble and complain, some of them, but watching them build the road, you will discover that the road is really building them." (Audretsch 2017)

And this excerpt from Rudy Polise, who had worked with a CCC company at High Point, New Jersey. Upon visiting his old camp area in 1976 and finding nothing there, he wrote an epilogue (part of which is quoted below), full of nostalgia. (Cohen 1980)

"...there was not one sign or anything telling tourists that the roads they were traveling on or the lakes they were fishing in were built by a depression army. For this I will always be sad. Then I felt glad and happy because after all these years a part of me will always be at Co. 1280, SP-8, High Point Park, New Jersey. Then I had no right to expect the camp and everything else to remain the same. Perhaps I went back there expecting to find my youth again, or something to rekindle a fire in a lamp that will for all outward purposes slowly dim, then go out. But until that light goes out, I will always remember the time spent in the CCC."

And finally, this one from Roy Lemons (1918–2002), one of the most eloquent of the ex-CCC boys. His is a statement full of passion.

"In the final years of my life, in assessing the most profound happenings, I find the CCC experience the most rewarding of all. Nothing had more impact than that. All that I am was shaped by that 2 1/2-year interval of my life and the 3 1/2 years of the depression that preceded it."

CCC CAMPSITES IN NEW MEXICO

During its 9 1/3-year lifetime (April 1933 through June 1942) the CCC operated a total of 119 camps in New Mexico at 90 physical locations. (*Appendices II, III, V,* and *Figure 0-1*) Some of these sites were used more than once and thus bear more than one number, hence the larger total. The camps were concentrated on the federal and state lands, of which New Mexico had plenty. The total number of camps operational annually varied according to federal funding levels. The number ranged from fewer than 20 to as many as 50, but usually about 30 to 40 in any one year. New Mexico was a major recipient of the benefits of the program. Almost 55,000 men served in New Mexico's CCC camps, over 32,000 of them residents of the state.

Some of the camps established temporary outlying tent camps, called "side," "fly," or "spike" camps, housing a small contingent of enrollees closer to their work sites, thus avoiding long transportation to remote sites. They were set up to do important work that was too far from their main, "mother" camps. These were typically 25-man operations, housing the enrollees in five canvas tents. The mess unit was also a tent. Given the camps' small size, they still had room for a centrally-placed flagpole. Although these were not main camps, a few were given their own camp numbers, thus adding to much confusion when tallying up camp names. For example, camps F-53-N (Glorieta in Santa Fe County), F-56-N (Coyote in Rio Arriba County), and SCS-24-N (Hatch in Doña Ana County), were "side" camps. Only the main camps are featured in this book.

At the outset of the program in the spring of 1933 the state was subdivided into three CCC administrative "districts": Albuquerque (northern New Mexico), Silver City (southwestern New Mexico), and Fort Bliss (southern and southeastern New Mexico and west Texas). In 1937 the first two were merged with the Fort Bliss District and thus became the New Mexico District. These terms are anachronistic, so for the purpose of this book I proffer a more user-friendly, simple geographic subdivision of the state into 11 areas of interest. These encompass 26 of the 33 counties that contain campsites, which are called "Areas" (*Figure 0-1*), as shown below:

Area A / Central: Bernalillo, Sandoval, Los Alamos, and Torrance Counties
Area B / Northwest: San Juan and Cíbola Counties
Area C / North-Central: Rio Arriba and Taos Counties
Area D / Northeast: Santa Fe, Mora, and Western San Miguel Counties
Area E / Southwest: Catron and Grant Counties
Area F / The Bootheel: Hidalgo and Luna Counties
Area G / Central-South: Socorro County
Area H / Southern Rio Grande Valley: Sierra and Doña Ana Counties
Area I / South-Central: Lincoln and Otero Counties

Area J / Southeast: Chaves and Eddy Counties
Area K / East-Central: De Baca, Quay, Roosevelt, Curry, and Eastern San Miguel Counties

Seven counties, McKinley, Colfax, Union, Harding, Valencia, Guadalupe, and Lea, had no camps and so are not included in the above list. The exact campsite locations, with their latitudes and longitudes taken from *Google Earth*, plus their land-system designations, are tabulated separately in *Appendix V*.

In the following discussion of the individual campsites by Area, within each Area I take one county at a time and then list the campsites in alphanumeric order, even if it requires jumping around a bit from place to place. Only for Bernallilo County do I list the campsites in a more undisciplined way.

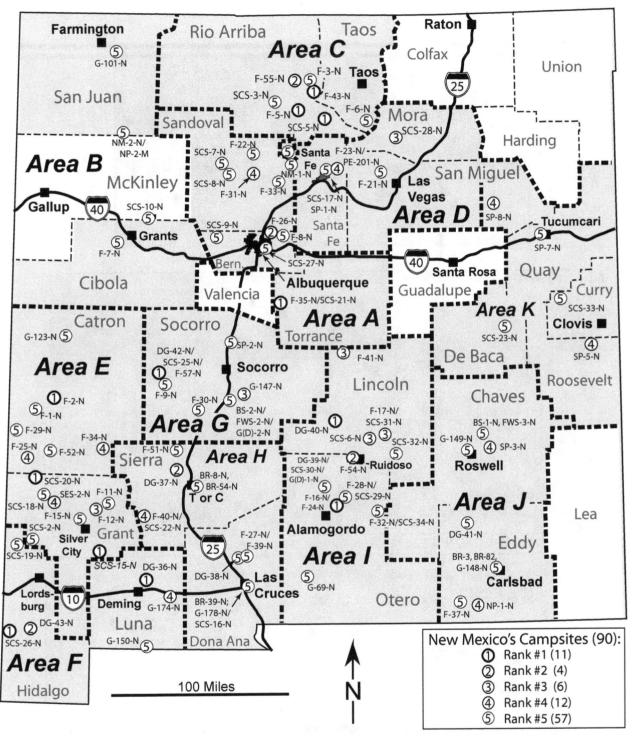

Figure 0-1. Civilian Conservation Corps Campsites (Various Circles) in New Mexico
in 11 AREAS (A through K).

A. F-37-N, Dark Canyon, Carlsbad (Photograph from L. Adkins).

B. DG-39-N/G-39-N/SCS-30-N/G(D)-N, Tularosa (Photograph from Author's Collection).

C. SP-7-N, Tucumcari (Photograph from J. Crocker).

Figure 0-2. Examples of Orderly Layout of CCC Camps.

A. Array of Four-Man, WWI-Vintage Tents (Camp Cody, Deming, ca. 1916, Photograph from M. Kremeke's Camp Cody Website).

B. Pre-Fabricated Barracks (NP-1-N, Rattlesnake Spring, 1930s, Photograph from R. Huff).

C. Pre-Fabricated Barracks (F-37-N. Dark Canyon, Carlsbad, 1930s, Photograph from L. Adkins).

D. Propped-Up and Leveled Pre-Fabricated Barracks (F-41-N, Corona, 1930s, Photograph from Author's Collection).

E. Moving Portable Building (DG-38-N, Jornada del Muerto, 1930s, Photo from Author's Collection).

Figure 0-3. Examples of Temporary Quarters for CCC Enrollees.

A. Interior of Barracks (DG-101-N/G-101-N, Bloomfield, ca. 1938).

B. Mess Hall (DG-101-N/G-101-N. Bloomfield, ca. 1938).

C. Daily Flag-Raising (G-101-N, Bloomfield, North View, ca. 1938).

D. Relaxing in Canteen (DG-42-N, Augustin, Photograph from Author's Collection).

Figure 0-4. Snapshots of CCC Camp Life.
(Photos A, B & C from San Juan County Archeological Research Center and Library)

A. Grease Rack (F-25-N, Glenwood, 2003, Photograph by Author).

B. Abandoned Concrete Slab (F-8-N, Sandia Park, 1999, Photograph by Author).

C. Root Cellar (F-43-N, La Madera, 2005, Photograph by Author).

D. Sturdy Supports for Heavy Equipment (F-8-N, Sandia Park, 1999, Photograph by Author).

E. Camp Entry Gate (SCS-15-N, Whitewater, 2003, Photograph by Author).

F. Camp Entry Sign (F-51-N, Montecello, 2017, Photograph by Author).

Figure 0-5. Typical Indicators of Former CCC Camps I.

A. Incinerator (Camp Cody, Deming, ca. 1916, Photograph from M. Kromeke's Camp Cody Website).

B. Feature Similar to A (DG-40-N, Carrizozo, 2006, Photograph by Author).

C. Showers/Bathhouse (with Tell-Tale Foot-Washing Basin at Center Left, F-5-N, El Rito, 2017, Photograph by Author).

Figure 0-6. Typical Indicators of Former CCC Camps II.

AREA A
Central New Mexico: Bernalillo, Sandoval, Los Alamos, and Torrance Counties
(Figure A-1)

This area includes four central New Mexico counties that contain 13 campsites, plus three additional sites of CCC interest (not camps) within the city of Albuquerque.

Bernalillo County:

    1. F-26-N, Juan Tabó area, northwestern Sandia Mountains (P.O. Albuquerque)
    2. SCS-27-N/A-SCS-1-N, East Mesa, Albuquerque (P.O. Albuquerque)
    3. F-8-N (#1), Sulphur Springs, East Mountain area (P.O. Albuquerque)
    4. F-8-N (#2), Sandia Park, East Mountain area (P.O. Albuquerque)
    5. SCS-9-N, Lower Rio Puerco Valley (P.O. Albuquerque)

Los Alamos County (Sandoval County in 1930s):

    6. F-19-N, Water Canyon, Jémez Mountains (P.O. Otowi)

Sandoval County:

    7. F-22-N, Camp Kearny, Battleship Rock, Jémez Mountains (P.O. Jémez Springs)
    8. F-31-N, Paliza Canyon, Jémez Mountains (P.O. Jémez Springs)
    9. F-33-N, Tent Rocks, Jémez Mountains (P.O. Peña Blanca)
    10. NM-I-N/NP-4-N, Frijoles Canyon, Bandelier, Jémez Mountains (P.O. Santa Fe)
    11. SCS-7-N, Middle Rio Puerco Valley (P.O. San Ysidro)
    12. SCS-8-N, Camp Catron Ranch, Rio Salado valley (P.O. San Ysidro)

Torrance County:

    13. F-35-N/SCS-21-N, Camp Red Canyon, Manzano Mountains (P.O. Manzano)

Albuquerque metropolitan area (non-CCC camps):

Sites of CCC interest in Albuquerque metropolitan area
Conservancy Beach side camp (P.O. Albuquerque)
Camp Albuquerque (POW camp)

F-26-N, Juan Tabó area, northwestern Sandia Mts., Bernalillo County
Rank 2 (I-B-1)

This campsite is located within the present Sandia Mountain Wilderness, just north of the Albuquerque metropolitan area, and therefore warrants special emphasis. (*Figures A-2* and *A-3*) The camp was constructed in October 1933, and operated only during the winter of 1933/34. A foreman and about 15 carpenters built two large barracks for 200 men, a headquarters structure, mess hall, and recreation building. A previous site in Juan Tabó Canyon was discarded because it was exposed to the sweeping winds. (*Albuquerque Journal*, 1933) Just below and southwest from the Juan Tabó Cabin (see below) is a 150x300-foot graded pad that held the two barracks, between which was an area that served as a parade ground. (*Figure A-4*)

In November a CCC company moved down from Sulphur Canyon in the East Mountains (see F-8-N below) to the Juan Tabó camp for its winter quarters. (*Figure A-5*) Work done there by the company included the camp road, installation of numerous check dams to halt erosion, retard runoff and recharge the area's springs. A forest service telephone line was installed from Alameda down in the valley up to the camp, and construction of the Jaral Ranger Cabin along Spring Creek.

The iconic Juan Tabó Cabin is a cipher. (*Figures A-4A* and *A-6*) It's construction, mainly of blocks of metamorphic rock (a hard, layered rock, rich in platy, mica minerals, probably quarried from the rock ridge just on the west side of FS-333), contrasts sharply with the surrounding stone wall made from blocks of the more massive Sandia Granite (probably quarried from some place near to the east). An undated photo of the camp, from sometime in the 1930s, shows a two-room cabin. A third room was evidently patched onto the north side sometime prior to 1944 because a photo that year shows the three-room edifice that exists today. (*Figure A-6*)

When the CCC company was moved out of the Juan Tabó Camp, bound for Camp F-35-N at Manzano (see below), work continued in June 1934 by the Transient Service of the Works Progress Administration (WPA). The WPA had been established in 1935 to participate in the government's work relief program. It was similar to the CCC except that the typical enrollee of the WPA was older than his CCC counterpart, often married, and (in this case) included many transients who were unemployed from out-of-state. A federal transient shelter had been established at 314 N. 1st Street, Albuquerque, for 350 men. (*Albuquerque Journal* 1934) WPA work included developing the Juan Tabó area as a recreation area for the city of Albuquerque, with the well-crafted picnic tables and shelters that exist today.

SCS-27-N/A-SCS-1, East Mesa, Albuquerque, Bernalillo County
Rank: 5 (III-D-1)

This late camp was operational from mid-1940 to early 1942. Its general location is known but its exact location (the focus of this book) to date is uncertain. (*Figure A-7*) The location has been described as "a mile east of the Fair Grounds, built on a 20-acre plot of ground, and housing 200 men." (*Albuquerque Journal* 1940) This vague description pins the place as near or just north of the corner of Wyoming Blvd. and Central Avenue. A tentative but very compelling choice is the site of National Guard Armory, a short distance north of Central Avenue, on the east side of Wyoming.

In the summer of 1940 the Conservancy Beach side camp (see below) was closed and consolidated with SCS-27-N. In May 1942, with war in Europe looming, the camp was renamed A-SCS-1 and the work focused on military tasks at the Army Air Base until that summer. (*Albuquerque Progress* 1940)

After Pearl Harbor in December 1941, many of the CCC structures at this camp were disassembled and trucked 115 miles south to the Trinity Site and reconstructed there about 11 miles from the first atomic bomb's ground zero. (Melzer 2000)

F-8-N, Sulphur Springs, East Mountains, Bernalillo County
Rank 5 (II-D-1)

Two camps with this name were established along the Sandia Crest Road in Sandia Park. (*Figure A-8*) In June 1933 a company of 150 juniors was sent up from Fort Bliss to establish a summer camp at Sulphur Springs, the first tent camp in the state. It was tasked with work in the Cibola National Forest, specifically the recreation areas of La Cienega, Doc Long, and Sulphur Springs. This camp is shown in a now-iconic photo of the camp taken from a hill to its south. (*Figure A-9*).

Today's realigned Sandia Crest Road, NM-536, passes where the southern row of tents was once located. The campsite is now occupied by three private residences. A keen eye will recognize a level area that was once the tent pad. The original, 1933 road is now a gravel residential path, Tejano Canyon Road, sometimes barricaded and with a "Road closed" sign. It is located just to the south of the Sandia Crest Road. and merges with it. When the barricade is down though the road is passable.

The camp was never used again after the first spring and summer of 1933. I suspect the reason had to do with drainage issues because the camp was located on sloping terrain, and perhaps due to limited space for expansion. In November 1933 the company moved to winter quarters at Juan Tabó. (see F-26-N above; *Official Annual – 1936, Albuquerque District*)

F-8-N, Sandia Park, East Mountains, Bernalillo County
Rank 5 (III-A-1)

Note: Despite this campsite being on private land and now generally inaccessible to the public, I have a special attachment because I personally knew three CCC-boys who actually worked at the camp. (A.B. Barela, d. 2009; F. Cabrera, d. 2009; and Max Trujillo. Also I personally mapped the campsite (with the help of a surveyor/geophysicist

David Hyndman), have numerous historic photos, and suspect (and hope) that the campsite will someday be accessible to the public. Therefore, I devoted some extra space to it here.

The camp was sited in the very southwest corner of the San Pedro Land Grant, only about 500 feet east of the previous Sulphur Springs site. (*Figure A-8*) In 1935 the grant was in the hands of the U.S. District Court following the bankruptcy of the previous owner (a mining company) in about 1930. In 1937, while the CCC was at the site, the grant was purchased from the Court by Thomas D. Campbell for his company, Campbell Farming Company (since renamed Campbell Corp.). The CCC used this as a summer tent camp from 1935 through 1941. (*Figures A-10A and 10B*)

The new F-8-N camp was divided into two sections, the "Technical" area to the north and the "Army" area to the south. (*Figure A-10B*) The former was administered by Forest Service personnel who commuted daily to the site. It was their responsibility to prioritize and oversee the work projects. The Army area was occupied by the CCC boys and their U.S. Army supervisors, who all lived at the site. During the winter the company migrated south to quarters at Monticello, camp F-51-N, northwest of Hot Springs (today's Truth or Consequences; see AREA H below).

The dormitory tents were constructed on wooden platforms. Some of the tents had concrete entry pads for stomping mud off boots, and a few of these pads remain today. A medical tent, and an education tent with a reading room, were integral parts of the camp. Other buildings such as administrative offices, storage and tool sheds were constructed either on wooden platforms or on concrete pads. Structures that required plumbing, such as the mess hall and the showers, were constructed on elevated concrete foundations. A diesel-fueled generator station provided electricity and was placed on a concrete platform to support the weight of the machinery. Water was piped in from a natural spring source at Sulphur Canyon, about a half mile to the west. Walkways were paved with fine gravel and neatly bordered by carefully-aligned fieldstones. The company conducted many projects in the Cíbola National Forest. One of the more visible of them today is the Kiwanis Cabin on Sandia Crest, built in 1936. (*Figure A-11A*)

The Tilton Store, down Sandia Crest Road east of the camp, sold picnic supplies and hot dogs to the CCC boys on their days off and to weekenders on their way up to the crest. (*Figure A-11B*) The building once housed the old Sandia Park Post Office that was moved to its present site east of San Antonito and NM-14 in 1982. The store had the only telephone in the vicinity and was understandably quite popular. It was closed in 1978 and is now a rather obscure private home.

Today's Tinkertown Museum, directly south of Sandia Crest Road, was built in the 1980s after the realignment and construction of the new highway. The CCC campsite entryway is immediately opposite and north of the Tinkertown Museum. The site entry is a locked gate, just past a private home to the east. The campsite is today off limits to the public.

The campsite languished until 1958 when a parcel around the old campsite was leased by the Girl Scouts of America (GSA) through 1979 as their Camp Campbell. The scouts painted "Singing Hill" on the side of the old CCC mess hall foundation, and also scavenged many of the old walkway perimeter stones for fire-hearth material. After 1979 the GSA established their new camp in the Jémez Springs area and never returned.

SCS-9-N, Lower Rio Puerco Valley, Bernalillo County
Rank 5 (III-D-3)

This site is located near the northwestern corner of Bernalillo County, 10.5 straight-line miles north-northwest of the intersection of the Rio Puerco and I-40. It operated from 1935 to 1939. There is nothing left of the campsite. It's located on Laguna Pueblo land and is not accessible.

F-19-N, Otowi, Water Canyon, Jémez Mountains, Los Alamos County
Rank 5 (III-D-2)

This was one of the very early camps, operating for only the spring and summer of 1933, and abandoned in November 1933. At the time this was in Sandoval County, since Los Alamos County was only created in 1949. The camp location has been described only generally as in Water Canyon, which runs northwest from the town of White Rock about halfway between Pajarito Road to the north and NM-4 to the south. There are very few reasonably level places in the canyon and no trace of a campsite is visible on *Google Earth*. Used only for a single period it was likely a tent camp, leaving little trace behind. A candidate location, now covered by a LANL facility, is located 1.1 miles northwest up the canyon from NM-4 at White Rock.

F-22-N, "Camp Kearny," Battleship Rock, Jémez Mountains, Sandoval County
Rank 5 (III-D-1)

A 1937 topographic map clearly shows the site of the CCC camp. (*Figure A-12A*) This early camp operated for only one period, so it's little surprise that it left little footprint. The CCC out of this camp did restoration at Jémez State Historic Site and work at the adjacent Battleship Rock Picnic Ground. Today the site is the YMCA's Camp Shaver, since 1945 a summer camp for boys and girls ages 7-14. (*Figure 12B*) It is not accessible to the public. The camp name "Kearny" shows up in only one reference (Kammer, 1994), and evidently refers to General Steven Watts Kearny (1794–1848), the occupier of Santa Fe in 1846.

F-31-N, Paliza Canyon, Jémez Mountains, Sandoval County
Rank 4 (I-C-2)

There is some confusion about the years of operation of this camp. One source (*Number of Camps in each County by Period*) has the camp established in spring/summer 1933–1934, but a second source (*Official Annual – 1936, Albuquerque District*) says it was set up in May 1936. The latter source indicates that the camp was occupied by a company moving north from camp F-35-N at Manzano.

Today the campsite is almost completely covered over by the modern Paliza Canyon Group Campground. (*Figure A-13*) The sole trace of the camp is on a hill at the northeast corner, a concrete slab that probably held a water tank. (*Figure A-13B*) Trees have filled in much of the site, making it impossible to get an "after" photo for a before-and-after comparison. The cliff profile to the west is clearly recognizable in both the 1930s and modern photos. (*Figure A-14*)

F-33-N, Tent Rocks, Jémez Mountains, Sandoval County
Rank 5 (II-D-2)

Years ago I was acquainted with an ex-CCC boy named George R. Walker (1913–2010). He had worked at this camp as a young man. When asked exactly where it was located at Tent Rocks (BLM's Kasha-Katuwe Tent

Rocks National Monument), he replied "right there." Not very helpful. At one semi-level spot, 0.8 miles west of the monument entrance and north of the gravel road that branches north from the "main" Indian Service Road 92, there is a single, sizable chunk of reinforced concrete. It may be a vestige of the general campsite area. The BLM made a thorough job of erasing all traces. There is accordingly nothing left to see.

NM-1-N/NP-4-N, Frijoles Canyon, Bandelier, Jémez Mountains, Sandoval County
Rank 5 (I-D-1)

(Most of the history for this site is from Harrison *et al.*, 1988.) Prior to arrival of the CCC the only human access to the canyon floor was via a steep foot trail. In 1907 a judge Abbott and his wife moved to the Rito de los Frijoles in the canyon and built a lodge, "The Ranch of the 10 Elders." All supplies had to be hauled down the trail by mule. The Abbotts hosted the approximately 400 tourists that braved the trail each summer. They moved to Santa Fe in 1919 and in 1925 George and Evelyn Frey bought and moved into the lodge. The cable tram, built by George, has an interesting history. It had a telephone at top and bottom. When tourists arrived in groups at the top from the AT&SFRR touring company, a wrangler rode up, loaded their baggage onto the tram, and brought the tourists down by horseback. Despite this difficulty, by 1929 tourists numbered about 3200

In early 1933, a month after the CCC was formed, the Park Service requested that a camp be established in the canyon. In November, in a blinding snowstorm, the company from the Otowi camp F-19-N moved eight miles south from Water Canyon down into Frijoles Canyon. (*Figure A-15A*) As mentioned above, the only way to get equipment down to the canyon floor was via the cable tram from the canyon rim. First, a truck, an electric-light plant, and tents were dismantled and sent down the tram and reassembled. In 30 days some 1,250 tons of equipment had been delivered, and camp construction was finished by December 1933.

The first order of business was construction of temporary CCC buildings and a water line. The second order was construction of a service road into the canyon, despite heated resistance from some in Santa Fe who wanted to keep the access "natural." The road was completed by December 1933. (*Figure A-15B*)

The first, temporary camp consisted of two large U-shaped buildings at the end of the service road, up against the north side of the canyon. From 1934 to 1941 the CCC constructed more than 20 permanent buildings in the Santa Fe Style. (*Figures A-16* and *A-17*) Construction materials gathered locally, including timber and quarried rock (*Figure A-18*). By the late 1930s the original U-shaped CCC buildings had been removed to make room for the new stone buildings.

The camp went by the name NM-I-N until 1939. That year saw a major reorganization of the CCC, whereby it lost a lot of its autonomy. The camp name was changed to NP-4-N for the duration. The name NP-I-N was already taken by Rattlesnake Spring, Carlsbad, and NM-2-N taken by Chaco Canyon. For some unknown reason the name NP-3-N was skipped.

The National Park staff is intensely proud of its CCC heritage. Much if not most of the structures are testament to the CCC's work. Excellent CCC displays can be found in the Visitor Center and a bronze CCC-Worker statue is located in the amphitheater/quarry area up on the north mesa top. (*Figure A-15A*) Despite all this, nothing remains of the campsite itself, so I reluctantly give this a low camp-interest ranking.

Rio Puerco CCC camps: SCS-7-N and SCS-8-N, Sandoval County

In 1935 these two "range" camps were sited in the 113,000-acre Ojo del Espiritu Santo Land Grant, which in 1934 had been sold by the Catron family to the Federal Government at a "fire sale" price. The grant had been wretchedly overgrazed and was in terrible shape. Each camp's mission was to stem soil erosion and bring the land back to health as much as possible via the construction of check dams, contour furrows, range re-seeding, etc. Located 7.4 miles apart, they were located in different watersheds—SCS-7-N in that of the Rio Puerco and SCS-8-N in that of the Rio Salado. Finding both sites was at first a challenge in that the only clue given was the name of their common post office—San Ysidro. (*Official Annual - 1936, Albuquerque District*) Both camps were salvaged in 1942, so only their concrete "non-removables" remain.

SCS-7-N, Middle Rio Puerco Valley, Sandoval County
Rank 5 (III-A-2)

This campsite is in the Middle Rio Puerco Valley. (*Figure A-19*) The good news about this one is that there is a wealth of information. The bad news is that it is located on Jémez Pueblo land and is closed to the public. Furthermore it is not visible from the main highway, US-550. The camp's specific mission was to stem the flow of an enormous amount of sediment flowing down the Rio Puerco to Elephant Butte Reservoir, placing the reservoir in danger of silting up and significantly decreasing its storage capacity.

In the mid-1930s a portion of the old highway, then NM-44 and now abandoned, passed by the west edge of the camp. (*Figure A-19A*) The key to locating this site was recognizing and identifying the profile of South La Ventana Mesa in a 1936 photo of the camp. (*Official Annual - 1936, Albuquerque District; Figure A-20*) Driving up US-550 to match the profile on the ground with that in the photo took me to the entrance of Dragonfly Recreation Area at mile 48. Access is west from there down the gravel road (now gated off) for 0.75 miles, and then south along a 4WD track for 0.6 miles to the site. The campsite had been studied intensively by Peter McKenna of the Bureau of Indian Affairs, and he had produced a comprehensive report. (McKenna 2006)

Being right next to a main highway, NM-44, delivery of food and general supplies was never an issue. Water supply however was a serious problem. Until a spring could be developed in the Nacimiento foothills, about three miles to the east, water had to be trucked in from camp SCS-8-N (see below). When a 9-inch diameter water line, made from old wood conduits contributed by the Santa Fe Railroad, was finally put in place, the camp had their water supply. Once the water issue was taken care of, time was available to spruce the place up and to relax a bit. (*Figures A-21B* and *A-21C*)

I had the good fortune of knowing a former CCC boy who had spent a six-month period in this camp. Archie Archuleta (1920–2017) was a farm boy from Turley, New Mexico (on the Río San Juan east of Bloomfield). He told me tales of camp life, including one tragedy about a truck that had missed a bridge over the arroyo north of camp, veering off into the arroyo and killing the young driver.

SCS-8-N, "Camp Catron Ranch," Rio Salado Valley, Sandoval County.
Rank 5 (III-C-1).

About 7.5 miles south of SCS-7-N was its twin camp, SCS-8-N, on the east side of US-550 (then NM-44) at mile 40.6. (*Figure A-22*) It was located on the old Espiritu Santo Ranch, also called the Catron Ranch. Like SCS-7-N, the camp was tasked with bringing the range back to health. This camp was larger than SCS-7-N, and operated longer, from July 1935 to the spring of 1940. At the outset this camp was also faced with the dilemma of water. Water haulage, probably from Holy Ghost Spring (also known as *El Ojo del Espiritu Santo*) about 1.75 miles to the north was necessary until a piping system could be developed from two springs at the mountain front (*Figure A-22*). The camp then became a large, well-organized affair. (*Figure A-23A*)

Researching this camp was made more interesting because I was personally acquainted with two men who had worked at the camp, though at different times. Rupert López (1916–2018) was the company clerk at the camp. He is pictured in the 1936 company portrait. (*Figures A-23B and 23D*) In early 2000 Rupert and I, armed by written permission from Zia Pueblo, scaled the gate and visited the campsite. This was his first time in 64 years. Memories came flooding back and brought the place alive to him again.

The second CCC boy was Alex Gallegos. (*Figures A-23C and 23D*) He told tales of hitchhiking down to Albuquerque and of serious hiking out to Cabezon Peak, which was visible out to the west of the camp. He was in the company when the camp was dismantled in 1940 and trucked in pieces north to Bayfield, Colorado (halfway between Durango and Pagosa Springs). Today there's only the tantalizing image of a couple of adobe buildings, once part of the motor pool and set back about 600 feet east of highway US-550. The campsite resides on Zia Pueblo land and is not accessible to the public.

F-35-N/SCS-21-N, "Camp Red Canyon," Manzano Mountains, Torrance County
Rank 1 (I-A-2)

The camp had two periods of occupation. First, as F-35-N, spring/summer 1934 to winter 1935–1936, and later as SCS-21-N, winter 1936–1937 to winter 1939–1940. Apparently it was a tent camp, which is hard to understand given that it spent those winters relatively high in the foothills of the Manzano Mountains at about 7,400 feet elevation. (*Figure A-24*) A fair number of structures remain scattered among the trees (which are today taking over) including an incinerator, a pair of some kind of concrete supports, and four concrete foundations. The largest of the latter is just off to the south of Forest Service Road 253. It matches up with a CCC company group portrait of 1938, with the mess hall to the rear, and thus identifying this slab. (*Figure A-25*)

Sites of CCC interest in the Albuquerque metropolitan area, Bernalillo County

A number of sites of interest can be found in the downtown area of Albuquerque. (*Figure A-26*) In 1935 the Army set up its Albuquerque District offices downtown to administer its large number of camps. The offices, located over the Albuquerque Gas and Electric Co. at 5th and West Central Avenue, replaced those previously used by the regional Forest Service. The city built a 30,000-square foot steel and concrete warehouse for the CCC, located on the east side of the Santa Fe RR tracks between Mountain Road and New York Avenue. (*Figure A-27A*) This structure was designed to handle perishable foodstuffs for the 3,600 men in the district's camps and to house a 20-man drafting department. No trace of this facility exists today. (*Albuquerque Progress* 1935a and 1935b) Also, there are two other sites of interest in the Albuquerque area that are not main camps, the Conservancy Beach Side Camp and Camp Albuquerque.

Conservancy Beach Side Camp

In late 1935 the Albuquerque District of the Division of Grazing (DG) felt the need to set up a side-camp in Albuquerque that would support its other DG camps. The city mayor and city manager acquired the site, at the southern end of today's Kit Carson Park, north of the zoo. (*Figure A-27B*) It was operational from at least 1935 until 1940 when it was consolidated with SCS-27-N on Albuquerque's "east mesa" (see above). It had permanent barrack-type construction, including a 30-man convalescence structure, and a school for cooks. (*The Grazette* 1936; *Official Annual – 1936, Albuquerque District*, pg. 77; *Albuquerque Progress* 1940) Not a trace of the side-camp remains today.

Camp Albuquerque

This was not a CCC camp, but is mentioned here because of the confusion it may cause. "Camp Albuquerque" was a WWII POW camp, at first located at the site of the Conservancy Beach Side Camp (see above). The original plans were to house POWs in the former CCC barracks. However, the camp was located next to a residential area and Mayor Clyde Tingley (with his ear ever to the political ground) went ballistic. The Army then suggested using the site only for Italian POWs because there were many Italian residents in the area. Italian inmates were moved into the camp in October 1943, but were moved elsewhere six months later. When word got out that the camp was then to be used for German POWs from the North African campaign, the local uproar increased. It was then agreed to house the Germans south of town, where no one lived, on a 8-acre tract just north of the Schwartzman meat-packing plant on the west side of South 2nd Street and 4.2 miles north of Rio Bravo Blvd. SE. (*Figure A-26*) The CCC barracks were moved to the new site and in July 1944 the first prisoners arrived. In 1945 there were 171 of them stationed at Camp Albuquerque. The camp was closed in March 1946. The Schwartzmans stuccoed over the CCC barracks and leased them out as 26 small apartments. In the mid-1960s the structures were all transported down to Los Lunas. (Spidle 1974; Smith 2005)

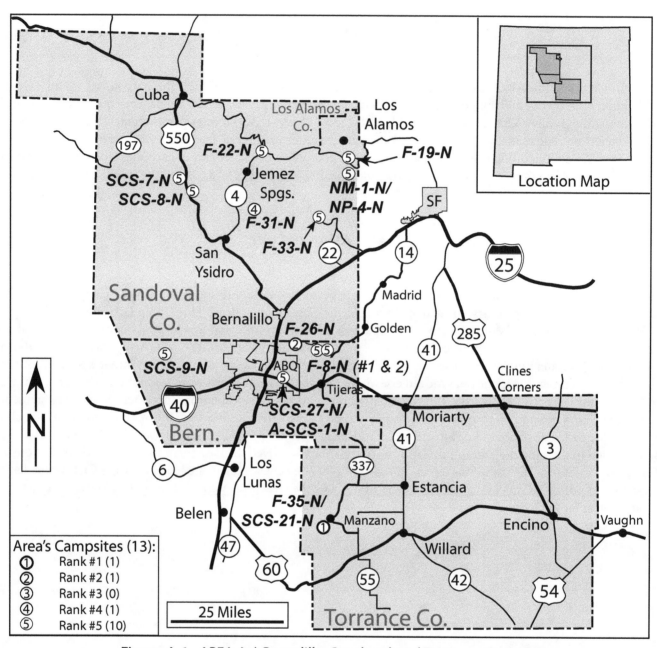

Figure A-1. AREA A / Bernalillo, Sandoval and Torrance Counties.

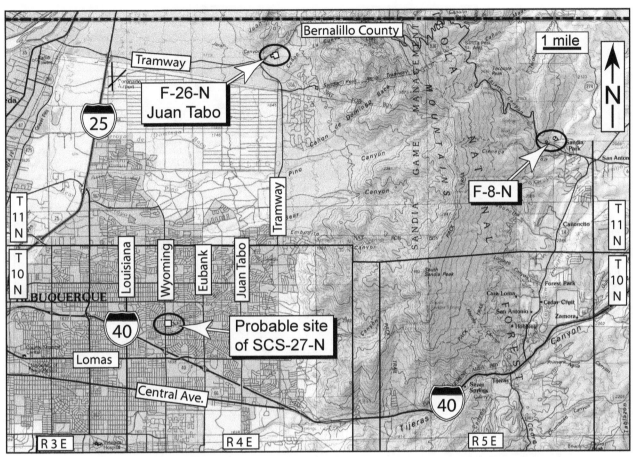

Figure A-2. Map of Eastern Albuquerque and its Three CCC Camps.

Figure A-3. Camp F-26-N, Juan Tabó I (*Google Earth* image).

A. Northeast view, ca. 1930s (Photograph from C. Benedict).

B. Same View as Above, 2003 (Photograph by Author).

Figure A-4. Camp F-26-N, Juan Tabó II.

A. CCC Company Portrait, 1933 (Photograph from Author's Collection).

B. Same View as Above, 2018 (Showing Ruins of Juan Tabó Cabin, Photograph by Author).

Figure A-5. Camp F-26-N, Juan Tabó III.

A. Juan Tabó Cabin, 1944 (Photograph from Cíbola National Forest).

B. Juan Tabó Cabin, 1998 (Photograph by Author).

Figure A-6. Camp F-26-N, Juan Tabó IV.

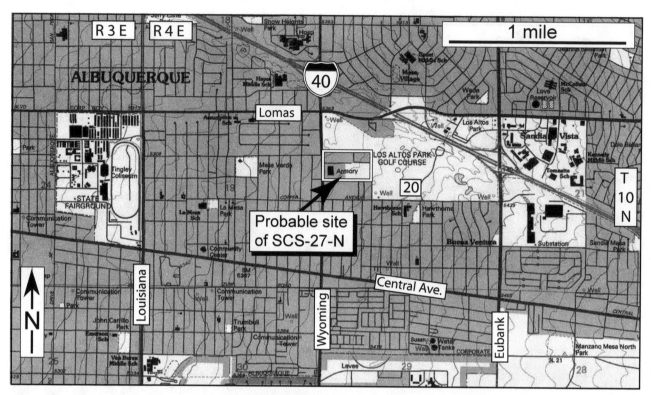

Figure A-7. Camp SCS-27-N, Albuquerque's East Mesa
(Probable site of National Guard Armory).

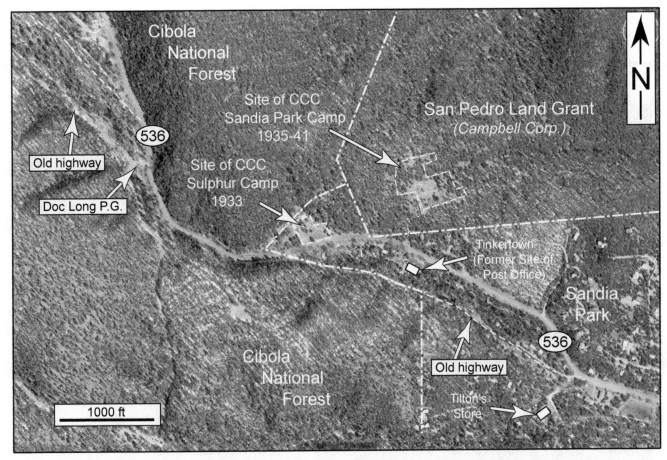

Figure A-8 *Google Earth* Overview of Camps F-8-N, Sulphur Springs and Sandia Park.

A. North Oblique View, 1933 (Photograph from Cibola National Forest).

B. North Oblique *Google Earth* Image.

Figure A-9. Camp F-8-N, Sulphur Springs.

A. West View, ca. 1940 (Photograph from Author's Collection).

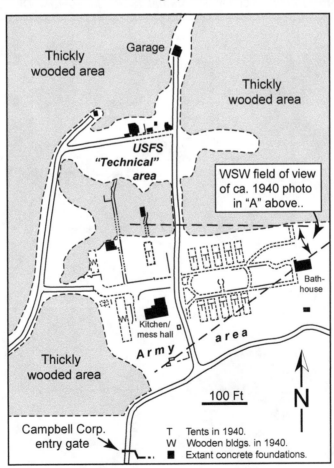

B. Map of Camp (Drawn by Author, 1998).

Figure A-10. Camp F-8-N, Sandia Park I.

A. Building the Kiwanis Hut on Sandia Crest, 1936
(Photograph from CCC *Official Annual-1936, Albuquerque District*).

B. The "Boys" Heading out on the Town, ca. 1939 (Photograph from Author's Collection).

Figure A-11. Camp F-8-N, Sandia Park II.

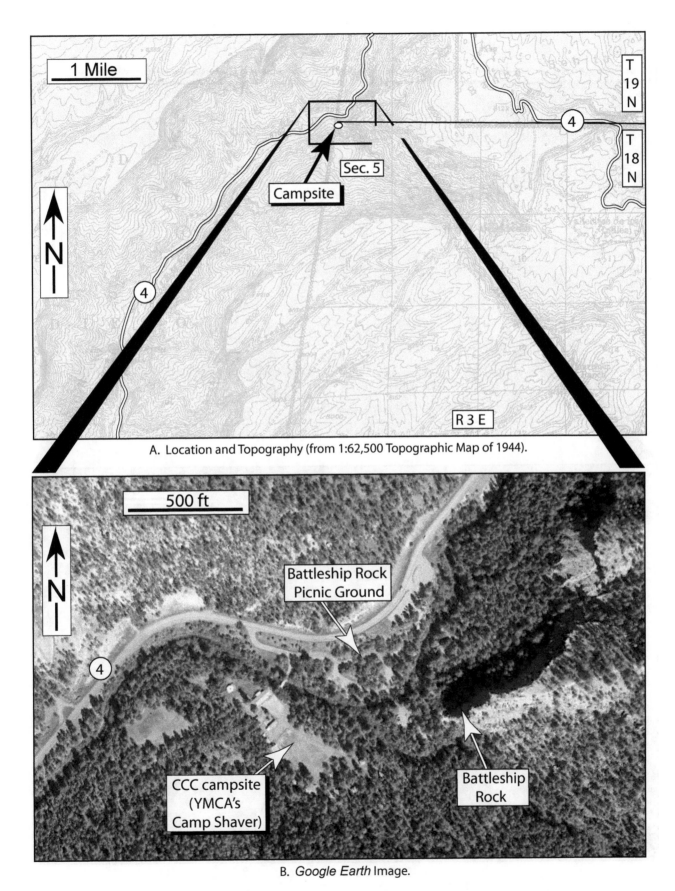

A. Location and Topography (from 1:62,500 Topographic Map of 1944).

B. *Google Earth* Image.

Figure A-12. Camp F-22-N, Battleship Rock, Jémez Mountains.

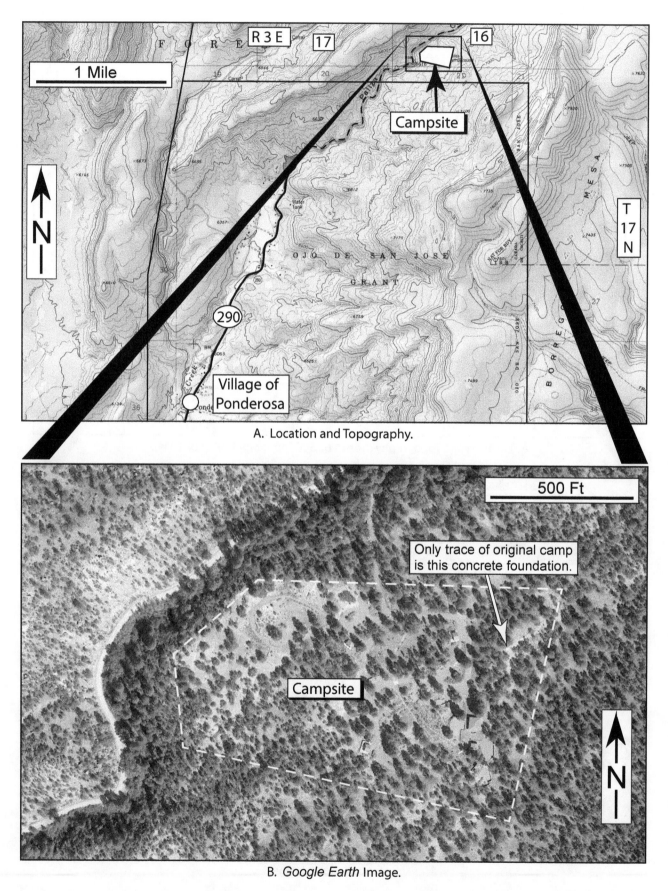

A. Location and Topography.

B. *Google Earth* Image.

Only trace of original camp is this concrete foundation.

Campsite

Figure A-13. Camp F-31-N, Paliza Canyon Group Campground, Jémez Mountains I.

A. East Oblique Aerial View of Camp, 1930s (Photograph from *Jemez Thunder*, Sept. 15, 1996).

B. West View of Camp and Canyon's West Wall, 1930s (Photograph by A. Newman).

C. West View of Canyon's West Wall from Campground, 2018 (Photograph by author).

Figure A-14. Camp F-31-N, Paliza Canyon Group Campground, Jémez Mountains II.

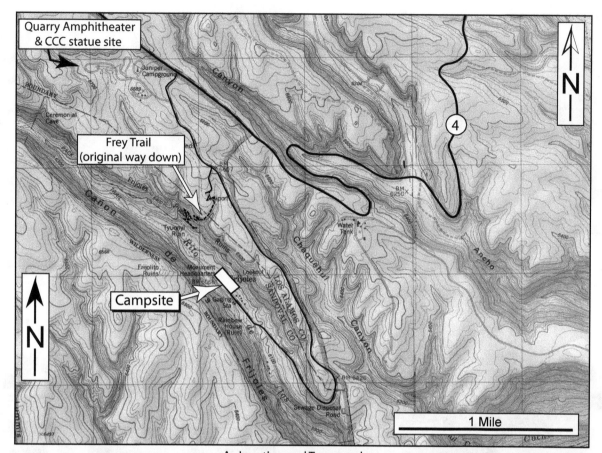

Quarry Amphitheater
& CCC statue site

Frey Trail
(original way down)

Campsite

A. Location and Topography.

A. Construction of Road into Canyon, 1933 (Photograph from National Park Service).

Figure A-15. Camp NM-1-N/NP-4-N, Bandelier I.

A. South View of Camp, 1930s (Photograph from National Park Service).

B. West View of Camp, 1938 (Photograph from National Park Service).

Figure A-16. Camp NM-1-N/NP-4-N, Bandelier II.

A. *Google Earth* Image (Showing Present Facilities and Part of Original Camp in White Outline).

B. Northwest View of Bandelier Lodge, 1930s (Photograph from National Park Service).

Figure A-17. Camp NM-1-N/NP-4-N, Bandelier III.

A. All that Soft Rock ("Tuff") from Local Quarry on North Rim (Photograph from National Park Service).

B. Park Hotel Under Construction, 1930s (Photograph from National Park Service).

Figure A-18. Camp NM-1-N/NP-4-N, Bandelier IV.

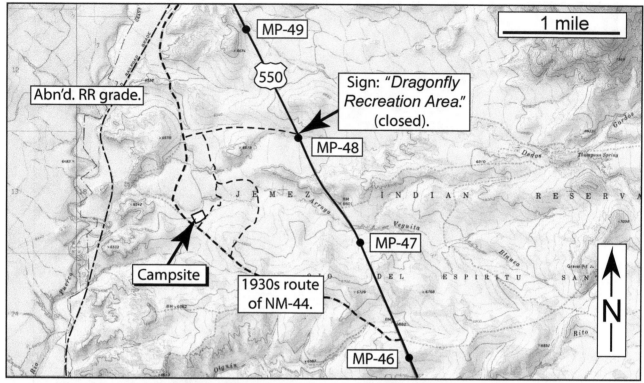

A. Location and Topography (Showing Highway Mile Posts, MPs).

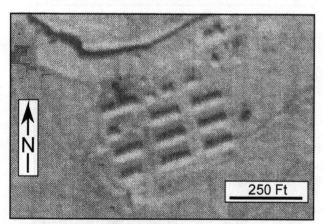

B. Fuzzy Enlargement of Fairchild 1935 SCS Aerial Image of Camp.

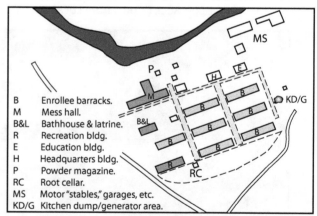

C. Interpretation of Function of Camp Structures in B (McKenna, 2006).

Figure A-19. Camp SCS-7-N, Rio Puerco I.

A. East-Northeast View of Camp, 1936 (Photograph from CCC *Official Annual-1936, Albuquerque District*).

B. Same View as in A, 2001 (Photograph by Author).

Figure A-20. Camp SCS-7-N, Rio Puerco - II.

A. A Fleet of trucks was Vital (and Had to be Faithfully Maintained).

B. East View of Camp (Showing Granite-Boulder Perimeters).

C. What Became of These Musicians?

Figure A-21. Camp SCS-7-N, Rio Puerco III
(Photographs from CCC *Official Annual-1936, Albuquerque District*).

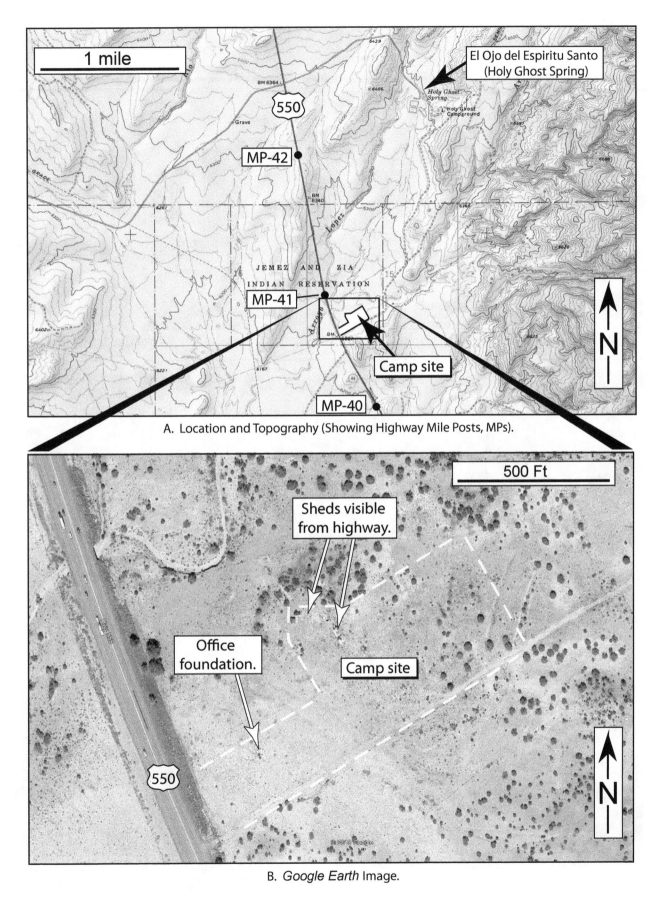

1 mile

550

BM 6364

Grave

MP-42

El Ojo del Espiritu Santo
(Holy Ghost Spring)

Holy Ghost
Spring

Holy Ghost
Campground

JEMEZ AND ZIA
INDIAN RESERVATION

MP-41

Camp site

MP-40

N

A. Location and Topography (Showing Highway Mile Posts, MPs).

500 Ft

Sheds visible
from highway.

Office
foundation.

Camp site

550

N

B. *Google Earth* Image.

Figure A-22. Camp SCS-8-N, Catron Ranch, Rio Salado I.

A. Northeast View of Camp, 1936 (Photograph from CCC *Official Annual-1936, Albuquerque District*).

B. CCC Company, Highlighting Rupert López, 1936
(Photograph from CCC *Official Annual -1936, Albuquerque District*).

C. Alex Gallegos, 1939 (Photograph from Author's Collection).

D. Alex Gallegos (1919-2018) and Rupert López (1916-2018), 2007 (Photograph by Author).

Figure A-23. Camp SCS-8-N, Catron Ranch, Rio Salado II.

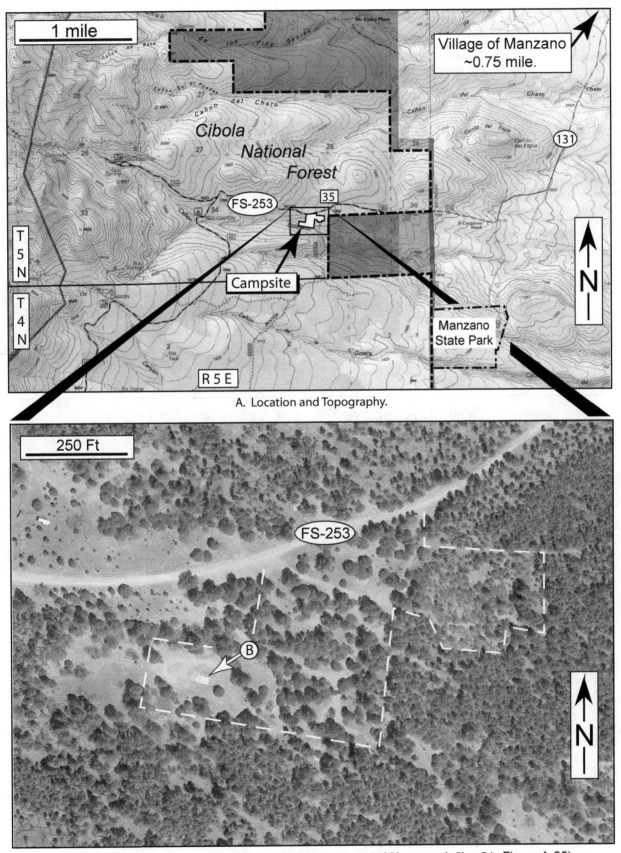

1 mile

Village of Manzano
~0.75 mile.

Cibola

National

Forest

FS-253

35

T 5 N
T 4 N

Campsite

R 5 E

Manzano
State Park

N

A. Location and Topography.

250 Ft

FS-253

B

N

B. *Google Earth* Image (Showing General Campsite Area and Photograph Shot B in Figure A-25).

Figure A-24. Camp F-35-N/SCS-21-N, Red Canyon, Manzano I.

A. CCC Company Portrait, 1938 (Photograph from Cíbola National Forest).

B. Same View as in A Above, 2017 (Photograph by Author).

Figure A-25. Camp F-35-N/SCS-21-N, Red Canyon, Manzano II.

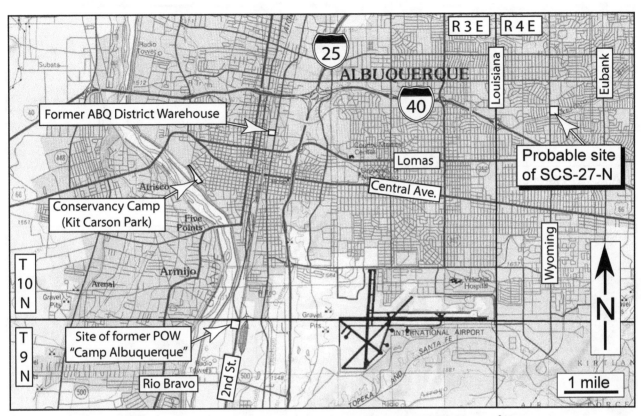

Figure A-26. Map of Central Albuquerque Showing CCC Sites of Interest.

A. CCC Warehouse, 1935 (Located East of SFRR Tracks Between New York Ave. and Mountain Rd., Photograph from *Albuquerque Progress*, September 1935b).

B. Conservancy Beach Side Camp, 1936 (Site of Present Kit Carson Park, Photograph from CCC *Official Annual-1936, Albuquerque District*).

Figure A-27. Downtown Albuquerque CCC Facilities.

AREA B

Northwest New Mexico: San Juan and Cibola Counties
(Figure B-1)

These two non-contiguous counties contain four CCC campsites. Little remains of the four today and access is a problem, so they all have a rank of 5.

San Juan County:

1. DG-101-N/G-101-N, Bloomfield (P.O. Bloomfield)

2. NM-2-N/NP-2-N, Chaco Canyon (P.O. Crownpoint)

Cíbola County:

3. SCS-10-N, San Mateo (P.O. San Mateo)

4. F-7-N, "Camp Soloman Luna," Mt. Sedgwick (P.O. Grants)

DG-101-N/G-101-N, Bloomfield, San Juan County
Rank 5 (II-D-1)

This camp started out in 1938 as a Division of Grazing (DG) facility, but in 1939 the agency was renamed the Grazing Division (G). The camp was located just south of the Rio San Juan and the town of Bloomfield, and west of US-550 on the north side of Mangum Road. (*Figure B-2* and *B-3*)

I have a letter written by ex-CCC boy, Charles Wilburn of Belton, Texas, dated July 1991, plus a collection of photographs relating his experiences at the camp during the halcyon summer of 1941. A photo of him at Bloomfield's west side is priceless. (*Figure B-3B*) Today not a trace of the campsite remains as it is completely built over by the Rio Vista Mobile Home Community.

NM-2-N/NP-2-N, Chaco Canyon, San Juan County, San Juan County
Rank 4 (I-C-1)

It is not generally known that there was a CCC camp in Chaco Canyon. The National Park Service does a marvelous job managing this world-class historic site. However, there is more in the park than the Anasazi ruins, although admittedly of lesser importance. The NPS has completely obliterated the site of Richard Wetherill's 1901 ranch, hotel and a post office (called "Putnam") immediately west of Pueblo Bonito. Wetherill's involvement began in 1895, initiating the archeologic work there by himself and later in conjunction with the Hyde Exploring Expedition. He was murdered in 1910 and almost disappeared from history. At least the NPS left his grave intact.

The CCC camp was originally designated NM-2-N, renamed NP-2-N, and operated as a rather late camp from August 1939 to November 1941. It lies only 0.7 miles southeast of the Visitor Center, and just west of NM-57 where the road forks east to the Pueblo Bonito area. (*Figure B-4*) The CCC led a failed attempt to stabilize "Threatening Rock," the enormous monolith that had loomed over Pueblo Bonito for centuries and, despite herculean preventive efforts, it came thundering down onto the northeast sector of the ruin in January 1941. Nothing of this engaging story is cited in the Visitor Center or in the site literature. *Google Earth* imagery clearly shows the CCC campsite outlines, although little remains on the ground.

A sidebar is warranted here. There was a second CCC camp at Chaco: an Indian Mobile Unit, camp CCC-ID, which was located just east of Pueblo Bonito. It was jointly administered by the Bureau of Indian Affairs and the National Park Service. Its purpose was to train Navajo men in stone masonry and ruin stabilization, and it was set up in July 1937 in advance of construction of the full-blown 200-man camp NP-2-N. The success of the Indian Mobile Unit led to the establishment of ruin-stabilization units at other parks in the Southwest. Camp NP-2-N was closed in 1941 and the Indian camp in 1942. (Van West and Schelberg 2015) Traces of both camps were obliterated in 1943. (Van West and Sebastian 2010)

SCS-10-N, San Mateo, Cibola County (then Valencia County)
Rank 5 (III-D-2)

This facility was located 23 miles north of Grants. It operated from spring/summer 1935 through most of 1937. Today only traces appear on *Google Earth*, and is located on the private Fernández Ranch. (*Figure B-5*) It has the unusual distinction of being marked on the modern USGS topographic map.

F-7-N, "Camp Solomon Luna," Mt. Sedgewick, Cibola County (then Valencia County)
Rank 5 (I-D-2)

F-7-N was an early camp, built near Malpais Springs in the Zuni Mountains, about 10.5 road-miles southwest of Grants, in what was then Valencia County. (Today's Cíbola County was formed in 1982.) It was probably a tent camp, and therefore left no footprint. The camp was disbanded in November 1933 and the company moved to the Jornada del Muerto north of Las Cruces. The camp's namesake, Solomon Luna (1858–1912) was the first of the Luna clan to settle in New Mexico. He bequeathed the family name to the town Los Lunas in Valencia County. (Kammer 1994)

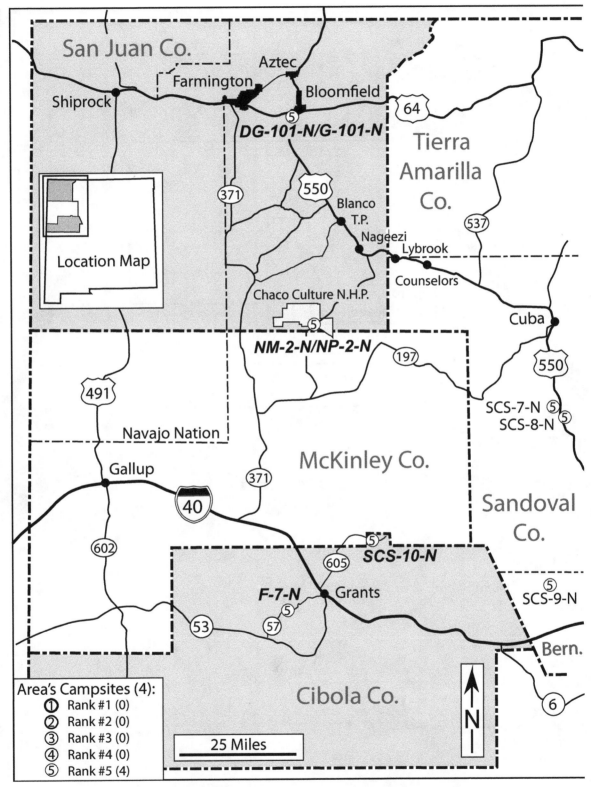

Figure B-1. AREA B / San Juan and Cíbola Counties.

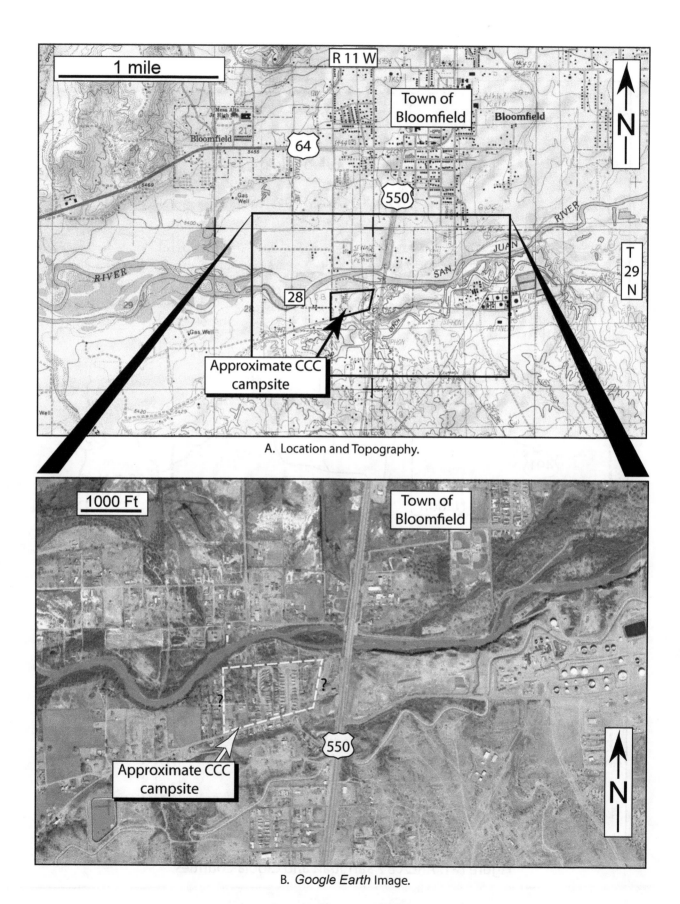

A. Location and Topography.

B. *Google Earth* Image.

Figure B-2. Camp DG-101-N/G-101-N, Bloomfield I.

A. North View of Camp, ca. 1938.

B. CCC-Boy Charles Wilburn on West edge of Bloomfield, 1941.

Figure B-3. Camp DG-101-N/G-101-N, Bloomfield II
(Photographs from San Juan County Archeological Research Center and Library).

81

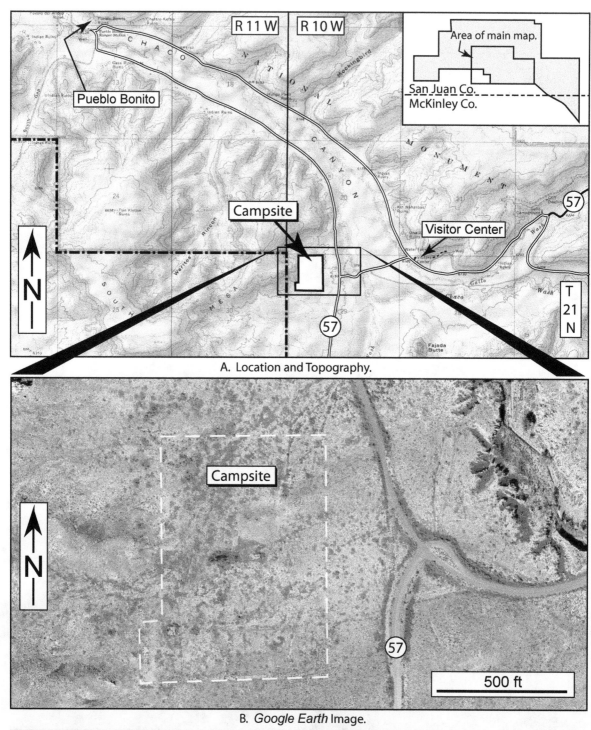

R 11 W   R 10 W

Area of main map.

San Juan Co.
McKinley Co.

Pueblo Bonito

Campsite

Visitor Center

N

T
21
N

57

57

A. Location and Topography.

Campsite

N

57

500 ft

B. *Google Earth* Image.

C. West View of Camp, Late 1930s (Photograph from Van West and Sebastian, 2010).

Figure B-4. Camp NM-2-N/NP-2-N, Chaco Canyon.

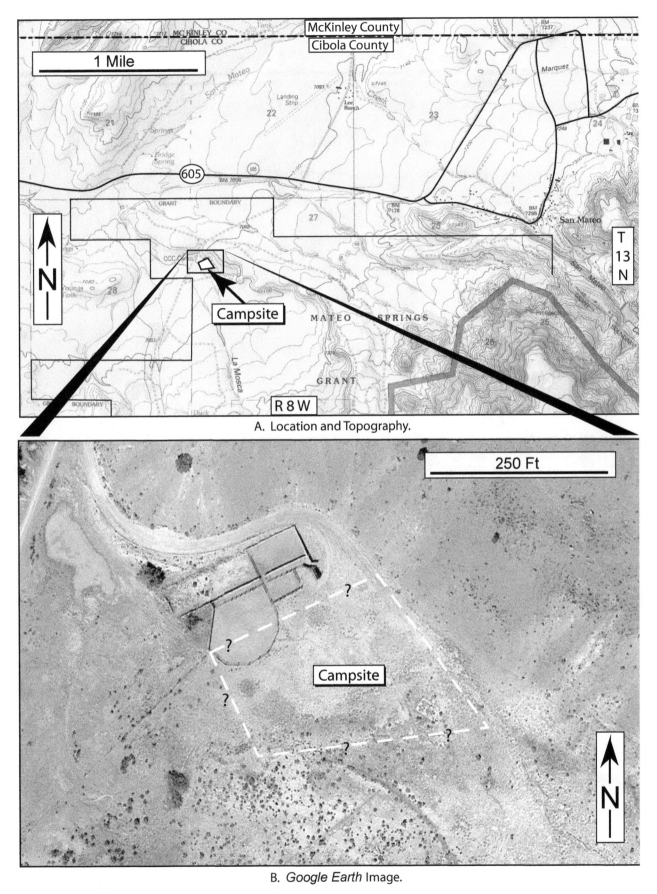

A. Location and Topography.

B. *Google Earth* Image.

Figure B-5. Camp SCS-10-N, San Mateo.

AREA C
North-Central New Mexico: Rio Arriba and Taos Counties
(*Figure C-l*)

This huge area covers the north-central part of the state. It holds a total of seven campsites.

Rio Arriba County:

1. F-3-N, "Camp Sterling Price," Vallecitos (P.O. El Rito)

2. F-5-N/SCS-4-N/F-36-N, El Rito (P.O. El Rito)

3. F-43-N, La Madera (P.O. La Madera)

4. F-55-N, El Rito (P.O. El Rito)

5. SCS-3-N, "Camp Piedra Lumbre," Ghost Ranch (P.O. Abiquiu)

6. SCS-5-N, Rio Truchas, Velarde (P.O. Española)

Taos County:

7. F-6-N, "Camp Kit Carson," Tres Ritos (P.O. Vadito)

F-3-N, "Camp Sterling Price," Vallecitos, Rio Arriba County

Rank 5 (I-D-2)

This camp's nickname, "Sterling Price" (Kammer 1994), was derived from New Mexico's territorial governor (1846–1847). Locating it has been an exercise in detective work. (*Figure C-2A*) For some time I had assumed that a camp named Vallecitos, F-55-N (see below), was a reoccupation and renaming of camp F-3-N, 12 miles northwest of El Rito, because I knew nothing of a camp near the village of Vallecitos located some 20 driving miles to the northeast. Then I found a superb photo from *Getty Images* on the Internet. (Note: Getty is an agency located in Seattle WA dealing with stock photo images. It would have been necessary to purchase a license to use the photo in this book.) The photo is labeled "A view of the Civilian Conservation Corps' Camp Vallecito, Carson, New Mexico, September 1933." However, the surrounding mountain profile on *Google Earth* does not match that of what I had identified as F-3-N.

Checking into and around the little community of Vallecitos, looking west from there via *Google Earth* in the Cañada del Borracho, I found a mountain profile that does indeed match up exactly with the Getty photo. (*Figure C-2B*) The valley was named after a famous old yellow steer named "Borracho" ("drunk" in Spanish) that once lived here. (Julyan 1996) However, there does not appear to be a trace of a campsite there. To muddy the waters even more, there is the discrepancy of the dates: the Getty photo is labeled September 1933, but F-55-N was established in May 1940. (CCC Legacy) Therefore, putting all the pieces together, I have concluded that the Getty image is of Vallecitos camp F-3-N, located just west of Vallecitos, 20 miles north of El Rito, and that an El Rito Camp, F-55-N, is the one located 12 miles northwest of El Rito. Worse yet, there is a second El Rito camp, F-5-N, five miles south of El Rito (see below).

F-5-N/SCS-4-N/F-36-N, El Rito, Rio Arriba County

Rank 1a (I-A-1)

This is one of the more accessible of the campsites. Its nearest settlement is Abiquiu, 11 miles to the southwest, and Española is about 25 miles to the southeast. The campsite is located at a roadside pull-off, on the east side of NM-554 at mile 6.7. Just to the east of the pull-off is a fenced enclosure, with a number of cryptic structures. (*Figure C-3B*) It can be accessed by taking a dirt road, 1/4 mile north of the pull-off for about 0.1 mile east, and then south on a dirt track about 0.3 miles to the east side of the site. There is a moderately large stone chimney, also seen from the highway (*Figure C-4A*), and an assortment of concrete foundations and the supports of a water tower. (*Figure C-4B*) A vintage photo of the camp (*Figure C-3C*) is of little help, other than that the profile of the background hills from *Google Earth* indicates a match and that the old photo was taken looking northeast.

Camp F-5-N was operational from spring/summers 1933 and 1934. It was resurrected as camp SCS-4-N, spring/summer 1935 through fall/winter 1937–1938, and then a third time as camp F-36-N, from spring/summer 1938 through summer 1939.

F-43-N, La Madera, Rio Arriba County

Rank 1 (I-A-2)

This very interesting site is located one mile south of the hamlet of La Madera. It lies atop a river terrace on the west side of highway NM-111, about 50 feet above road level and out of sight from the highway. (*Figure C-5*) The terrace is underlain by cobbly gravel, remains of an ancestor stream above the present Ojo del Caliente Creek, and some of the camp structures are made from this stuff. The "road" leading up to the site was originally paved with these cobbles and infilled with finer material, but years of rain and runoff have removed the fines and left a very bumpy, cobbly mess. Do not attempt to drive up except with a high-clearance, 4WD vehicle. However, it's only about a 100-yard walk up, where there is the reward of finding an assortment of fascinating camp structures. (*Figure C-6*) This site is the exemplar of New Mexico's lost history, known only by a handfull of local folks.

F-55-N, El Rito, Rio Arriba County

Rank 2 (I-A-3)

The site of F-55-N is not known for its convenience. It's a 12-mile drive over a gravel road through the Carson National Forest northwest of the little college town of El Rito. (*Figure C-7*) However, it is definitely worth the effort as some interesting features appear on both sides of the forest road. One of the concrete slabs is probably what is left of the mess hall, and an incinerator is close to it. A cluster of rounded field cobbles suggest what's left of a possible root cellar. One of the larger slabs is sometimes used as a platform for a large RV.

SCS-3-N, "Camp Piedra Lumbre," Ghost Ranch, Rio Arriba County

Rank 5 (III-C-1)

This camp was set up in August 1935. Like camp SCS-10-N above (see AREA B above), it is actually marked on the modern USGS topographic map. (*Figure C-8A*) Restricted access to the campsite is 0.4 miles through locked gate on the south side of US-84, 3.5 miles northwest of the intersection of NM-96 to Abiquiu Dam. This land is today owned by Ghost Ranch. When the camp was built Abiquiu Lake did not exist, and the original access to the camp was from the south, much of which is now underwater.

In June 2016 my wife and I gained permission from Daniel Manzanares (Chief Operations Officer, Ghost Ranch) to tour the site. A stone wall, at the north side of the site, tantalizingly visible from US-84, seems to be part of the camp's motor pool. A root cellar, with a collapsed roof, some path-perimeter stones, and part of a south-entry portal are all that remains. (*Figures C-8B* and *C-9*)

SCS-5-N, Rio Truchas, Velarde, Taos County

Rank 1B (I-A-2)

This little-known campsite is located east of Velarde, only about 0.9 miles east of NM-68 on CR-435. (*Figure C-10*) It operated from spring/summer 1935 through 1940. This easy-to-get-to site occupies a little river terrace on the north side of the Rio Truchas. A variety of features provides a challenge to fit them together into a functional whole. A rather large, possible office complex is on the east side of the county road. It is worn down to the base of the walls. The rest of the campsite is on the west side of the road. A large slab that was probably a mess hall is suggested by the nearby kitchen dump of coals. Various drainage features indicate that flood threat was a consideration. A flag-pole support near the west-east access trail off the county suggests that the camp extended to the north as well. At the northwest corner of the site is a large shower/bathhouse site that visible on *Google Earth*. This is a very worthwhile easy detour off the main road north to Taos.

RANK 5 (III-C-1)

Camp F-6-N at Vadito is today occupied by the Tres Ritos Boy Scout Camp on the south side of highway NM-518, in Carson National Forest. (*Figure C-11*) There is little level ground in this area so it is quite reasonable to assume that the BSA took advantage of a CCC camp clearing for their facility and built over it. Nothing is visible on *Google Earth*.

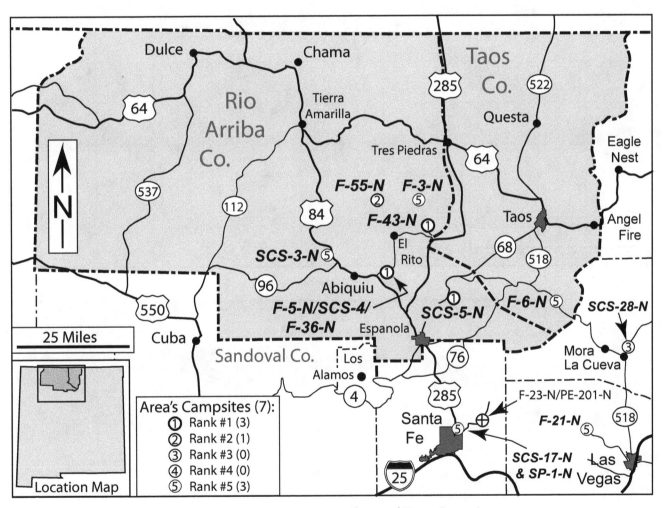

Figure C-1. AREA C / Rio Arriba and Taos Counties.

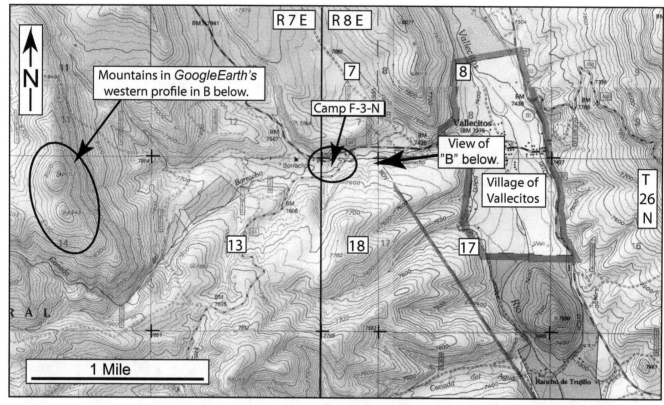

A. Location and Topography.

B. West Oblique *Google Earth* Image.

Figure C-2. Camp F-3-N, Cañada del Borracho, Vallecitos.

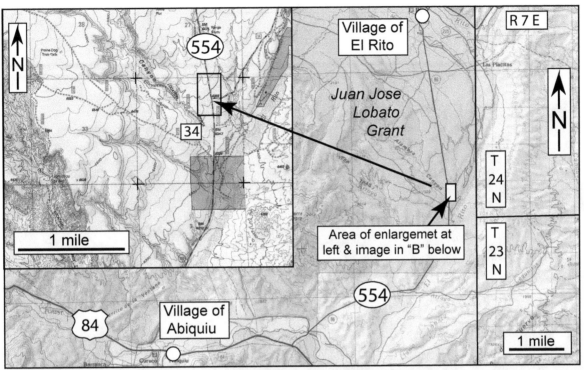

A. Location and Topography.

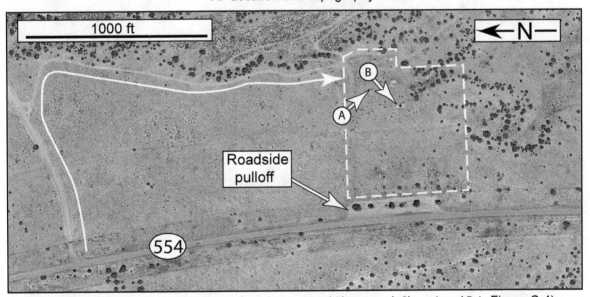

B. *Google Earth* Image (Showing Preferred Access and Photograph Shots A and B in Figure C-4).

C. Camp in 1936 (Photograph from CCC *Official Annual-1936, Albuquerque District*).

Figure C-3. Camp F-5-N/SCS-4-N/F-36-N, El Rito I.

A. Southeast View of Fireplace Chimney, 2017 (Photograph by Author).

B. Southwest View of Enrollee Bathhouse/Shower, 2017 (Photograph by Author).

Figure C-4. Camp F-5-N/SCS-4-N/F-36-N, El Rito II.

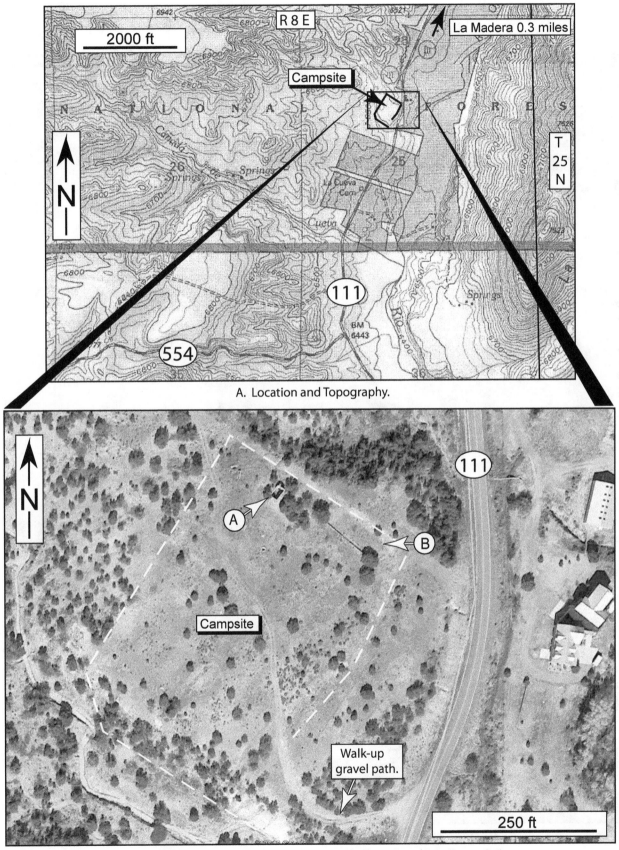

A. Location and Topography.

B. *Google Earth* Image (Showing Photograph Shots A and B in Figure C-6).

Figure C-5. Camp F-43-N, La Madera I.

A. Northeast View of Remains of Root Cellar, 2003 (Photograph by Author).

B. West View of Camp's Eastern Border Wall, 2003 (Photograph by Author).

Figure C-6. Camp F-43-N, La Madera II.

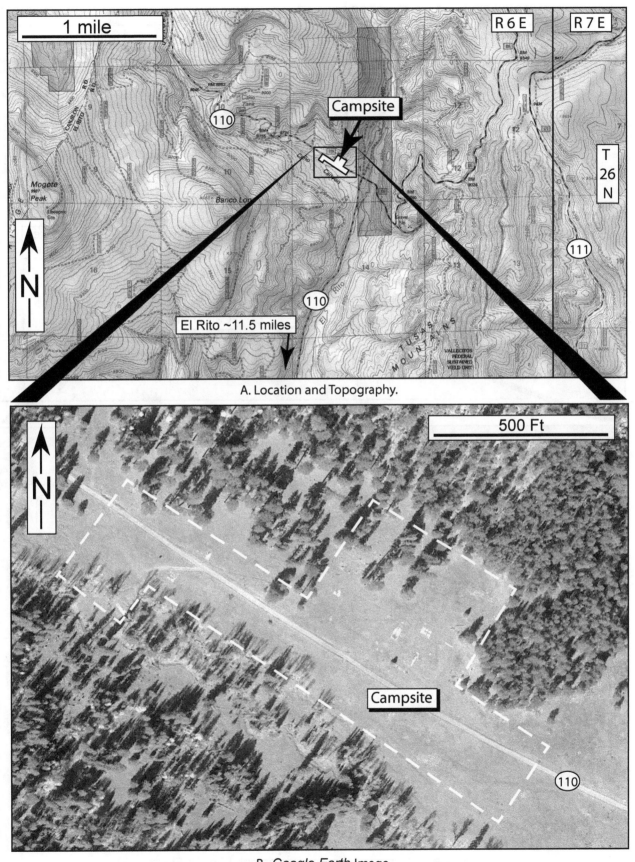

A. Location and Topography.

B. *Google Earth* Image.

Figure C-7. Camp F-55-N, El Rito.

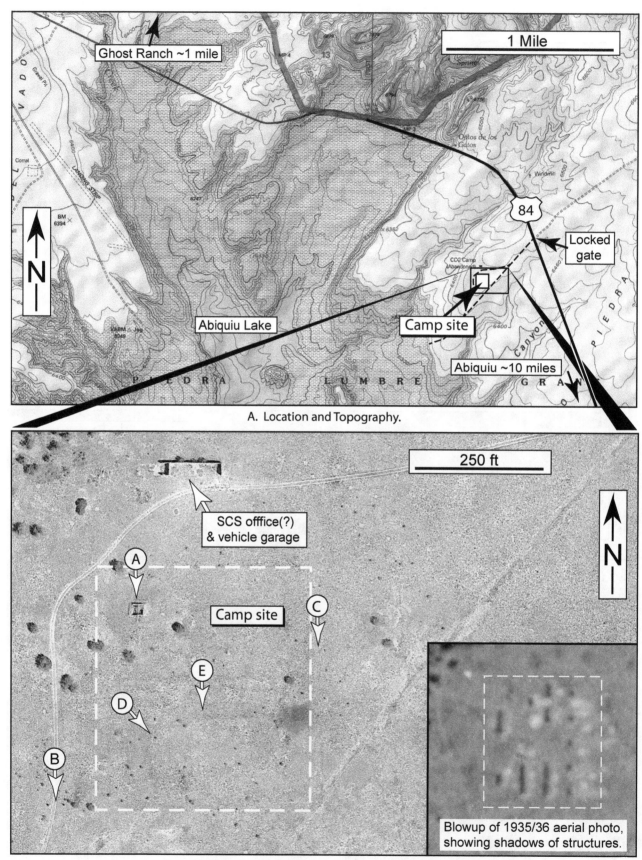

A. Location and Topography.

Ghost Ranch ~1 mile

1 Mile

84

Locked gate

CCC Camp (Abandoned)

Camp site

Abiquiu Lake

Abiquiu ~10 miles

N

B. *Google Earth* Image (Showing Photograph Shots in Figure C-9).

250 ft

SCS offfice(?) & vehicle garage

Camp site

N

Blowup of 1935/36 aerial photo, showing shadows of structures.

Figure C-8. Camp SCS-3-N, Ghost Ranch I.

A. South View of Root Cellar and Iconic Pedernal Peak, 2016 (Photograph by Author).

B. South Vew of Camp's Southern Entryway, 2016 (Photograph by Author).

C. South View of Camp's Eastern Perimeter, 2016 (Photograph by Author).

D. Probable Flagpole Support, 2016 (Photograph by Author).

E. South View of Flagpole and Enrollee Barracks, 1936 (Photo from CCC *Official Annual-1936, Albuquerque District*).

Figure C-9. Camp SCS-3-N, Ghost Ranch II.

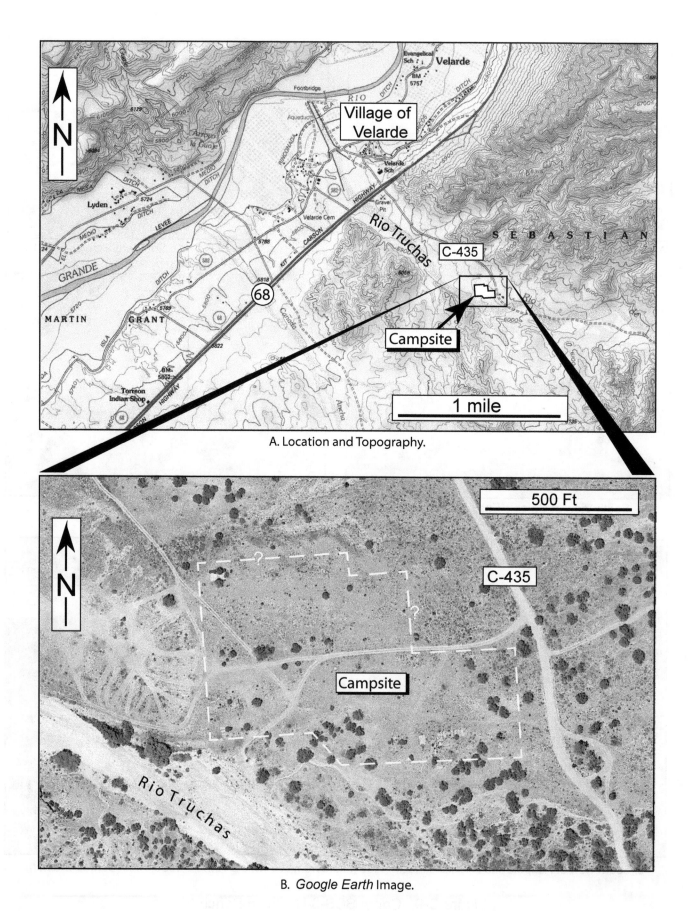

A. Location and Topography.

B. *Google Earth* Image.

Figure C-10. SCS-5-N, Rio Truchas, Velarde.

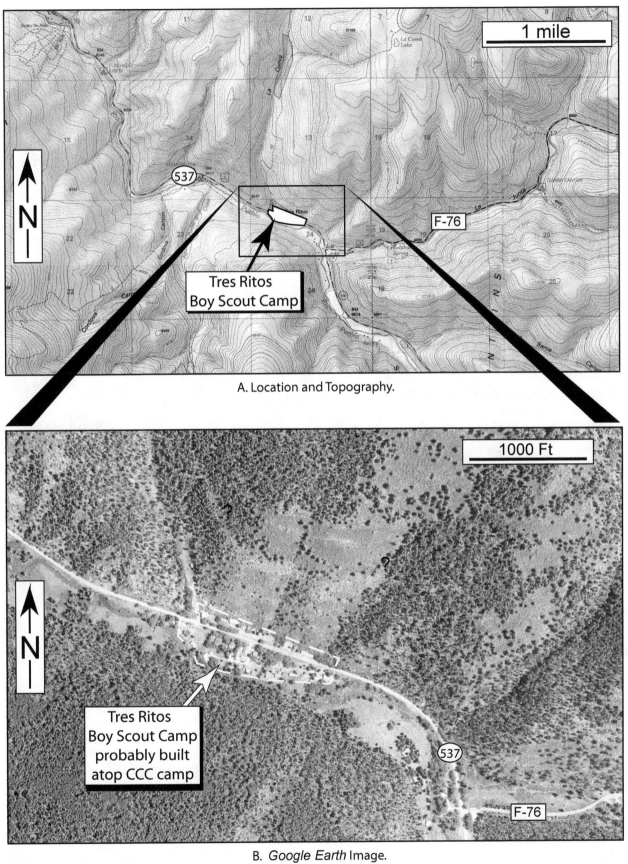

A. Location and Topography.

B. *Google Earth* Image.

Figure C-11. F-6-N, Tres Ritos.

AREA D

NORTHEAST NEW MEXICO: SANTA FE, MORA, AND WESTERN SAN MIGUEL COUNTIES
(*FIGURE D-1*)

Area D includes the Santa Fe and Las Vegas metropolitan areas. Five camps operated in this general area.

Santa Fe County:

1. F-23-N/PE-201-N, "Camp de Vargas," Little Tesuque Canyon, Hyde Memorial State Park (P.O. Santa Fe)

2. SCS-17-N, Santa Fe (P.O. Santa Fe)

3. SP-I-N, Santa Fe (P.O. Santa Fe)

Mora County:

4. SCS-28-N, La Cueva (P.O. Mora)

San Miguel County (western):

5. F-21-N, "Camp E.V. Long," Gallinas Canyon (P.O. Las Vegas)

F-23-N/PE-201-N, "CAMP DEVARGAS," HYDE MEMORIAL STATE PARK, SANTA FE COUNTY

RANK 4 (I-C-1)

This was an early camp, the last of the first wave of 17 that were rushed into existence in the spring of 1933. After the first period this Forest Service camp was renamed a Park Erosion Control camp, PE-201-N. It was located in Little Tesuque Canyon in the Santa Fe National Forest in an area that later became Hyde Memorial State Park.

The exact site of the camp center is elusive. Since there are very few level spots in the canyon, the camp might have been a tent facility in a less-than-ideal spot. A strong and likely candidate is the Hyde Memorial State Park Group Campground. (*Figure D-2*) This site exhibits abundant CCC work such as sturdy walls and a fireplace, that was once part of a cabin and used for many years afterwards. (*Figure D-3*) A suspicious concrete foundation off to the south side, today used as a trash platform, seems very much out of place and may have supported something heavy, and is at least a suggestion of a CCC camp structure. The State Park Visitor Center has a very nice CCC display.

SP-1-N AND SCS-17-N, SANTA RE, SANTA FE COUNTY

RANK 5 (III-D-1)

These two camps were established side-by-side, although administered by different agencies. Both camps occupied a broad swath of land just downslope and southeast from today's Frank S. Ortiz Dog Park in northwest Santa Fe. (*Figure D-4*) Together they formed a "town" of some 450 people. SP-1-N was the first. It was established in November 1933 by a company just formed and moved down from Wyoming. The company's most notable task was construction of the Old Santa Fe Trail Building between 1937 and 1939 in Spanish-Pueblo Revival style, the largest adobe-brick building (more than 280,000 bricks.) ever built in the country. The building is today used as offices for the National Park Service and serves to remind us of the CCC's significant contribution to the National Park Service.

The adjacent camp to SP-1-N, SCS-17-N, was occupied three weeks after the first one by a company that had also been moved down from Wyoming, first to PE-201-N at Hyde Park, and then six months later to Santa Fe. There seems to have been at least some kind of cooperation between the two neighboring camps, but of an unknown extent. One of SCS-17-N's tasks was construction of the adobe bricks to be used in the Old Santa Fe Trail Building. (Rupert López, whom we met earlier, worked at this camp as well and was a brick maker.) The bricks were made from material excavated for the building's foundation. Someone arranged for the *vigas* and corbels for the building to be harvested from the CCC camp area PE-201-N at Hyde Park. SCS-17-N was closed in January 1936 and the company moved to camp SCS-6-N at Fort Stanton.

The area of the two camps has an infamous later history. In March 1942, a large group of Japanese civilians, many U.S. citizens, were rounded up and incarcerated at the two abandoned CCC camps. In contrast to the CCC population of about 450, the Japanese population by 1945 eventually reached about 2,000. All in all, about 4,555 passed through its gates. Today a large stone monument, erected only in 2002 on the hill above the campsite, documents the sad chapter. The area was built over by the Casa Solana housing subdivision during the 1950s. Nothing remains of this multilayered history, except that big rock on the hill overlooking the site.

SCS-28-N, LA CUEVA, MORA COUNTY

RANK 3 (II-B-1)

Locating this campsite was another adventure. I have a single reference for the location of this site. It is from a personal letter, ca. 1992, written by Robert H. True, an ex-CCC boy who worked at this camp. He had revisited the site in 1988 and described it in his letter as "about seven or eight miles to the south of Mora, New Mexico," and, "The main road goes right along the side of some of the barracks pedestals." The letter had a return address in Grove, Oklahoma. (True, ca. 1992) I wrote to that address and had the great fortune of contacting Linda True. She graciously loaned me a set of the photos that Robert had taken during his 1998 CCC-camp visit. Matching up the profile of the background ridge in his photos, using *Google Earth* oblique views, I was able to locate it, but about five miles *east* of Mora. (*Figure D-5*) It goes to show that even first-hand descriptions must be occasionally taken with a grain of salt. The campsite is actually 1/2 mile *north* of the tiny community of La Cueva, on the west side of NM-442. It is fenced off, on private property, but very visible from the highway. *Google Earth* reveals six large foundations plus some smaller ones, and the outline of the entire campsite. It is frustrating that such an interesting site is apparently off limits.

F-21-N, "Camp E.V. Long," Gallinas Canyon, Las Vegas, San Miguel County

Rank 5 (II-D-1)

The location of this camp is vaguely described as along the Rio Gallinas. (*Official Annual–1936, Albuquerque District, p. 8*) One publication though indicates that this camp was also named the E.V. Long Camp. Lo and behold, today there is an E.V. Long Campground in Gallinas Canyon, west of Las Vegas in the Santa Fe National Forest. (Kammer 1994) Not a trace reveals itself on *Google Earth*, but considering that this was an early, one-period camp, likely a tent camp, that is not surprising. One might conclude though that this modern campground is the site of the CCC camp.

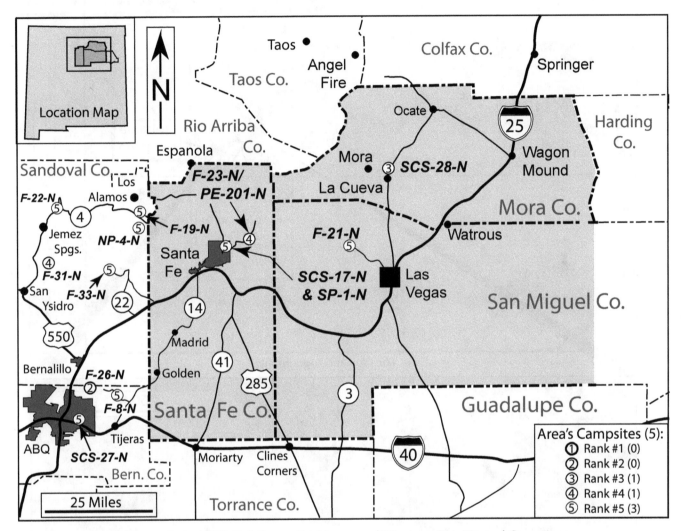

Figure D-1 AREA D / Santa Fe, Mora, and Western San Miguel Counties.

101

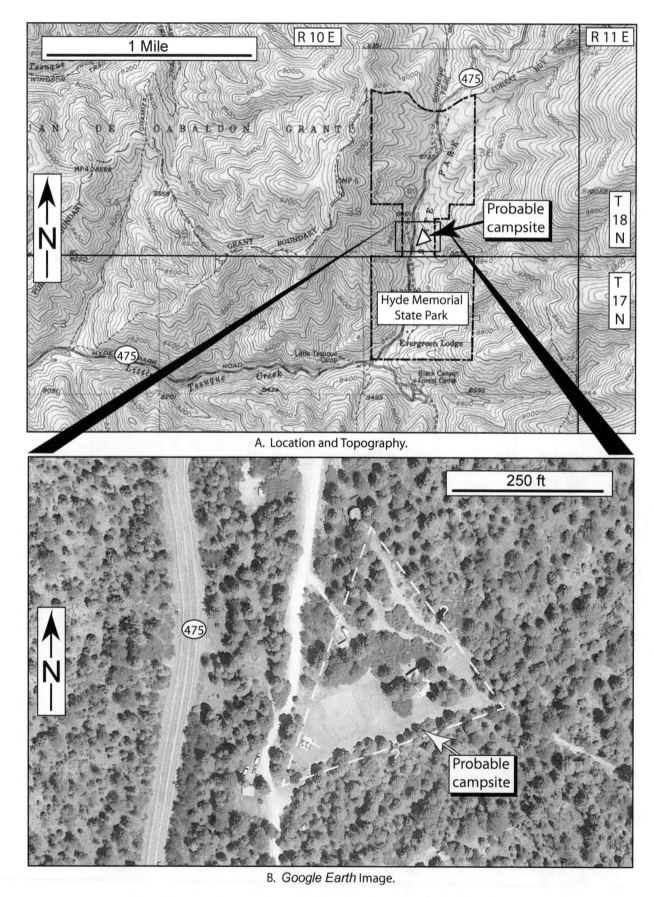

A. Location and Topography.

1 Mile

R 10 E   R 11 E

Probable campsite

Hyde Memorial State Park

Evergreen Lodge

T 18 N

T 17 N

250 ft

475

Probable campsite

B. *Google Earth* Image.

Figure D-2. Camp F-23-N/PE-201-N, Hyde Memorial State Park I.

A. Northeast View of Camp, 2017 (Photograph by Author).

B. West View of Group Cabin, 2017
(Photograph by Author.)

C. Group Cabin, 1941
(Photograph #1985, State Archives of NM).

D. Suspicious Concrete Slab, South Side of Site, 2017 (Photograph by Author).

Figure D-3. Camp F-23-N/PE-201-N, Hyde Memorial State Park II.

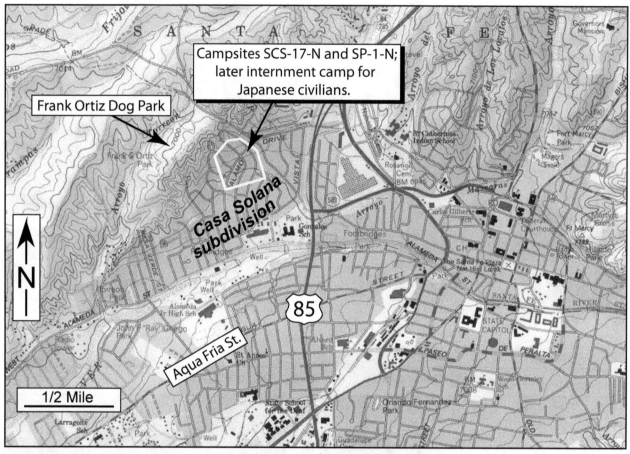

Frank Ortiz Dog Park

Campsites SCS-17-N and SP-1-N; later internment camp for Japanese civilians.

Casa Solana subdivision

N

1/2 Mile

Aqua Fria St.

85

A. Location and Topography.

B. West Composite View of Japanese Internment Camp (Photograph from Internet).

C. West View of Camp Area, 2017 (Photograph by Author).

Figure D-4. Camps SCS-17-N and SP-1-N, Northern Santa Fe
(Later Japanese Internment camp, 1942-1946).

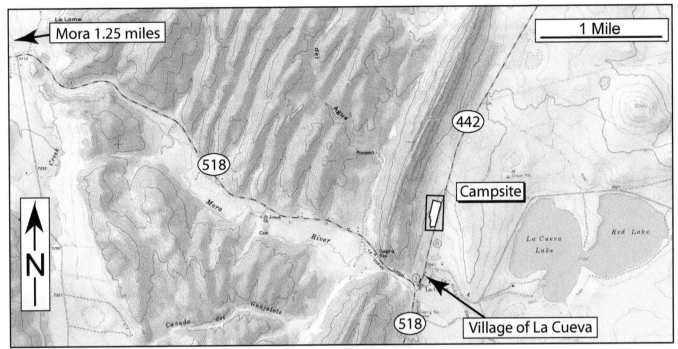

A. Location and Topography.

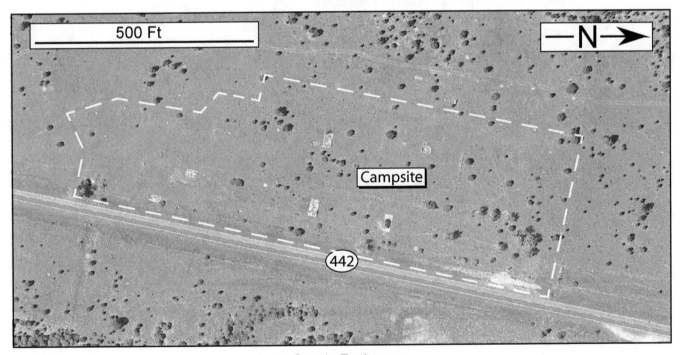

B. *Google Earth* Image.

Figure D-5. Camp SCS-28-N, La Cueva.

AREA E

Southwest New Mexico: Catron and Grant Counties
(Figure E-l)

These counties were administered by the Silver City District, which had its headquarters located in Silver City at the northeast corner of Bullard and 6th Avenue. Containing much public land, these two counties contain a total of 15 campsites.

Catron County

1. F-1-N, "Camp Beale," Reserve (P.O. Reserve)

2. F-2-N, "Camp Chaffee," Apache Creek (P.O. Reserve)

3. F-25-N, Glenwood (P.O. Glenwood)

4. F-29-N, "Camp Emmit Crawford," Pueblo Park (P.O. Alma)

5. F-34-N, Beaverhead (P.O. Silver City)

6. F-52-N, Willow Creek (P.O. Mogollon)

7. G-123-N, Quemado (P.O. Quemado)

Grant County:

8. F-11-N, "Camp Sully," Mimbres (P.O. Mimbres)

9. F-12-N, "Camp Jack Fleming," Redstone (P.O. Silver City)

10. F-15-N/PE-202-N/SCS-14-N, "Camp Little Walnut" and "Camp Whitehill" (P.O. Silver City)

11. SCS-2-N, Redrock (P.O. Redrock)

12. SCS-15-N, Whitewater (P.O. Whitewater)

13. SCS-18-N, Buckhom (P.O. Silver City)

14. SCS-20-N, Mangas Canyon (P.O. Silver City)

15. SES-2-N/SCS-1-N, Gila (P.O. Cliff)

F-1-N, "Camp Beale," Reserve, Catron County

Rank 5 (I-D-1)

The camp's namesake, Edward F. Beale (1822–1893), surveyed a wagon road in the late 1850s from Fort Smith Arkansas across New Mexico to Fort Defiance. The route later was later coopted by the railroad, then US-66, and finally I-40. The CCC camp operated from spring/summer 1933 through the winter to 1934, and then during the winter of 1934–1935.

I visited the site in 2005. Back then what little left of the campsite was a mile west of Reserve on route NM-12. On the north side of the highway I found a few concrete posts, tapering somewhat to the top, maybe 5-feet tall, supporting a thick steel cable. One had the date 1934 sketched into it. Incredibly I neglected to take a photo. Revisiting the site in September 2018 there was nothing left. Lesson: always take a photo.

F-2-N, "Camp Chaffee," Apache Creek, Catron County

Rank 3 (I-B-1)

The name for this camp, "Chaffee," is cited by Kammer (1994), and also by Tom Holland, who was a first lieutenant on active duty with the CCC from 1935 to 1940. (Holland 1991) However, neither specified just who "Chaffee" was. This campsite is located a quarter of a mile south of NM-12 from the little hamlet of Apache Creek, along Tularosa Creek. (*Figure E-2*) (The creek's name can be easily confused with the town of Tularosa in Otero County, southern New Mexico.) F-2-N was one of the first camps, set up in the spring of 1933. A modest but fascinating inventory of concrete and rock structures exist in this informal hunters' campground, as well as on the north side of the gravel road. (*Figure E-3*) Camp Chaffee is an interesting and easy place to visit.

F-25-N, Glenwood Catron County

Rank 4 (I-C-1)

This campsite is now the site of Glenwood's municipal park, about a mile northeast of the town center. (*Figures E-4, E-5, and E-6*) It is one of the first camps set up in the national forests in 1933. The camp had a long occupation history extending for eight winters and three summers, into early 1942. Despite this, little remains today, except the conspicuous grease rack at the north end of the municipal park, a possible water fountain to its southwest, and some kind of concrete trough across the road to the north.

About a mile northeast of the campsite is the home of an independent geologist. When he acquired the property he discovered an unusual building on it. (*Figure E-7*) After some research he learned that it was a CCC building from the camp down the road, possibly a mess hall that had at some time been hauled to his place. Typically, all removable structures from CCC camps were long ago stripped off their foundations and salvaged, so it is difficult to recreate the story behind this one. The owner had/has plans to someday restore the building and convert it into something useful.

F-29-N, "Camp Emmet Crawford," Pueblo Park, Catron County

Rank 5 (I-D-2)

The name "Emmet Crawford" is to commemorate an American captain (1844–1886) in the U.S. Army who was killed by the Apache in Mexico. This remote place is now the site of the Pueblo Park Campground, located 24 miles from its post office in Alma. It operated for only the winter of 1933–1934, so it left little, if any, footprint. Nothing remains today.

F-34-N, Beaverhead, Catron County

Rank 5 (I-D-2)

The location of this campsite is probably near the Beaverhead Ranger Station. (*Figure E-8A*) I poured over the *Google Earth* imagery and found nothing at the station, nor on the flat areas near the station that are on the flood plain of Corduroy Creek and its tributaries. A 1930s vintage photo of the CCC camp shows the tent camp nestled against a low ridge. (*Figure E-8B*) About a half mile southwest of the station *Google Earth* does reveal a very subtle rectilinear pattern on the ground, and although questionable, might be a candidate. The location of this campsite must remain indeterminate. The location of the ranger station is listed in *Appendix V.*

F-52-N, Willow Creek, Catron County

Rank 5 (I-D-3)

This site is something of a mystery. I suspect its first winter (1937–1938) was a learning experience for everyone involved because from then on it was used only as a summer camp. The nearest settlement is Reserve, hardly a metropolis, 49 miles away. I can't imagine a camp of about 200 souls at an elevation of 8,000 feet being supplied by truck from a far-away depot during the winter. Importantly, the camp's post office is recorded as located at Mogollon. This important fact locates the camp somewhere east of Mogollon, because if it had been west of there it would have used a more convenient post office down the hill at Glenwood or Alma. The closest level spot east of Mogollon is at Willow Creek, 11 hard miles away, where two campgrounds, Willow Creek and Ben Lilly, are today.

In short, this campsite is accessible via both a west and a north route. The first is a wonderful winding nine-mile drive from US-180 on the west, over paved NM-159 east up to the old mining town of Mogollon, then followed by an 11-mile, bone-and-spirit-crushing drive up onto the Mogollon Mountains at over 9,000 feet, and then gradually down into the valley of Willow Creek at 8,000 feet. There is virtually nothing there to reward the intrepid driver, except a single, cryptic step-like rock structure a couple of feet tall near the Ben Lilly Campground. Fortunately, the less tortuous escape route (probably the original supply route for the camp) is the 49-mile route north to Reserve via the much-less-trying continuation of NM-159, connecting to NM-435. This site can be skipped.

G-123-N, Quemado, Catron County

Rank 5 (I-D-1)

Several visits to the Gila National Forest Ranger Station in Quemado to locate this site met with little success. *Google Earth* shows no trace of a campsite. A man who visited the camp in 1938 (Holland 1991) described the area thusly: Quemado at that time "consisted of US-60, a narrow two-lane, a dilapidated run-down adobe hotel with outside plumbing on the north side of the road, and a filling station and a cluttered general store on the south side. The CCC camp was a quarter mile or so south of the highway, and like Quemado itself, in the middle of nowhere." Another description, from since-retired ranger Bob Schiowitz in 2003, places the campsite in the open field south of the Quemado post office, somewhat compatible with the first description. Nothing is evident on *Google Earth* and I was unable to find a trace of the site on the ground during several visits. The camp operated from the fall of 1939 to the spring of 1941. Evidently the camp left little footprint.

F-11-N, "Camp Sully," Mimbres, Grant Comity

Rank 5 (III-D-1).

This camp was located at the Three Circle Ranch on the Mimbres River. In August 1933 an order came down to rename three camps, F-1 I -N, F-12-N, and F-15-N to do honor to prominent men who played historic roles in the area. Mimbres, for some reason, was accordingly named "Sully" for John M. Sully (1863–1933), who had formed the Chino Copper Co. in 1909 and who was a well-known figure in the Silver City area. The camp is located in the Gila National Forest. It was one of the first camps set up in 1933 and it operated for the first two periods. From then it was a winter camp from 1934–1935, and then 1937–1938 through 1940–1941. In 1948 a Christian church group leased the land from the Forest Service and constructed Camp Thunderbird, which formally opened in 1950 and is today private property.

F-12-N, "Camp Jack Fleming," Redstone, Pinos Altos, Grant County

Rank 3 (I-B-3)

Despite its number F-12-N, this was the first camp established in the 8th Army Corps area. Like F-11-N (above), in August 1933 the camp was renamed "Jack Fleming," who was one of the owners of the Old Man Mine, discovered in 1882. The little settlement of Fleming, about 11 miles west of Silver City, was named in his honor. The mine was worked until 1888 and dribbled on until 1893, after which it withered away to a ghost town. (Sherman 1975)

Locating this campsite on the ground was a challenge. (*Figure E-9*) While fruitlessly searching for the site a local farmer told me that "some foundations" were in an area called Meadow Creek. Unfortunately, the road to Meadow Creek is not marked and I could not find it. Later, with the help of *Google Earth* I learned that Meadow Creek Road is in fact an unmarked, graveled turnoff 3.2 miles north of Cherry Creek Campground on NM-15. Following Meadow Creek Road for 3.7 miles east and then north takes one to a group of concrete foundations. These remnants are what is left of the campsite.

Because this CCC camp was in the vanguard of the CCC movement, setting it up had an element of "winging it." According to the new commanding officer, "There will be several permanent buildings, constructed at Redstone. They will be the mess hall and storerooms. The men will live in hospital ward tents with 24 to each tent. Hot and cold running water will be provided. This is largely experimental and exact details are not definitely known. These will be worked out, however, as the men become settled." (Holland 1991) Sounds quite comfortable, but being an early tent camp, built on uneven terrain, it may have been less than that. (*Figure E-10*)

F-15-N/PE-202-N/SCS-14-N, "Little Walnut," later "Camp Whitehill," Grant County

Rank 5 (I-D-I)

The camp was established in May 1933 as Camp Little Walnut, F-15-N, about six miles north of Silver City on Little Walnut Road. (*Figure E-11*) It was at first a tent camp. As at F-11-N and F-12-N above, in August 1933 the camp was renamed, this time to "Whitehill." In the summer of 1934 it operated as camp PE-202-N (Park Erosion Service). There was a hiatus until 1935 when the camp was given the new designation of SCS-14-N, with an expanded mission and winterized with permanent buildings. Today the campsite occupies the Little Walnut Group Picnic Area and is fully accessible. However, nothing remains of the camp itself, although much of the CCC's work is evident. The mess hall, looking to the southwest to the conical Gomez Peak, today is a wide spot in the access road into the picnic ground. (*Figure E-12*) A superb photo of the CCC company is displayed on a sign at the group site.

Although emphasis of this book is on the physical campsites and their locations, an additional word about this camp's work is appropriate. Their mission was to restore the watershed that drains southward into the city of Silver City from the Gila National Forest. Old timers remembered the year 1895 as that of the "big flood" that ravaged the town, and they never forgot. Intensive erosion on the heels of overgrazing and the resultant ponding of flood-waters in the watershed led to the disaster. No one wanted to ever experience that again. The Little Walnut CCC company set to work to construct the appropriate structures to stem the flow of water down the drainage. The boys of Little Walnut were the saviors of Silver City. (Holland 1991)

SCS-2-N, Redrock, Grant County

Rank 5 (Ill-C-2)

The camp operated on the south side of the Gila River. When I visited the site in 2003, the property owner, Mrs. Cabral, showed what she called the "transient" camp on her land. There was nothing to see, despite its rather long occupation.

SCS-15-N, Whitewater, Grant County

Rank 1 (I-A-2)

This relatively well-preserved and extremely interesting campsite is located three miles due south of the Silver City/Grant County Airport, on the east side of a gravel road, on a little raised hill 0.3 miles north of the railroad. (*Figure E-13*) It seems to be on private land, but is not posted and discretion is called for. The camp's post office was at the now abandoned railroad station of Whitewater. It had a rather long, year-round occupation from 1935 until its abandonment in the latter part of 1939. This is a fascinating place, with much to see and explore. (*Figure E-14*)

SCS-18-N, Buckhorn, Grant County

Rank 5 (III-C-1)

The campsite of SCS-18-N is located on private property just off and to the east of US-180, about 2.5 miles northwest of the tiny community of Buckhorn. It is nestled between the modern US-180 on the west and the old, abandoned concrete highway on the east. Only a root cellar and a concrete foundation are visible north from highway US-180. (*Figure E-15*)

SCS-20-N, Mangas, Grant County

Rank 1 (I-A-2)

This quite interesting and easy-to-get-to site is only a little off the beaten track, about 1.6 miles east of US-180 on the graveled Sacaton Road with a couple of gentle drainage crossings, on the south side of the road. (*Figure E-16*) It had a long occupation, from spring/summer 1935 into early 1941. There are some intriguing features, including a concrete stairway structure and adjoining shaft of unknown use, plus some concrete platforms and walkways.

SES-2-N/SCS-1-N, Gila, Grant County

Rank 5 (III-C-1)

This camp was tasked to work along the Gila River for the Soil Erosion Service. In 1935 the agency became the Soil Conservation Service (SCS), so that year the camp was duly renamed SCS-1-N and it operated until 1937. The site was, and is, located on private land on the southeast side of NM-153, two miles northeast of the little town of Gila and about 4.5 miles from the equally little town of Cliff. Only a part of one concrete foundation is visible from the road.

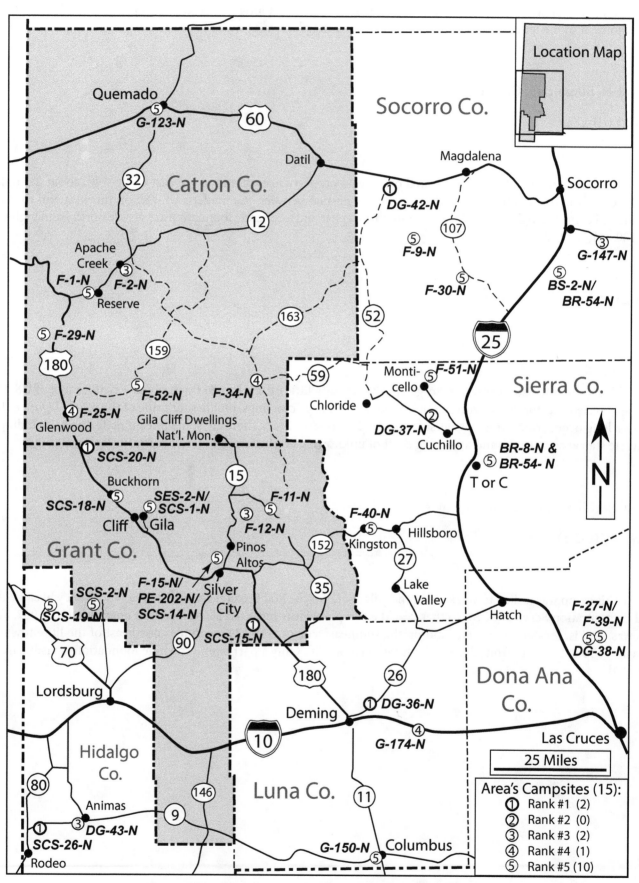

Figure E-1. AREA E / Catron and Grant Counties.

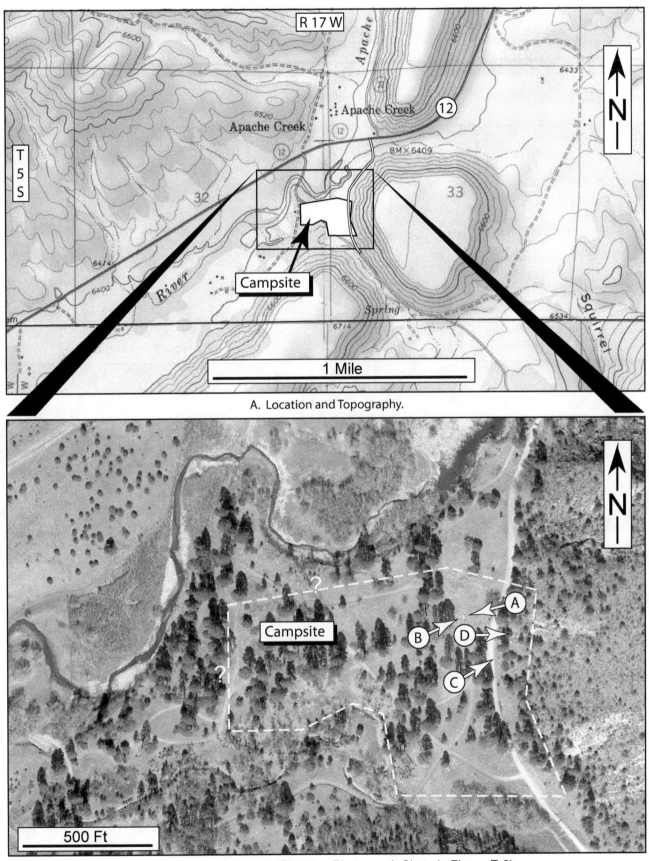

A. Location and Topography.

B. *Google Earth* Image (Showing Photograph Shots in Figure E-3).

Figure E-2. Camp F-2-N, Apache Creek I.

A. Campground and CCC Structures, 2005
(Photograph by Author).

B. Probable Remains of Mess Hall, 2018
(Photograph by Author).

C. The Ubiquitous Incinerator, 2018
(Photograph by Author).

D. Typical Fancy CCC Masonry Work, 2005
(Photograph by Author).

Figure E-3. Camp F-2-N, Apache Creek II.

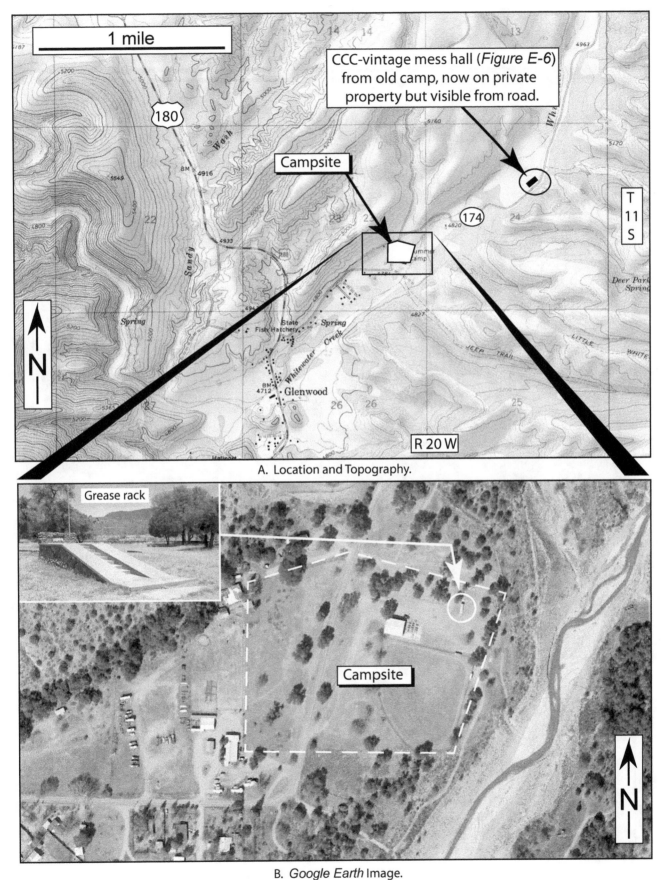

1 mile

CCC-vintage mess hall (*Figure E-6*) from old camp, now on private property but visible from road.

Campsite

N

A. Location and Topography.

Grease rack

Campsite

N

B. *Google Earth* Image.

Figure E-4. Camp F-25-N Glenwood I.

A. Southeast View of Camp, 1930s (Photograph from Internet).

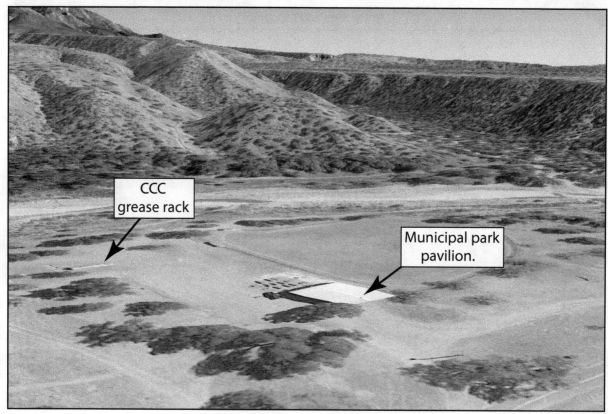

B. Southeast Oblique *Google Earth* Image.

Figure E-5. Camp F-25-N, Glenwood II.

A. CCC Company Portrait with Mogollon Mountains in Background , 1934
(Photograph by A. Newman).

B. Inset of Photograph in A Above (Showing Standardized Nature of Frame-Building Construction).

Figure E-6. Camp F-25-N, Glenwood III.

Figure E-7. Camp F-25-N, Glenwood IV, CCC-Vintage Possible Mess Hall, 2005
(Now on Private Property, Photograph by Author).

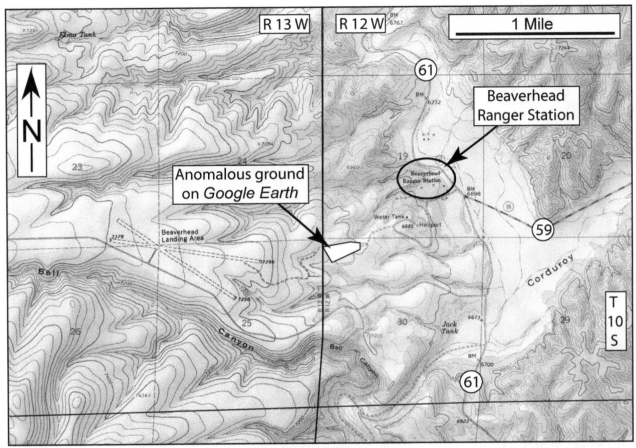

A. Location and Topography.

B. Summer Tent Camp, 1930s (U.S. Forest Service, Photograph #290235).

Figure E-8. Camp F-34-N, Beaverhead.

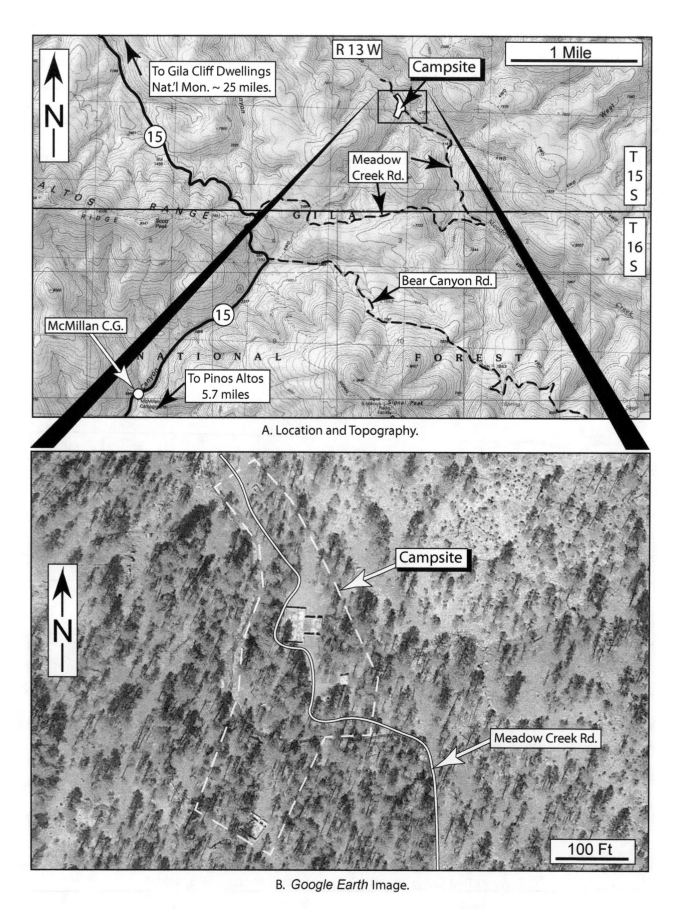

A. Location and Topography.

B. *Google Earth* Image.

Figure E-9. Camp F-12-N, Redstone/Jack Fleming I.

Figure E-10. Camp F-12-N, Redstone/Jack Fleming II
(a Crowded Early Tent Camp, Photograph #279898 from National Archives).

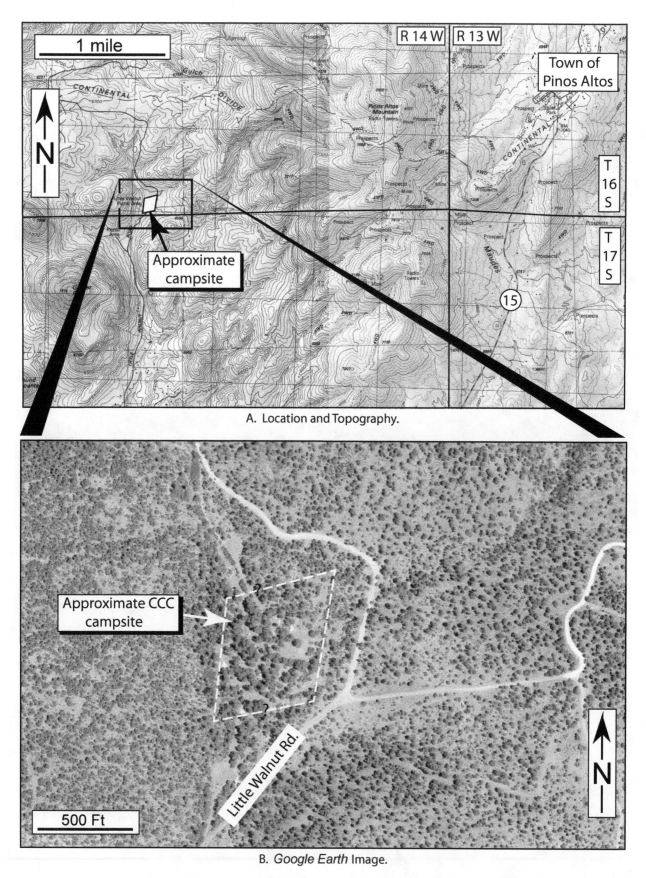

A. Location and Topography.

B. *Google Earth* Image.

Figure E-11. Camp F-15-N/PE-202-N/SCS-14-N, Little Walnut/Whitehill I.

A. Mess Hall with Gomez Peak in Background, 1936
(Photograph from *CCC Legacy* Website: Archives New Mexico/Lloyd Warford Collection).

B. Interior of Mess Hall, 1936
(Photograph from *CCC Legacy* Website: Archives New Mexico/Lloyd Warford Collection).

Figure E-12. Camp F-15-N/PE-202-N/SCS-14-N, Little Walnut/Whitehill II.

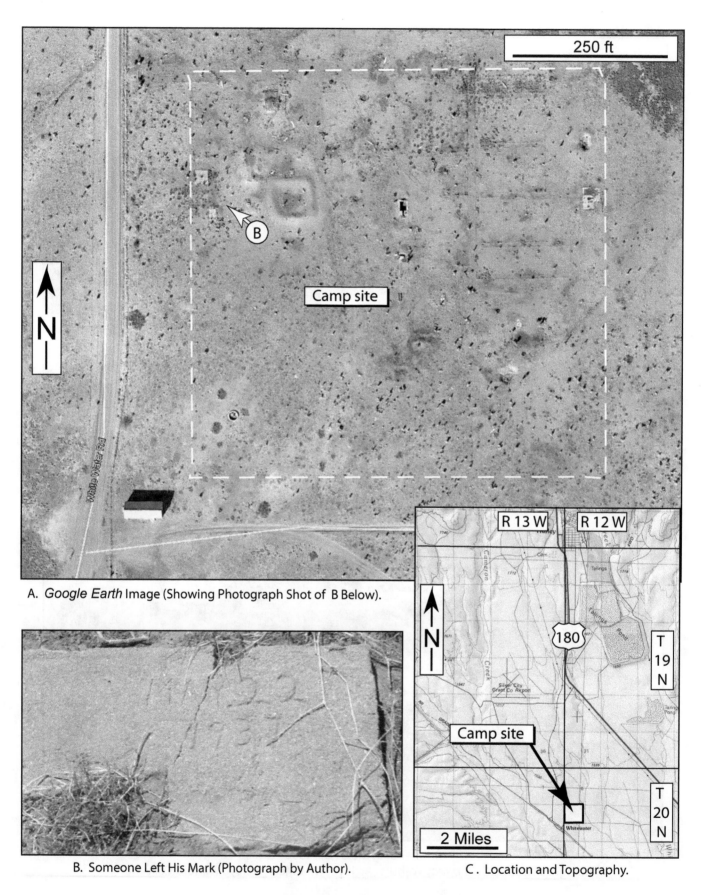

A. *Google Earth* Image (Showing Photograph Shot of B Below).

B. Someone Left His Mark (Photograph by Author).

C. Location and Topography.

Figure E-13. Camp SCS-15-N, Whitewater I.

A. Northwest View of Entry Gate.

B. Tell-Tale Walking-Path Perimeter Stones.

C. What's This?

D. Incinerator.

E. Some Sort of Water Fountain.

F. Root Cellar.

Figure E-14. Camp SCS-15-N, Whitewater II (Photographs by Author, 2014).

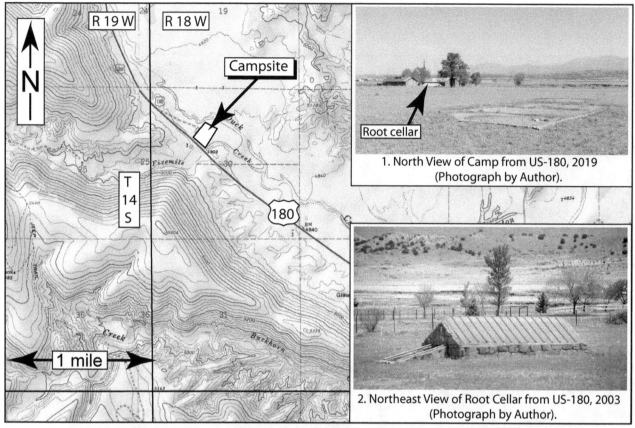

Root cellar

1. North View of Camp from US-180, 2019
(Photograph by Author).

2. Northeast View of Root Cellar from US-180, 2003
(Photograph by Author).

A. Location and Topography.

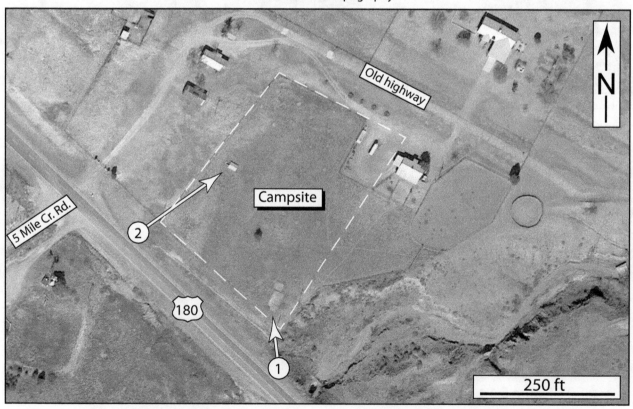

B. *Google Earth* Image (Showing General Campsite Area and Photograph Shots of Insets in A Above).

Figure E-15. Camp SCS-18-N, Buckhorn.

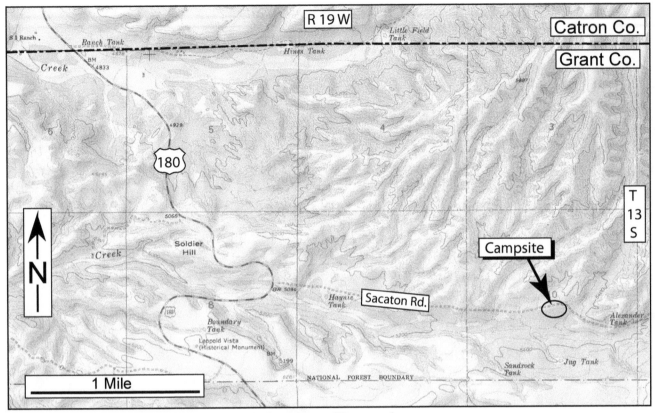

A. Location and Topography.

B. Site Was Obviously Built to Last a While, 2018
(Photograph by Author.)

C. Possible Root Celler Entrance, 2005
(Photograph by Author).

Figure E-16. Camp SCS-20-N, Mangas Canyon.

AREA F

The Bootheal of New Mexico: Hidalgo and Luna Counties
(*Figure F-1*)

Six sites are contained in this large two-county area.

Hidalgo County:

    1. DG-43-N, Animas (P.O. Animas)

    2. SCS-19-N, "Camp Mesquitita," Virden (P.O. Duncan, Arizona)

    3. SCS-26-N, Rodeo (P.O. Rodeo)

Luna County:

    4. DG-36-N, "Camp Mirage," Mirage (P.O. Deming)

    5. G-150-N, Columbus (P.O. Columbus)

    6. G-174-N, Cambray (P.O. Cambray)

DG-43-N, Animas, Hidalgo County

Rank 4 (I-C-1)

Locating this site was a problem. (*Figure F-2*) During the search, an amiable woman I spoke to at the Valley Telecom office in Animas insisted that the campsite was located several miles west of Animas on NM-9. We visited that area, about five miles west, where we found two suspicious sites on opposite sides of NM-9. The first of the two is on the south side of NM-9 at mile 8.5, Clay Mine Road (CO-52). A large concrete foundation of unknown function sits just to the southeast of the intersection. But the feature was alone and may have had something to do with the old railroad grade just to the south.

The second site is on the north side of NM-9 at mile 8.6 where it intersects with Washburn Road. (CO-79). The site has an obviously man-made pile of gigantic hunks of basalt rock. This is where the woman-in-the-know told us to look. About 250 feet east of Washburn, south of the building that looks like a one-story triplex apartment, are four short (about 2-feet tall) concrete rectangular columns of unknown function, in a row. The area is heavily littered with old metal cans—unlike most CCC campsites. The area did not seem right. Oddly, 1/4 mile north of NM-9 at this intersection is a very odd array of white, one-story buildings, each with some sort of wooden roof-support structures jutting off to the west. This is *Dark Sky*, a natural-light (versus radio, like the VLA west of Socorro) observatory. The roofs of the buildings slide off onto the supporting frames to expose the telescopes inside. This is one of the rare, perfectly dark places in the country–perfect for an observatory. But it is not a CCC site.

A vital clue is that the mountain profile evident in a west-northwest oblique *Google Earth* image at this site does not match up with an oblique 1930s photo of the camp that I have. (*Figure F-3A*) It is too close to the mountains, i.e., too far west. A second oblique *Google Earth* image, though, looking west-northwest from a location near the center of Animas just west of NM-338, does indeed match up perfectly. (*Figure F-3B*) I tentatively identify the second site as the correct one (with apologies to the nice woman at Valley Telecom).

SCS-19-N, "Camp Mesquitita," Virden, Hidalgo County

Rank 5 (Ill-C-2).

"Little Mesquite" is located 1/4 mile east of NM-92, on the south side of the Gila River. This is the site of the private Dixon Ranch, built directly on top of the campsite. (*Figures F-3* and *F-5*) The Dixon family took my wife and me on a cook's tour of what's left of the campsite and availed us of vintage photos. Two original CCC buildings survive and are used by the Dixons today. The base of a possible grease rack rounds out the sparse surviving inventory of this camp. The family has owned the ranch since the early 1940s, which is about the time the CCC moved out of the area.

SCS-26-N, Rodeo, Hidalgo County

Rank 1a (I-A-1)

The Rodeo campsite is one of the best preserved and easiest to visit. It is located just south of NM-9, 1.2 miles east of the intersection with NM-80. (*Figures F-2A* and *F-6*) The campsite occupies about eight acres between NM-9 and an electrical power station to the south. The site is fenced, on State Land, and not posted.

The site hosts a wealth of CCC structures, including a grease rack, incinerator pit, several concrete foundations, possible fuel-tank supports, an array of four concrete blocks that possible supported a water tower, and numerous path-perimeter stones that mark connecting paths. (*Figure F-7*) It's a fun challenge to mentally assemble everything into a functional camp.

DG-36-N, Mirage, Luna County

Rank 1b (I-A-2)

This is another nicely-preserved campsite, right off the well-traveled NM-26 (the road that connects Deming with Hatch), at mile 7.1 and immediately north of the old railroad siding of Mirage. (*Figure F-8*) The triangular, approximately five-acre site is apparently State Land, fenced, and not posted. I had originally ranked this site as a

I-A-1, but after visiting the site the third time in September 2018, downgraded it to an I-A-2. The reason was the well-maintained, very tight barbed-wire fence separating the site from the highway. I fortunately have a small gut and—ever so carefully—was able to thread between the strands. That situation is definitely a deterrent. A large fireplace lies just north of the fence, along with a large foundation. About 500 feet northwest of the fence is another foundation, a fine grease rack, and next to the grease rack five vertical structures that likely supported a large garage. (*Figure F-9*)

G-150-N, COLUMBUS, LUNA COUNTY

RANK 5 (I-D-1)

The CCC campsite in Columbus is now covered over by Pancho Villa State Park. It has two layers of history that are difficult to unravel: 1) the US Army's Camp Furlong of 1916 to the early 1920s, and 2) the CCC camp of 1939–1942. Camp Furlong, so named because it seemed to be only about a furlong (1/8 mile or 660 feet) north of the Mexico border. Actually it was about three miles north. (*Figures F-10, F-11* and *F-l2*) The camp was constructed by the army under the command of General John "Blackjack" Pershing in response to Pancho Villas' raid on Columbus in March 1916. Its site was largely determined by the conveniently adjacent El Paso and Southwestern RR (EP&SW). Very soon after the raid, Camp Furlong became a base and supply camp for the 1916–1917 punitive expedition into Mexico. This was the first "modern" military expedition, based primarily on motor vehicles rather than exclusively on horses. The camp housed about 5,000 men, first the New Mexico National Guard, and later by some regular units, and supported a large fleet of trucks with their supply and repair facilities.

Today the area is known as the Camp Furlong National Historical Landmark District. Structures remaining from Camp Furlong times are the 1902 Customs House (just east of the Visitor Center for the Pancho Villa State Park, *Figure F-11A*), a pair of adobe structures, a large grease rack probably re-used by the CCC (*Figure F-12A*), and the Camp Furlong Recreation Hall built in 1916. (*Figure F-12B*) The recreation hall was also reused by the CCC, and then restored in the 1980s.

The CCC established its camp G-150-N at the site in October 1939. The EP&SW was still operational (although hurting since the drop in copper prices after WWI), and that may have been a factor in locating the camp here. No recognizable CCC structures can be found at the site. The excellent Visitor Center tells the story of Camp Furlong, but nothing about the CCC. Furthermore, State Park personnel seem to know little of the CCC presence here. Despite this lack of input, it still remains a fascinating place.

G-174-N, CAMBRAY, LUNA COUNTY

RANK 4 (I-C-2)

This easy-to-reach site is a wedge-shaped parcel sandwiched between NM-549 and the Union Pacific railroad tracks. (*Figure F-13* and *F-14A*) It was originally built along the main drag of US-80, an interstate highway between the east and west coasts. It was just west of the little town of Cambray, which served as a watering stop for the Union Pacific Railroad. Only a nicely-preserved grease rack sticks up in the middle of the campsite. (*Figure F-14B*) A small ranch is located just to the west of the site, with what appears to be the ruin of an old store. The town's fate was sealed when Interstate I-10 bypassed it in the early 1960s. (Julyan 1996)

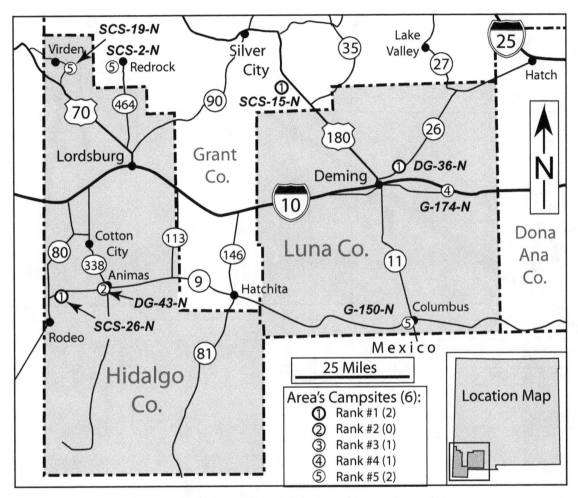

Figure F-1. AREA F / Hidalgo and Luna Counties.

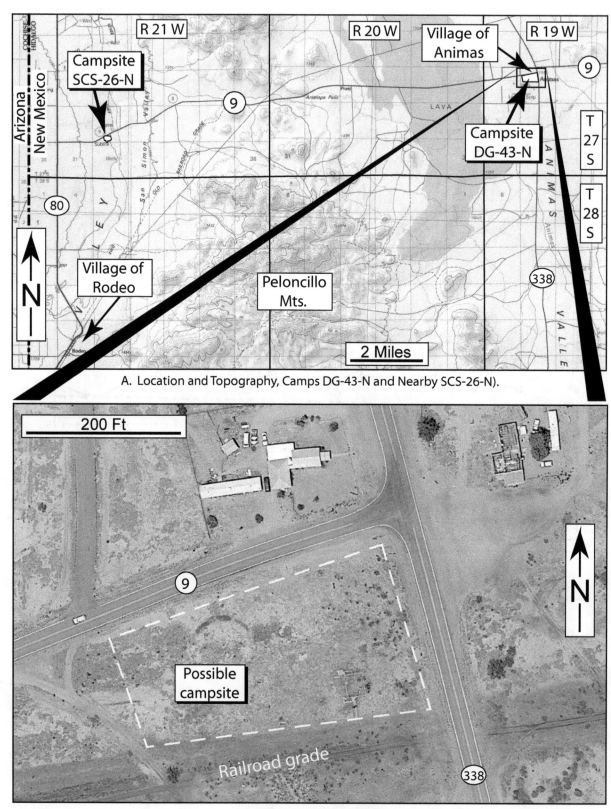

A. Location and Topography, Camps DG-43-N and Nearby SCS-26-N).

B. *Google Earth* Image.

Figure F-2. Camp DG-43-N, Animas I.

A. West-Northwest View of Camp, 1930s (with Faint, but Diagnostic Mountain Profile in Distance, Photograph from Nolte, 1990).

B. West-Northwest Oblique *Google Earth* Image (from just West of Village of Animas).

Figure F-3. Camp DG-43-N, Animas II.

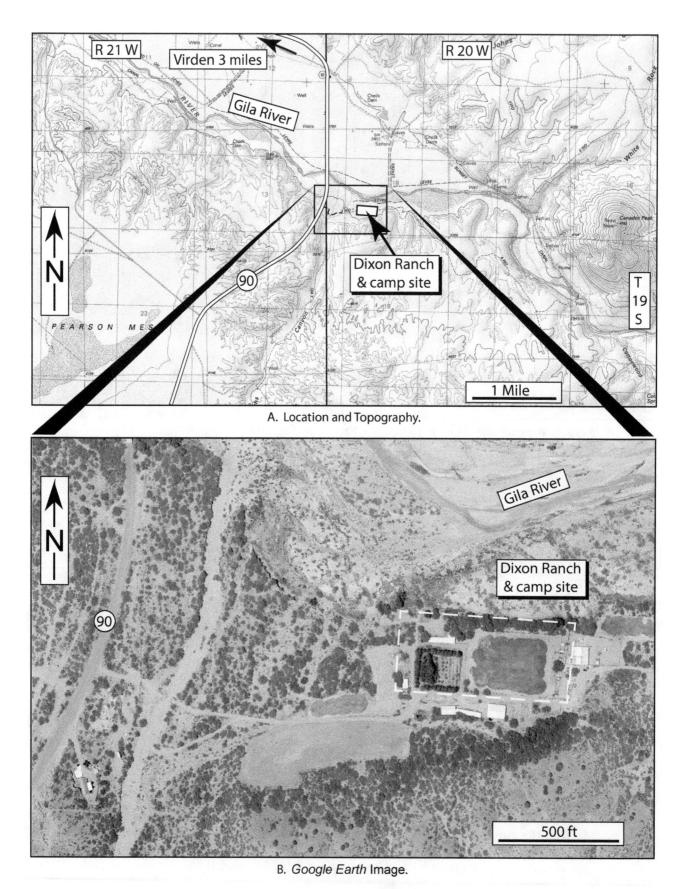

A. Location and Topography.

B. *Google Earth* Image.

Figure F-4. Camp SCS-19-N, Virden I.

A. West View, 1935 (Photograph from Dixon, 2018).

B. West Oblique *Google Earth* image.

Figure F-5. Camp SCS-19-N, Virden II.

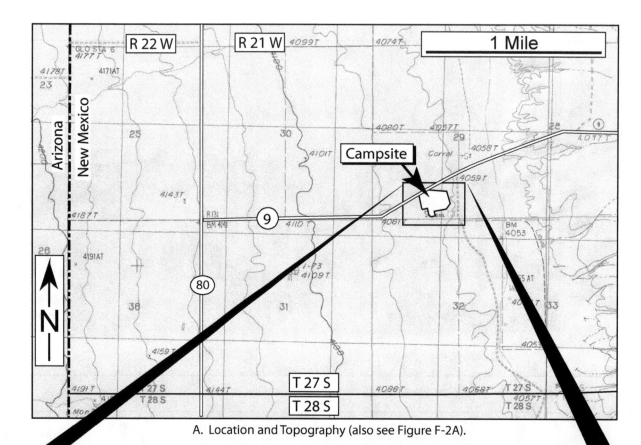

A. Location and Topography (also see Figure F-2A).

B. *Google Earth* Image (Showing Campsite Outline and Photograph Shots in Figure F-7).

Figure F-6. Camp SCS-26-N, Rodeo I.

A. Southeast View of Unknown Structure, 2003 (Photograph by Author).

B. West View of Large Concrete Slab and Grease Rack, 2003 (Photograph by Author).

C. South View of Grease Rack, 2003 (Photograph by Author).

D. West-Northwest View of Cryptic Structure, 2003 (Photograph by Author).

E. Northwest View of Incinerator, 2003 (Photograph by Author).

F. South-Southeast View of Walking-Path Perimeter Stones, 2003 (Photograph by Author).

Figure F-7. Camp SCS-26-N, Rodeo II.

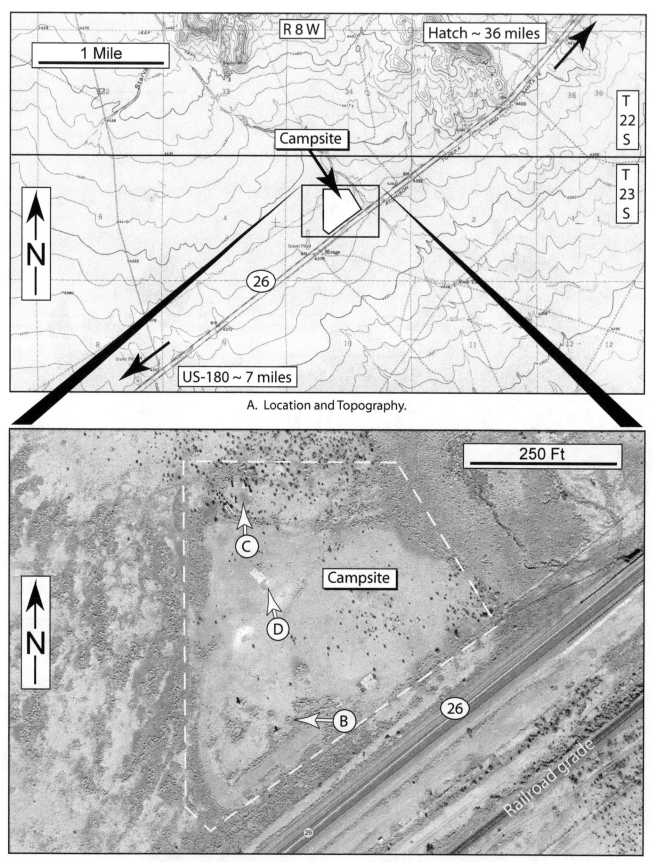

A. Location and Topography.

B. *Google Earth* Image (Showing Photograph Shots in Figure F-9).

Figure F-8. Camp DG-36-N, Mirage I.

A. Northeast View, ca. 1935 (Photograph from Luna County Museum Archives).

B. Northwest View of Masonry Structures, 2003
(Photograph by Author).

C. North View of Truck Garage, 2003
(Photograph by Author).

D. North View of Large Foundation, with Grease Rack and Truck Garage in Distance, 2003 (Photograph by Author).

Figure F-9. Camp DG-36-N, Mirage II.

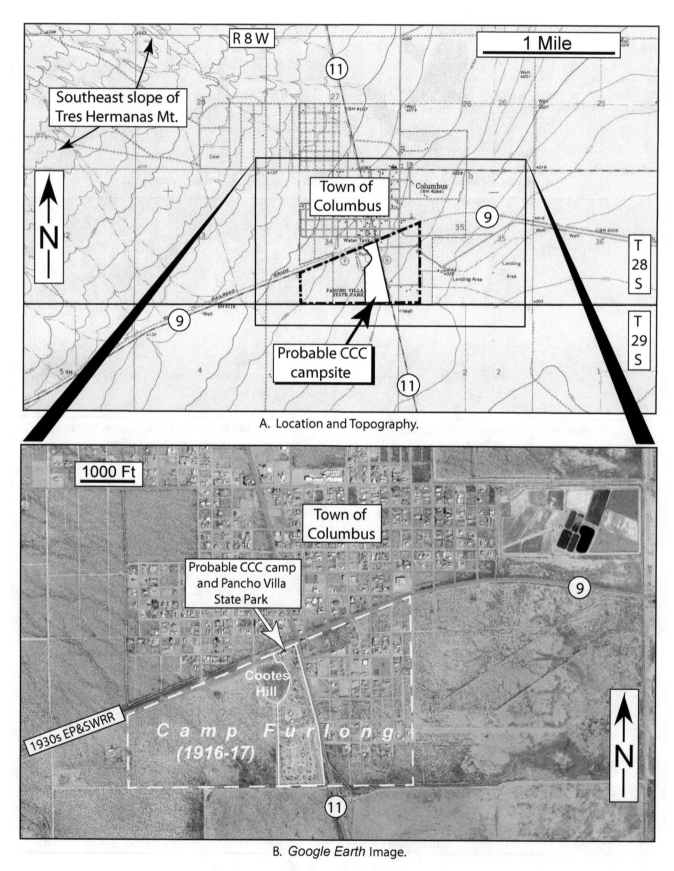

A. Location and Topography.

B. *Google Earth* Image.

Figure F-10. Camp G-150-N, Columbus I.

Cootes Hill

A. Southwest View over 1902 Customs House (Center Foreground) and U.S. Army Camp Furlong, 1916-1917.
(CCC camp G-150-N Later Occupied Area Between Customs house and Cootes Hill, South to the Left.)

B. North View of West Side of U.S. Army Camp Furlong, 1916-1917
(Photograph is of Area in Background of A Above).

Figure F-11. Camp G-150-N, Columbus II.
(Photographs from website: *demingnewmexico.genealogyvillage.com*)

A. Southwest View of Army Grease Rack, 2017 (Probably Later Used by CCC, Photograph by Author).

B. Southwest View of 1916 Fort Furlong Recreation Hall, 2017 (Later Used by CCC, Photograph by Author).

Figure F-12. Camp G-150-N, Columbus III.

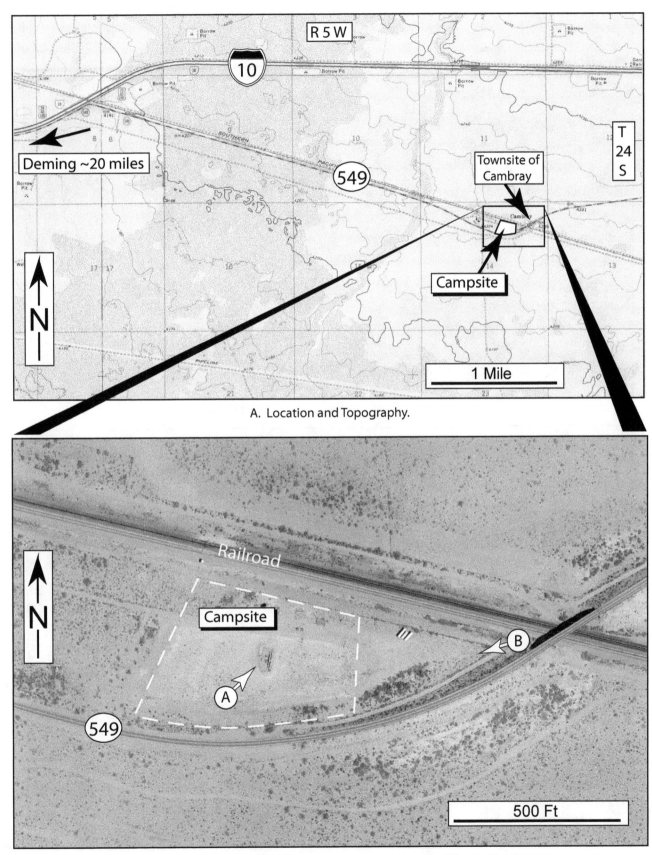

A. Location and Topography.

B. *Google Earth* Image (Showing Photograph Shots in Figure F-14).

Figure F-13. Camp G-174-N, Cambray I.

A. West View of Campsite Area, 2003 (Photograph by Author).

B. Northeast View of Lonely Grease Rack, 2003 (Photograph by Author).

Figure F-14. Camp G-174-N, Cambray II.

AREA G

Central-South New Mexico: Socorro County

(Figure G-l)

The county hosts six CCC campsites:

1. BS-2-N/FWS-2-N, Bosque del Apache (P.O. San Antonio)

2. DG-42-N/SCS-25-N/F-57-N, "Camp Augustin" (P.O. Magdalena)

3. F-9-N, "Camp Monica," Bear Trap Canyon (P.O. Magdalena)

4. F-30-N, "Camp 76" Ranch (P.O. Magdalena)

5. G-147-N/G(D)-2-N, Tokay (P.O. San Antonio)

6. SP-2-N, La Joya State Park (P.O. Socorro)

BS-2-N/FWS-2-N, Bosque del Apache National Wildlife Refuge (NWR), Socorro County

Rank 5 (III-D-1)

This camp was at the north edge of the Bosque del Apache National Wildlife Refuge. In 1940 the Biological Survey (BS) moved from the Department of Agriculture to the Department of Interior and combined with the new Fish and Wildlife Service (FWS). Its location is described as 250 feet south of the northern Refuge line, 250 feet west of highway NM-I (Bosque del Apache NWR, 2018), and hugs the western edge of the Rio Grande flood plain. (*Figure G-2*) Not a trace remains today.

DG-42-N/SCS-25-N/F-57-N, "Camp Augustin," Magdalena, Socorro County

Rank 1 (I-A-2)

This is one of the most interesting and intriguing campsites. It's easy to visit, and is almost right next to a premier tourist attraction—the Very Large Array, or VLA. (*Figure G-3*) DG-42-N had its post office at Magdalena, and confusedly sometimes went by that name. The site is located on the old alignment of US-60, 2.5 miles south of the modern one via NM-52, and then 0.6 miles east on the old highway to an old windmill and a cluster of scraggly trees that do not seem to belong there. DG-42-N was the camp's name for spring/summer 1935 to summer 1939, SCS-25-N for fall 1939 to spring 1941, and F-57-N for winter 1941–1942.

In 2003 I visited the site with a pair of ex-CCC boys, Keith Creveling (1922–2017) and James Langley (1913–2007). James had worked at this camp and was here for his first time in 64 years. (*Figure G-4*) He and his crew had planted those trees. The effect of being at this place "out of the past" right next to an enormous, moveable VLA radio telescope is, stunning. (*Figures G-4A* and *4B*) A stroll over the remains, armed with old photographs of the camp, provided an experience like that of a time machine.

F-9-N, "Camp Monica," Bear Trap Canyon, Socorro County

Rank 5 (I-D-3)

The camp was nicknamed "Monica" (from a topographic divide called "Monica Saddle"), and was located in Bear Trap Canyon in the San Mateo Mountains southwest of Magdalena. This was one of the earliest camps, and operated for only Period 1 (spring/summer 1933). It was probably a tent camp, set up in an area with little level ground. Probably for these reasons, in November 1933 the company of men packed up and moved to a new location that was designated F-30-N (see below). Nothing remains.

F-30-N, "Camp New Monica," Old 76 or Woofter Ranch, Socorro County

Rank 5 (III-D-3)

In November 1933 the company from camp F-9-N moved to this new location, designated F-30-N, at the headquarters of the "Old 76 Ranch," a.k.a. the "Woofter Ranch." (Churches, undated.) Confusingly, an oral history of an ex-CCC boy who worked there, Ernest Portwood, described this camp as the "San Marcial" camp, probably because that flooded-out town was the nearest named place. (J.F. Justin CCC Museum website) In another oral history, Paul Woofter described his ranch as being 52 to 53 [driving] miles from Socorro, which puts it at the foot of the San Mateo Mountains, just east and outside of the Gila National Forest. (Soccoro County Historical Society ca. 1993) The camp operated at that location for only one early period (#2), but *Google Earth* shows a suspicious group of foundations, 1/2 mile west of the Woofter Ranch house, and that is tentatively concluded to be the campsite.

G-147-N/G(D)-2-N, Tokay, Socorro County

Rank 3 (II-A-2)

The CCC camp was located to the east of the old coal-mining town of Tokay, established in 1915. For the first few years Tokay had no formal name. The Post Office Department insisted that whatever name was chosen could not conflict with existing ones. A mining engineer, who had organized the district, looked at a case of Tokay grapes on the store counter and suggested the name Tokay. (Julyan 1996; Hook 2015) The postal inspector agreed and so it came to be. Coal mining ceased in 1940, and the town's frame buildings were moved to Socorro.

The CCC campsite is now on the Fite Ranch. (*Figures G-5* and *G-6*) The ranch is located 1.8 miles south of US-380 on Fite Ranch Road. The Fites sold the ranch in 2002 to Dewey and Linda Brown, who now operate the ranch, plus a delightful B&B just northwest of their ranch house. The CCC campsite is easily accessible from the B&B, 0.4 miles southeast of the ranch house. The campsite is on ranch property, so permission should be sought at the house. There are concrete foundations on either side of the road at the site. On the west side, 300 feet from the road, are four concrete supports for a water tower and the remains of a water well. Well worth a visit, and a stay.

SP-2-N, La Joya, Socorro County

Location unknown; Rank 5 (III-1)-1).

This, the site of the second New Mexico state park after Hyde Park north of Santa Fe, operated for just a short time, Period 2, on land owned by the State Game and Fish Department. (Kammer 1994) It was tasked with constructing a migratory game bird sanctuary and manned by a company of homesick boys from Wyoming. (Richardson 1966) The CCC made many improvements to the drainage infrastructure. However, I have been unable to find a trace of this campsite along the Rio Grande flood plain.

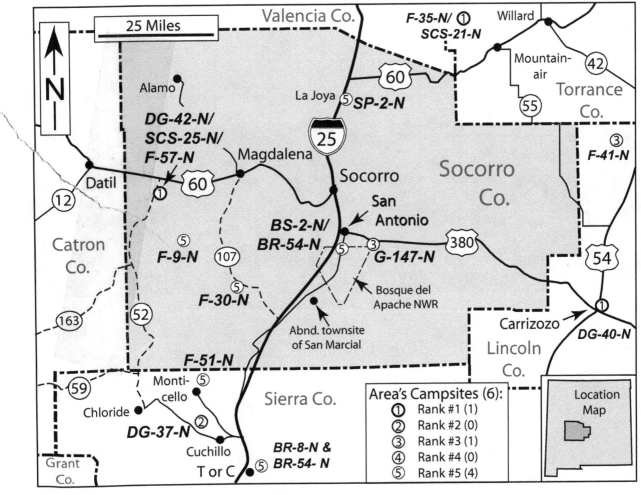

Figure G-1. AREA G / Socorro County.

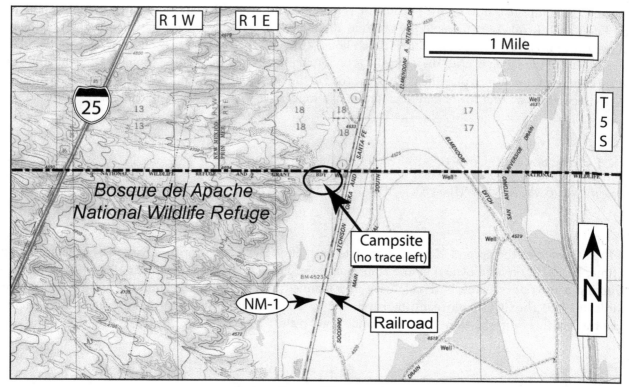

A. Location and Topography.

B. Northeast View, Late 1930s (Photograph from Bosque del Apache National Wildlife Refuge).

Figure G-2. Camp BS-2-N/FWS-2-N, Bosque del Apache.

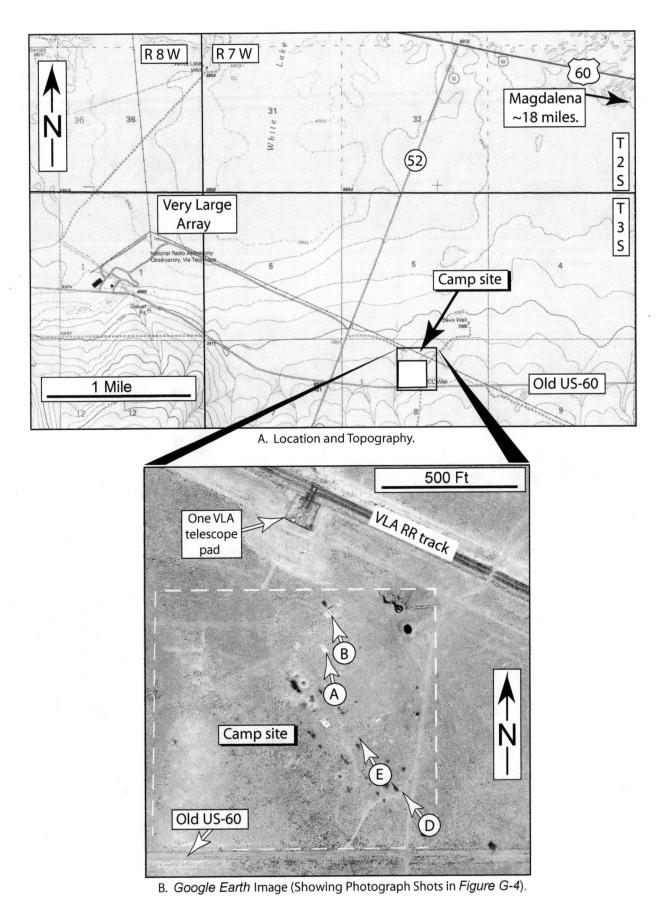

A. Location and Topography.

B. *Google Earth* Image (Showing Photograph Shots in *Figure G-4*).

Figure G-3. Camp DG-42-N/SCS-25-N/F-57-N, Augustin Plains I.

A. North View of Large Concrete Slab, 2003
(Photograph by Author)

B. North View of Grease Rack, 2003
(Photograph by Author)

C. North View of Camp Windmill, Late 1930s.
(Photograph from Author's Collection).

D. North View of Camp Windmill, 2003
(Photograph by Author).

E. North-Northwest View of Camp from Windmill, Late 1930s
(Photograph from Author's Collection)

F. CCC-Boy James Langley, Late 1930s.
(Photograph from Author's Collection).

Figure G-4. Camp DG-42-N/SCS-25-N/F-57-N, Augustin Plains II.

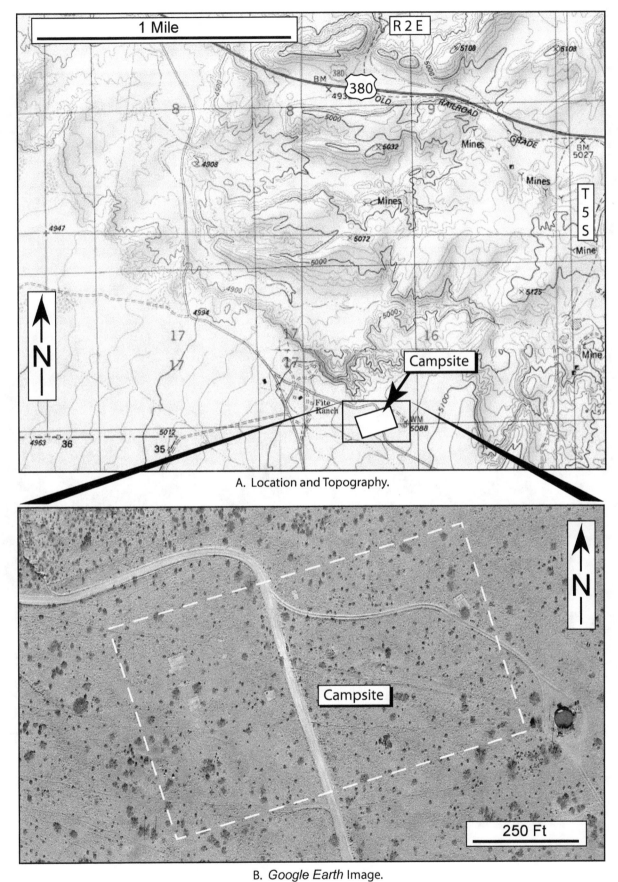

A. Location and Topography.

B. *Google Earth* Image.

Figure G-5. Camp G-147-N/G(D)-2-N, Tokay I.

A. CCC Company Portrait, 1939. (Note Water Well/Windmill in Background--Remains of Which Exist Today Photograph from A. Newman).

B. One Can Only Wonder What Became of These "Boys," Who Would Become the "Greatest Generation."

Figure G-6. Camp G-147-N, Tokay II.

AREA H
Southern Rio Grande Valley: Sierra and Doña Ana Counties
(Figure H-1)

These two counties host nine CCC campsites:

Sierra County:

    1. BR-8-N, Elephant Butte Dam (P.O. Hot Springs)

    2. BR-54-N, Elephant Butte Dam (P.O. Hot Springs)

    3. DG-37-N/G-37-N, Cuchillo (P.O. Hot Springs)

    4. F-40-N/SCS-22-N, Kingston (P.O. Kingston)

    5. F-51-N, Montecello (P.O. Montecello)

Doña Ana County:

    6. BR-39-N, Las Cruces (P.O. Las Cruces)

    7. DG-38-N, Jornada del Muerto (P.O. Mesilla Park; Radium Springs)

    8. F-27-N/F-39-N, Jornada Experimental Range (P.O. Las Cruces)

    9. SCS-16-N/G-178-N, Alameda, Las Cruces (P.O. Las Cruces)

BR-8-N, Elephant Butte Dam, Sierra County

Rank 5 (I-D-1)

There were four CCC camps assigned to the Bureau of Reclamation's Rio Grande Project of New Mexico and Texas: BR-4-T, BR-8-N, BR-39-N, and BR-54-N. Two of them, 8 and 54, were located at Elephant Butte Dam, the headquarters for the storage division of the project. (*Figure H-2*) The CCC focused on improving facilities for the operation, maintenance, and administration of the dam and reservoir, and on providing enhancement to the recreation facilities. Because the construction of the dam was primarily for irrigation storage, enhancement of recreation facilities was far down on the list of priorities. (Pfaff 2010)

Camp BR-8-N was built in 1934, and was operated cooperatively with the National Park Service, State Parks, and CCC. Because some buildings already existed at Elephant Butte Dam, fewer new ones had to be constructed. When the Bureau of Reclamation built the dam in 1910–1911, they constructed a permanent government headquarters one mile east of the dam. The headquarters included 14 residences, a two-story hotel building, an office building, mess hall, testing laboratory, and hospital. These buildings provided an economic and convenient locale for the CCC camp. The hospital was converted to apartments. The office building was initially used as a concession building and then converted to a modern 18-room hotel. The old hotel was used as the company headquarters, recreation hall, and much more. Electricity, water and sewerage were already in place. Therefore, very little new construction was needed. It included a bath house, latrine, mess-hall extension, and group of barracks. Because of the money thus saved it was possible to construct 21 cabin-type barracks to accommodate six CCC enrollees each, and only two of the usual four or five 50-men barracks. (*Figure H-3*) This was done in anticipation of relocating the cabin-barracks along the lake shore for use as tourist cabins at the termination of the CCC program. (Pfaff 2010)

The CCC did a significant amount of stone work around their camp. Due to the uneven terrain they terraced the landscape with carefully placed rock that remains today and gives the area a decidedly "crafty" look. (*Figure H-4*)

BR-54-N, Elephant Butte Dam, Sierra County

Rank 5 (III-C-1)

The second camp, BR-54-N, was built in 1935 on land under the jurisdiction of the BR and only about 1/4 miles southwest of BR-8-N. (*Figure H-3C*) The BR commissioner had no objection to a second camp as long as it did not preclude the establishment of a camp at Las Cruces (BR-39-N), which had already been requested. Buildings at the camp were all wood frame and for the most part of "rigid" construction. (Pfaff 2010)

By 1939 it was no longer deemed necessary to have the two camps in place, and BR-8-N was approved for termination during spring/summer 1939. BR-54-N remained active until May 1941 when it was closed. Prior to the closure of BR-8-N in August 1939, permission was requested to allow the Army to salvage the camp buildings for CCC purposes, except for the 22 cabin-type barracks. It was requested that the cabins be turned over to the BR for use in the recreational development at Elephant Butte, and the permission was granted. The remainder of the buildings were salvaged by the Army. (Pfaff 2010)

DG-37-N/G-37-N, Cuchillo, Sierra County

Rank 2 (I-A-3).

The Cuchillo campsite is off the beaten track but well worth the modest effort. (*Figure H-5*) West of the village of Cuchillo for 4.3 miles on NM-52 is a gravel road turnoff to the north auspiciously labeled "CC Camp." (aka CR-17; *Figure H-5A* inset) Take it for 2.6 miles. Just shy of the usually-dry drainage called Willow Spring Draw is the campsite on the east side of the road. (*Figures H-6* and *H-7*) Most conspicuous are the remains of what appears to be a food-storage structure. (*Figures H-7A* and *7B*) Several foundations, a masonry sign (reminiscent of the one at F-51-N), and—most interesting—a drinking fountain adjacent to a little masonry pool. (*Figure H-7E*) Etched into the concrete mortar of the pool wall is the inscription, "T.A. Funderburg." (*Figure H-7F*) The Fort Bliss 1936 Annual enrollee list for this camp includes a "T.A. Funderburg, Bwd. Tex." One wonders if the Funderburg clan in Brownwood ever knows that one of their great-grandfathers, as a boy, left his little mark behind in a desolate place way out in far-off New Mexico.

F-40-N/SCS-22-N, Kingston Ranger Station, Sierra County

Rank 5 (III-B-1)

F-40-N is located on the north side of NM-152 at Milepost 41, 1.1 miles east of the village of Kingston. (*Figure H-8*) At one time the Gila National Forest had a ranger station on the south side of the highway at this point, but it was deactivated. A 1935 photo of the CCC company shows them gathered around a big sign that says, "Kingston Ranger Station Camp." (*Figure H-9A*) On the north side of the highway is a massive stone entryway with a locked gate. (*Figure H-9B*) Both sides of the impressive entryway are constructed of rounded stream cobbles, nicely cemented together. Just to the west of the gate is a concrete grease rack visible from the highway (*Figure H-9C*), with a concrete slab located just west of it. These features are all that are left of the campsite. A resident whose home is just east of the campsite, but is not the owner of the campsite, surprisingly knew nothing of the campsite located right next door.

In the hamlet of Kingston, about 600 feet east of the large Black Range Lodge (a B&B) and on the south side of Main Street is an abandoned frame house, gated off with a little sign of pink letters saying "The Little House." I suspect that at least a part of this house may have been salvaged from the CCC camp.

F-51-N, Montecello, Sierra County

Rank 5 (III-A-3)

This camp served as the winter camp for the company that occupied the Sandia Park camp F-8-N in Bernalillo County during the summers. From NM-142 at the little town of Montecello, the well-graded gravel FS-139 leads to the northeast for 4.4 miles to the Red Rock Ranch, then past it for a total of 4.9 miles to the north turnoff on Luna Park Road, and finally north for about 500 feet. (*Figure H-10*) The campsite is on the west side of the road. What is left of the original, masonry stone camp sign is just off the road. (*Figure H-11B*) A cable barrier is marked "Private Property, No Trespassing." A bonus though awaits one back in the village of Montecello. At the east edge of town, just east of the little plaza, take CR-32 south, past the plaza, for only 0.1 mile. At that point there is the very large, white adobe Montecello Public School, built in 1935 by the WPA. Its roof is gone and the structure is decrepit, but it continues to fascinate.

BR-39-N, Las Cruces, Doña Ana County

Rank 5 (III-D-1)

There were two camps in the city of Las Cruces. BR-39-N was located at 535 South Melendres Street—few CCC camps have street addresses. (*Figure H-12*) This was one of four CCC camps established for the Rio Grande Project. It was occupied in August 1935. Seventeen buildings of rigid frame construction, including six barracks, were erected. In addition, there was the masonry schoolhouse that stands today opposite the campsite on the east side of Melendres Street.

After the CCC abandoned the camp in May 1942 the site was used to train U. S. Navy sailors. Next, the former CCC buildings were used to house Italian and German POWs. (Guzman 2001) The site is now that of the Human Systems Research, Inc. facility. The facility's office is the former CCC company's schoolhouse mentioned above. (*Figure H-12C*) The building is listed on the National Register of Historic Places.

An interesting sidebar for this camp was reported in a March 21, 1939 newspaper article in the *Las Cruces Sun*. At the time the camp's enrollees were from Pennsylvania. They had never been out west before. To many of them a "cattle guard" meant a policeman that guarded cows. They soon learned otherwise. (Snyder 2002)

DG-38-N, Jornada del Muerto, Doña Ana County

Rank 5 (III-D-3)

This camp was established in August 1935. Locating this site has been an interesting exercise. (*Figure H-13*) Very fortunately there are photographic data. In the Fort Bliss 1936 Annual there is a montage of photos of CCC activities. One of the little inset photos shows a prominent mountain peak in the background. (*Figure H-13A*) An intensive search of similar features via *Google Earth* in this part of the county came up with a single candidate, but something did not seem right. Then I acquired a vintage photo of a "Jornado del Muerto" camp, showing that distinctive mountain, but something still did not seem right. However, when I reversed the image (the compiler for the publication got it wrong) I was able to match that mountain in that photo with the reversed image of the known camp. (*Figure H-14B*)

I still needed the exact site. Moving around, using *Google Earth* and taking an oblique view to the west-northwest reveals the exact same profile as in both images. The peak is Summerford Mountain, a high point in the Doña Ana Range. Finessing the correct perspective angle in the *Google Earth* image and moving back farther to the east lands on a large area that has been bladed over. I interpret this "restored" area as the site of the old camp DG-38-N. There is no remaining trace of a camp footprint.

By 1936 most of the camp's scheduled work had been completed, and in the spring the camp was moved to a new location several miles to the east on the western slopes of the San Andres Mountains. (*The Grazette* 1936, see below)

F-27-N/F-39-N, Jornada Experimental Range, Doüa Ana County

Rank 5 (II-D-2)

DG-38-N, discussed above, was located just east of the Jornada Experimental Range. I believe that there was a second CCC campsite located on the Range east of DG-38-N. This site is F-27-N (used winter 1933–1934 through winter 1934–1935) and F-39-N (used spring/summer 1935 through winter 1936–1937 or perhaps summer 1937). These occupations are time-sequential, suggesting a single site used twice. Importantly, this site is one of the very few locations in the area with an adequate supply of water.

I have a 1930s photo taken of a water tower at camp F-27-N. (*Figures H-15B* and *H-15C*) It was taken by Ben E. Hodges, a CCC-boy who worked at the camp. The photo shows a ridge line in the distance of the San Andres Mountains to the east. The match of the line with a *Google Earth* oblique view is not perfect, which is worrisome, but according to Brandon Brestelmeyer of the Jornada Experimental Range, there was nowhere else on the range that a tower like that would have been built. I therefore conclude that the camp was probably at or near that spot.

Margaret Page Hood, of *New Mexico Magazine*, visited the site in 1934 and described the camp as a "very permanent, but neat affair of wooden barracks, canteen recreation hall, hospital, offices and mess hall clustered around a central area. a flag pole dominated the scene and a bit of landscaping had been attempted with cacti, yuccas, and queerly shaped stones." (Holland 1991)

SCS-16-N/G-178-N, Alameda, Las Cruces, Dona Ana County

Rank 5 (III-D-1)

The exact location of SCS-16-N is elusive, but clues do exist. The first clue is from camp BR-39-N's newsletter (*Organ Echoes* 1938), which states that the camp was located about 2 ½ miles from camp BR-39-N. The second is from the CCC Legacy's website, which compatibly lists this camp as "Alameda 2 mi NE." The camp operated from spring/summer 1935 through winter 1940.

The second camp G-178-N operated during spring/summer 1941 to spring 1942. Most of what is known about it is from an oral history by Alfonso Guzmán. (Guzman 2001) As a kid he was the camp's paperboy when it was used as a POW camp after the CCC had left. He rode his bike to the camp on Lohman Avenue, near *present-day* (my italics) Young Park to deliver the Sunday newspaper twice a week and hand the papers to the guards. In that same interview Guzmán mentioned a Montezuma Dance Hall and a Grandview Hall located at 1203 E. Lohman, which is also near Young Park. Importantly he doesn't identify this as the site of G-178-N. I suspect that these two camps, SCS-16-N and G-178-N, occupied the same site because it seems unlikely (very wasteful, but not impossible) to construct a second camp if an earlier abandoned campsite was readily available. The 1203 E. Lohman address is tenuous, but I do believe that the camp was located on Lohman Avenue, near Young Park.

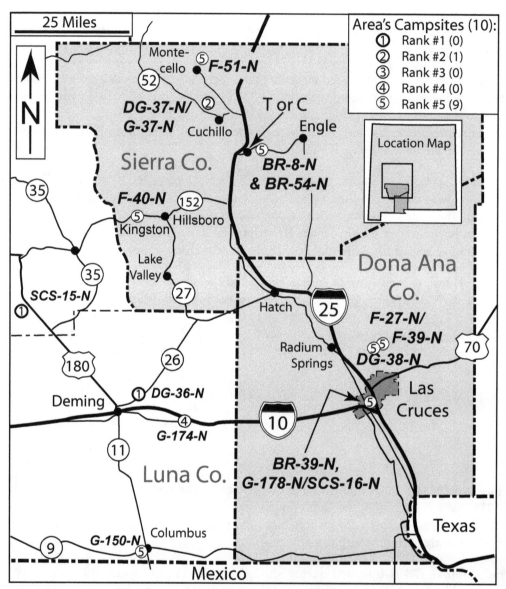

Figure H-1. AREA H / Doña Ana and Sierra Counties.

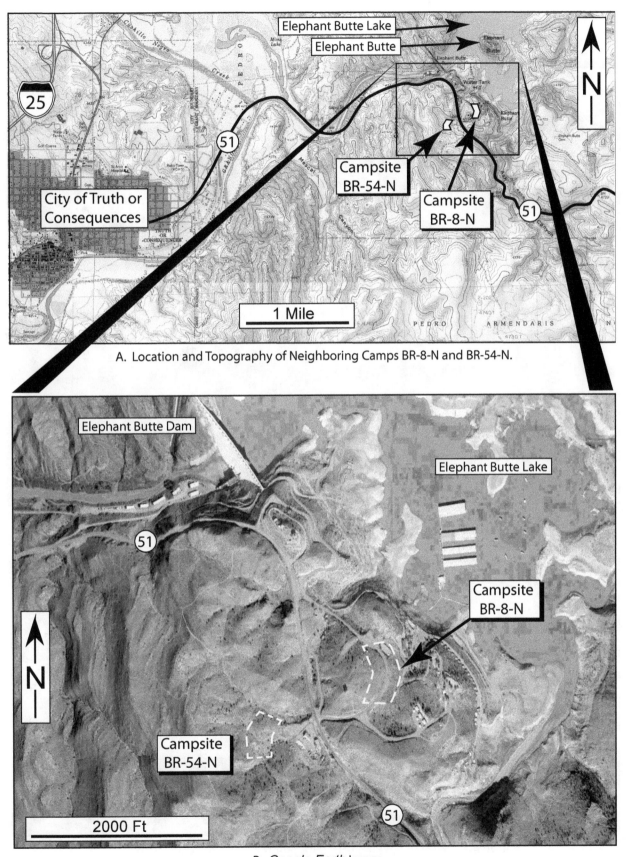

A. Location and Topography of Neighboring Camps BR-8-N and BR-54-N.

B. *Google Earth* Image.

Figure H-2. Camps BR-8-N and BR-54-N, Elephant Butte I.

A. West View of Camp BR-8-N, 1930s (Photograph from Pfaff, 2010).

B. West View of Camp BR-8-N as in A, 2017 (Photograph by Author).

C. West View of Camp BR-54-N, 1930s (Photograph from Pfaff, 2010).

Figure H-3. Camps BR-8-N and BR-54-N, Elephant Butte II.

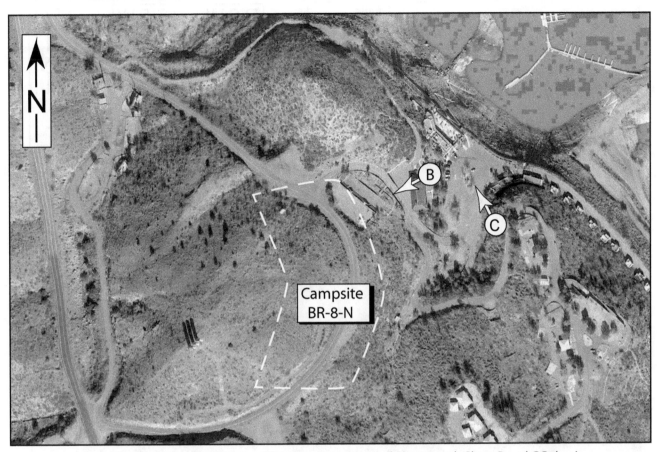

A. Detailed *Google Earth* Image (Showing Campsite and Photograph Shots B and C Below).

B. Southwest View of Camp Masonry, 2017 (Photograph by Author). C. New Mexico's First CCC-Worker Statue, 2017 (Photograph by Author).

Figure H-4. Camp BR-8-N, Elephant Butte III.

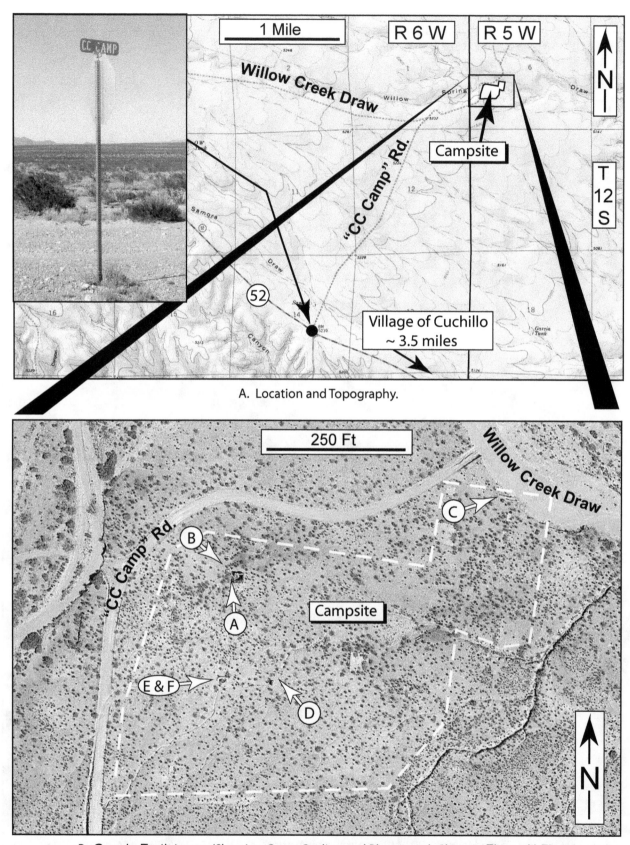

A. Location and Topography.

B. Google Earth Image (Showing Camp Outline and Photograph Shots in Figure H-7).

Figure H-5. Camp DG-37-N/G-37-N, Cuchillo - I.

A. North View of Forlorn Site, 2018 (Photograph by Author).

B. North-Northeast View, Late 1930s (Photograph by A. Newman).

C. North-Northeast Oblique *Google Earth* Image.

Figure H-6. Camp DG-37-N, Cuchillo II.

A. North View of Stone Building and Distant Vicks Peak, 2018 (Photograph by Author).

B. South-Southeast View of Stone Building in A, 2018 (Photograph by Author).

C. East View of Part of Possible Grease Rack, 2018 (with Front End Calved off into Arroyo, Photograph by Author).

D. Northwest View of Some Sort of Camp Sign, 2018 (Photograph by Author).

E. East View of Fountain, 2018 (Photograph by Author).

F. Graffiti on Fountain in E (by CCC-Boy T.A. Funderburg of Brownwood, Texas, Photograph by Author).

Figure H-7. Camp DG-37-N, Cuchillo III.

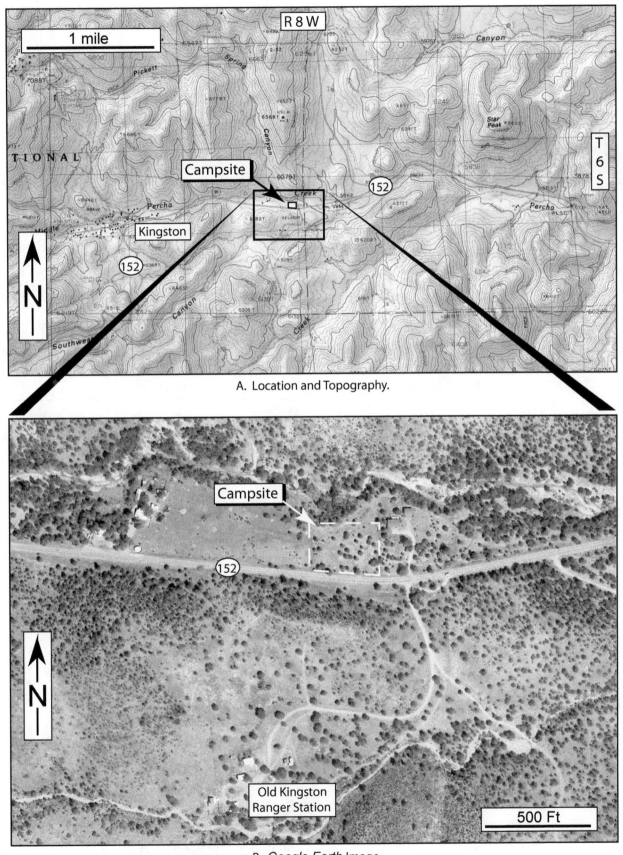

A. Location and Topography.

B. *Google Earth* Image.

Figure H-8. Camp F-40-N/SCS-22-N, Kingston I.

A. CCC Company Portrait, 1935 (Photograph from Internet).

B. Sketch of Typical CCC-Camp Entry Gate, 1935
(North Platte, Nebraska, from Pfaff, 2010).

C. North View of Camp Entry Gate, 2018
(from Highway NM-52,
Photograph by Author).

D. North View of Grease Rack, 2018
(from Highway NM-52, Photograph by Author).

Figure H-9. Camp F-40-N/SCS-22-N, Kingston II.

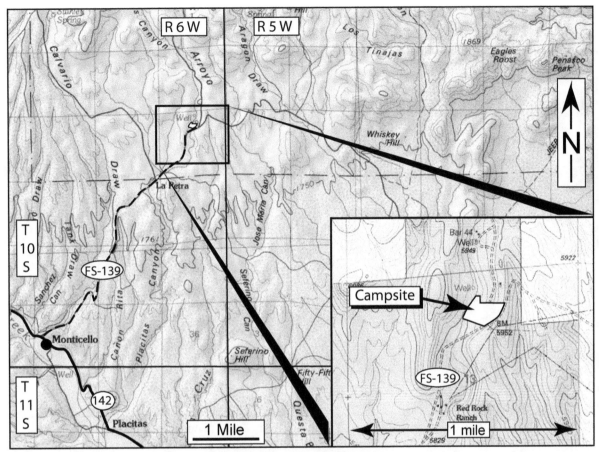

A. Location and Topography .

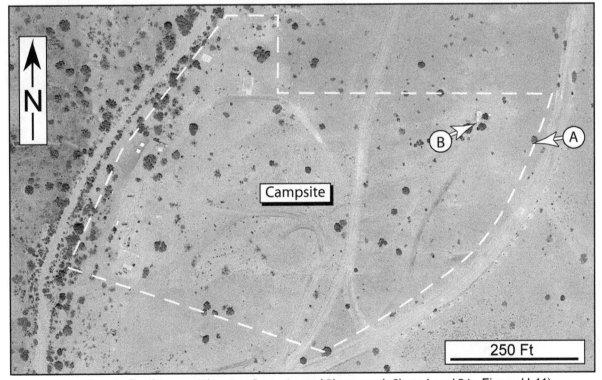

B. *Google Earth* Image (Showing Campsite and Photograph Shots A and B in Figure H-11).

Figure H-10. Camp F-51-N, Montecello I.

A. West View Downhill to Camp on Private Property, 2017 (Photograph by Author).

B. Northwest View of Former Camp Entry Sign, 2017
(Showing Space for Missing Bronze Plaque, Photograph by Author).

Figure H-11. Camp F-51-N, Montecello II.

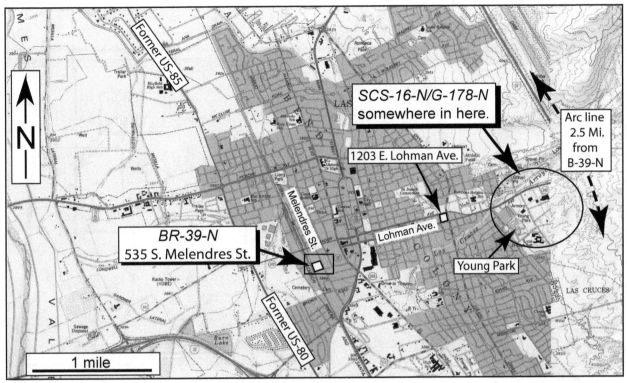

A. Location and Topography.

B. *Google Earth* Image of BR-39-N.

C. East View of 1938 CCC Schoolhouse
(Across Street from BR-39-N,
from Website *humansystemsresearch.org*).

D. West View of Camp BR-39-N, 1930s
(from Website *humansystemsresearch.org*).

Figure H-12. Camps BR-39-N and SCS-16-N/G-178-N, Las Cruces.

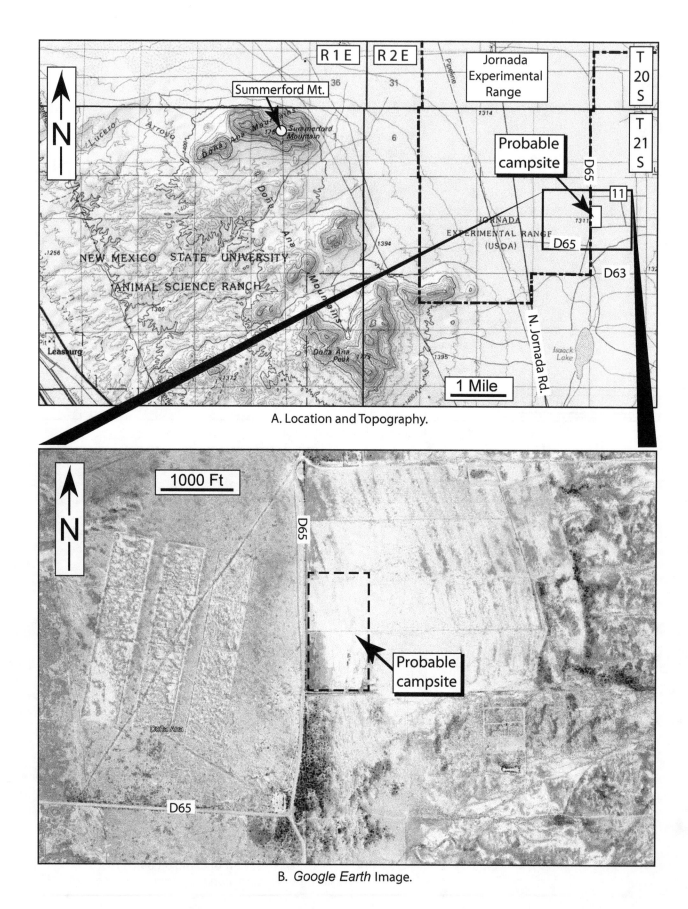

A. Location and Topography.

B. *Google Earth* Image.

Figure H-13. Camp DG-38-N, Jornada Experimental Range I.

A. CCC-Boys at Work, 1936, (Reversed Image from CCC *Official Annual-1936, Ft. Bliss District*).

B. West View of Camp from Water Tower, 1930s (Photograph from Internet).

Summerford Mt.

C. West-northwest Oblique *Google Earth* Image Toward Summerford Mountain, Doña Ana Mountains.

Figure H-14. Camp DG-38-N, Jornada Experimental Range II.

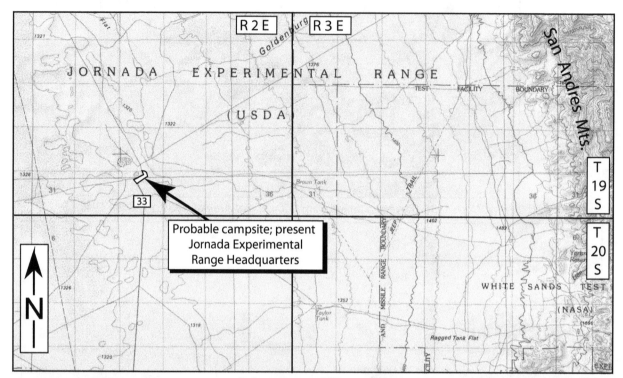

A. Location and Topography.

B. Northeast View of Camp's Water Tower, 1930s
(Photograph from Author's Collection).

C. CCC-Boy Ben Hodges atop Water Tower,
1935 (Photograph from Author's Collection)

Figure H-15. F-27-N/F-39-N, Jornada Experimental Range III.

AREA I

SOUTH-CENTRAL NEW MEXICO: LINCOLN AND OTERO COUNTIES

FIGURE I-1)

These two heavily forested counties contain 11 campsites.

Lincoln County:

    1. DG-40-N, Carrizozo (P.O. Carrizozo)

    2. F-17-N/SCS-31-N, Baca Campground, Capitán (P.O. Capitán)

    3. F-41-N, "Camp Gallinas," Gallinas Mountains (P.O. Corona)

    4. F-54-N, Cedar Creek, Ruidoso (P.O. Ruidoso)

    5. SCS-6-N, Fort Stanton (P.O. Fort Stanton

    6. SCS-32-N, Hondo (P.O. Hondo)

Otero County:

    7. DG-39-N/G-39-N/SCS-30-N/G(D)-1-N "Camp Mescelero," Tularosa (P.O. Tularosa)

    8. DG-69-N/G-69-N, "Camp Little America," Orogrande (P.O. Alamogordo)

    9. F-16-N/F-24-N/SCS-29-N, High Rolls (P. O. High Rolls)

    10. F-28-N, La Luz Canyon (P.O. High Rolls)

    11. F-32-N/SCS-34-N, "Camp Peñasco," Mayhill (P.O. Mayhill)

DG-40-N, Carrizozo, Lincoln County

RANK 1A (I-A-1).

The campsite lies along the north-south US-54, a scant 0.4 miles north of its intersection with the west-east US-380. On the west side of the former is a historical road marker extolling the virtues of Carrizozo, the Lincoln County Seat, which begins just south of the intersection. Immediately east of US-54, visible from the historical marker, is the campsite, with its very obvious fireplace chimney and an extensive array of foundations and other structures. (*Figures I-2* and *I-3*) There is not a word on the sign about the campsite, and this omission is the exemplar of that lost history mentioned earlier. The campsite occupies the area between the railroad tracks and the original old trace of US-54 on the east side and the modern US-54 on the west.

In 1935 the city of Carrizozo donated their old city dump as a site for a CCC camp. The camp was constructed on top of the dump in July 1935. The site was studied in detail. (Bullock 1998) The report claims that detritus from the dump—broken glass, pottery and metal—constantly worked its way to the surface and thus impossible to bare-foot around. Even after lawns were planted there was a smell of decay. At the end of the final period the camp was moved up north to Tokay. (G-147-N)

The area is today enclosed by the US-54 right-of-way fence, but the barrier is easily crossed. It is on State Land and is "accessible." The word is in quotes because State Land is not public land. To put a very fine point on it, permission from the state is required. Here I go out on a limb and state that with discretion the site can be easily visited from the highway.

Much remains to be seen at the site, and the *Google Earth* image is revealing. (*Figure I-2B*) The brick fireplace and chimney for the recreation building still stand. (*Figure I-3A*) Across and south from it is what is left of the camp's masonry bulletin board, along the west-east main "avenue." (*Figures I-3B* and *13E*) Foundations are everywhere, probably from offices of some sort, as well as showers, mess facilities, etc.—things that needed a sound base. Wood-frame dormitories were typically jacked up on temporary supports and were hauled away when the camps were moved, so their only trace is compacted earth. On the south edge of the site is what I once thought (similar structures occur at many campsites) was a "BBQ pit." (*Figure I-3C*) I got my comeuppance when I came across a photo of a similar feature from Camp Cody (a huge WWI training facility near Deming), in which it was clearly identified as an incinerator. (*Figure 0-6A*) A large rectangular cement bin in the southeast side of the campsite was not part of DG-40-N. This was a railroad coal bin that was already there when the camp was built. (*Figure I-3F*) The CCC boys used it as a swimming pool. The camp bell was hauled off and now resides in the yard of a private residence in Carrizozo. (Bullock 1998) Wandering across this campsite, trying to put the pieces together, is a fascinating exercise. In short, this site is one of the very best examples of a CCC camp "footprint."

F-17-N/SCS-31-N, Baca Campground, Capitán, Lincoln County

RANK 3A (I-B-2)

This site has a layered past. It was first established as a CCC camp in the summer of 1933 and named "Camp Saturnino Baca." (*Figure 1-4*) Baca (1830–1925) is known as the father of Lincoln County. As a member of the Territorial Legislature (1869) he introduced a bill to create the county. The camp operated only through the winter of 1933–1934, when the Forest Service condemned it as not suitable for use again as a winter camp.

It was then occupied starting in 1935 for one period as "Camp Capitán," a camp for unemployed girls. President Franklin Roosevelt had formed the CCC at the end of March 1933 to help unemployed young men. That program was wildly successful. FDR's wife, Eleanor, thought that young women should have the same opportunity. She lobbied vigorously for girls' camps modeled on those of the CCC. It was very much an uphill struggle, but she persevered—sort of. She got one camp at first, Camp Tera (later named Camp Jane Addams) in Bear Mountain State Park, New York, in June 1933. She wanted more than that crumb tossed her way. She continued her lobbying but passed the torch. (Adkins 2008)

In 1935 a new federal agency was created, the National Youth Administration (NYA), that gave needy young men manual work projects, and gave young women domestic jobs in public facilities, for a small stipend. Under the NYA the people all lived at home. Eventually a residential-camp program for women was put in place. The media derisively called this a "She She She" camp. Eventually at least eight of these were established nationwide. (Adkins 2008)

F-17-N in Baca Canyon was a nice place for a camp, with an active spring that still flows today. Fortunately, all the camp buildings had been left behind when the CCC abandoned the site in 1934, but other supplies were scant. When the girls occupied the site in September 1935 the camp acquired a new name, "Camp Capitán." (*Figure 1-5*) Technically it was similar to a CCC camp. In the summer of 1936 it was shut down due to budget problems. (Adkins 2008) In September 1940 the CCC boys from Fort Stanton (SCS-6-N) were moved to the abandoned Camp Capitán, this time designated as SCS-31-N (McBride 2008), and stayed until May of 1941.

After the bombing of Pearl Harbor, 32 Japanese immigrant railroad workers from Clovis, and their families–the entire Japanese population of Clovis–were rounded up in January 1942 by the Immigration and Naturalization Service and put into detention "for their own protection" at the abandoned camp that was this time renamed "Old Camp Raton." After almost a year of this, the detainees were transferred to a camp in Utah. None ever returned to Clovis.

The large foundation dominating the site is that of the CCC mess hall for F-17-N, and later used for Camp Capitán. (*Figures I-5A* and *5B*) The stone fireplace and chimney west of the foundation were built by the girls. (*Figure I-5C*)

F-41-N, "Camp Gallinas," Gallinas Mountains, Corona, Lincoln County

Rank 3 (I-B-3)

F-41-N was set up in August 1935 for road construction and range improvement. (*Figure I-6*) Finding this campsite proved to be quite elusive. The available information indicated that it was located at the Red Cloud Campground in the Gallinas Mountains, southwest of Corona. However, a thorough search of the campground revealed nothing. A local camper there reported that the present Red Cloud was a replacement campground, and that the original Red Cloud was up to the north and was burned out in one of the devastating forest fires during the last 20 years. A search back up to the north, on a hill on the west side of the road A023, revealed a chimney. (*Figures I-7A* and *7B*) I had one of those A. Newman wide-angle CCC company photographs, but could not match it up with the present terrain. (*Figures I-7C* and *7D*)

Oddly, down the hill a bit just to the north was a mobile home covered by a shade canopy that seemed to be empty at the time. There was a sign at A023 road below it identifying it as the "Lee Patsy Mulkey House." Back up at what might be left of the campsite is a strange little burial plot with a tombstone reading "George B. James, Jan. 18, 1938, April 9, 1983," and a little sign on the enclosure saying, "Mulkey-James Memorial Garden (There are no Actual Graves Here)." A sad little place, holding Lee Patsy's grim memories. All in all, it's a strange CCC campsite, but I believe it is the location of the camp.

Rank 2 (I-B-1)

I had seen the name Cedar Creek mentioned in conjunction with this camp. When I conducted my search up Cedar Creek Drive and at Cedar Creek Campground, I found nothing. A surprise came at the Lincoln National Forest's Smoky Bear Ranger Station just west of the main highway, NM-48. (*Figure I-8*) When I asked about foundations, etc., I was told, "Oh yeah, right across the street." The campsite lies directly across from the Station, on the north side of Cedar Creek Drive. The outline of the camp is not recognizable but a number of large foundations remain that are easily overlooked while driving by. (*Figure I-9*) This late facility was used for summers 1938 to 1940, and then summer 1941 through winter 1941–1942.

SCS-6-N, Fort Stanton, Lincoln County

Rank 3 (I-B-2)

This site has a multilayered and intriguing history. The first part is Fort Stanton itself, on the south side of the diminutive Rio Bonito (*Figure I-10*), but it is only incidental to this narrative. Next is the CCC camp SCS-6-N on the north side of the river, and then there is the German POW camp. (*Figure I-11*)

Fort Stanton was established in 1855 as a military post to protect settlers from the Apache. After the Indian Wars came to an end in the 1890s the camp's importance dwindled and it closed in 1896. In 1899 the fort was used as a merchant marine hospital for TB patients—the only such hospital in the nation at the time. The hospital underwent a major upgrade from 1938 to 1941 to become a modern facility.

Back in the summer of 1935 the Soil Conservation Service built its camp SCS-6-N on the north side of the Rio Bonito, opposite Fort Stanton. Its proximity to the fort was important because the camp received continual electric service from a power plant there. (*Figure I-11*) By the end of 1940 the camp was turned over to the Immigration and Naturalization Service and the CCC boys moved a few miles to the east to the Girls' Baca Camp. (See F-17-N/SCS-31-N above.)

What follows is taken from a superb little book titled *Interned*, by James McBride. (McBride 2008) In September 1939 the German luxury liner, *SS Columbus*, had the misfortune of being on a cruise in the Caribbean when Germany invaded Poland. The ship's captain tried to slip back to Germany but was intercepted at sea by a British destroyer. The captain, as per his orders, scuttled the ship. His crew of 576 seaman abandoned ship and were picked up by a trailing American cruiser. Since the U.S. and Germany were not yet at war, the crew became "guests," who no one quite knew what to do with. The crew was entrained to the West Coast with the idea of putting them on a Japanese ship bound for home. That didn't pan out, and for the year 1940 the crew languished on Angel Island in San Francisco Bay. By year's end a fire at the site reduced the island's capacity and it was decided to house them at the old CCC camp, sitting vacant in Fort Stanton. A few of the original crew were repatriated, but the 410 military-age members were entrained east to Carrizozo and bussed to Fort Stanton. On a snowy day in January 1941 they occupied the abandoned CCC camp.

During the year 1941 they spruced the place up and added desirable features, particularly an Olympic-size swimming pool at the foot of the hill that they soon dubbed "Columbus Hill." But their hearts were not fully in the work because they expected the allies to make peace with Hitler and for them to be repatriated soon. That changed after Pearl Harbor on December 7, 1941, and Germany's declaration of war on the U.S. on December 11. They suddenly were no longer guests, but POWs for the next three years. The camp was enclosed by a fence, guards were posted and guard towers built. In the summer of 1944 the men built the large recreation hall that stands today. Only after the Allied victory over Germany in May 1945 was the crew free to go home. By August 1945 the camp was empty.

The Marine Hospital at Fort Stanton later used some of the buildings for storage and the people there availed themselves of the nice swimming pool. Most of the buildings have since been salvaged and the campsite is returning to nature. A trail today leads to a little bridge across the Rio Bonito to the campsite. The first structure to be seen at the southeastern part of the campsite is the guardhouse. Next, to the west, is the big recreation hall, with the German words *Erbaut 1944* ("built 1944") engraved over the main entrance. (*Figures I-12A* and *12B*) The roof collapsed, probably in stages, sometime between 1982 and 1995 (McBride 2008), spelling the beginning of the *Erbaut's* demise. The infirmary sits among a group of trees at the southwestern end, and some substantial foundations line the western end. At the north side, at the foot of Columbus Hill is what remains of that fine pool, the pride of the crew of the *SS Columbus*. (*Figure I-13B*)

SCS-32-N, HONDO, LINCOLN COUNTY

LOCATION UNKNOWN

This late camp existed for only two periods, spring/summer 1941 to early 1942—hardly enough time to make a mark on the land. The only hint I had of its location is from hand-written notes by Art Roman, Archivist at the Deming Luna Mimbres Historical Museum, in which he writes that it was "ten miles south of Lincoln." That less-than-precise description puts the site in the community of Hondo, but nothing is visible via *Google Earth* in that area. It may have been a "mobile camp," i.e., structures mounted on wheeled trailers, leaving no trace. Its location remains indeterminant. This is one of the few remaining SCS camps shut down in the spring of 1942 due to the war effort.

DG-39-N/G-39-N/SCS-30-N/G(D)-1-N, "CAMP MESCALERO," TULAROSA, OTERO COUNTY

RANK 5 (I-D-1)

The campsite is just off and to the north of US-70, 4.5 to 5 miles east of the intersection of US-54 and US-70 in Tularosa. (*Figures I-14* and *I-15*) It is easy to miss because there is nothing left among the desert scrub. It started as DG-39-N, was redesignated G-39-N in 1940, replaced by SCS-30-N, and finally commandeered by the military as G(D)-1-N.

DG-69-N/G-69-N, "CAMP LITTLE AMERICA," OROGRANDE, OTERO COUNTY

RANK 5 (III-D-1).

Locating this tent camp is problematic because there are two possible sites. (*Figure I-16*) A note by Norman McNew (*Albuquerque Journal* 1984), who had lived with his parents on their ranch near the site, is informative. "My parents, Mr. and Mrs. R.J. McNew, owned the ranch then and the CCC tents were about a quarter of a mile northwest of our ranch headquarters. We furnished water for the camp, and we collected their garbage to feed to our hogs." The article continues, "McNew, although he was quite young when the CCC camp was in operation, said he can easily pinpoint the site, five miles north of Orogrande on U.S. 54. No visible signs remain on the site since there were no foundations or concrete works poured there. Only weeds grow now where the wooden-walled tents were pitched back in 1939."

This description directly conflicts with a topographic map, the 1943 Orogrande 15" quad (surveyed in 1940), which shows a CCC camp about four miles *south* of the McNew Ranch, just west of US-54 and north of the little community of Orogrande. (*Figure I-16B* inset) Neither location reveals any recognizable campsite features via *Google Earth*.

F-16-N/F-24-N/SCS-29-N, High Rolls, Otero County

Rank 1 (I-A-2)

This campsite is also tricky to find. It looks down on the little town of High Rolls from the north. (*Figure I-17*) On my first pass, using the geographic coordinates gathered from *Google Earth*, I somehow missed the site. Fortunately I stumbled onto Anthony Hyde, a retired New Mexico State University professor and owner the little shop *ClayWorks* in High Rolls. He and his neighbor, George Alexander, took me up the hill above the town and led me off the road to the campsite. (*Figure I-18A*) One is struck by the redness of the ground, inherited from the red Permian bedrock below the area. Several foundations are scattered about, but the most interesting feature is what appears to be a large food storage structure. (*Figures I-18B, 18C, 18D*) It has a concrete foundation, is surrounded by masonry walls, and is attached to a separate root-cellar-like room. A puzzle. The camp had a sporadic operation: as F-16-N during the summer of 1933; as F-24-N during winter of 1937–1938 through winter 1938–1939, and then winter 1939–1940; lastly as SCS-29-N during spring/summer 1940 through winter 1940–1941. Winters must have been a challenge up there.

F-28-N, La Luz Canyon, Otero County

Rank 5 (III-D-3)

There are few level spots within La Luz Canyon for a camp. The strongest candidate is the site of the Aspen Valley Ranch with its grand house. The young residents I queried when I visited knew nothing of a CCC camp on their property, but it is suspected that their big house is atop the site. The camp operated during the winter of 1933–1934, then the winter of 1934–1935 with its post office each time at High Rolls, and then through spring/summer of 1935 with the post office down the hill at La Luz. No trace of a campsite is visible today.

F-32-N/SCS-34-N, "Camp Peñasco," Mayhill, Otero County

Rank 5 (III-C-1)

This camp had the nickname "Peñasco". (*Figures I-19* and *I-20*) I had the good fortune of having access of the photo collection of Ralph Cericola. (Lincoln National Forest undated, *Figures I-20A* and *I-21*) He worked at this camp in 1940 and evidently was an enthusiastic photographer. The SCS took it over and ran it as SCS-34-N during spring/summer 1941 through winter 1941–1942. Unfortunately, the site is inaccessible because it is covered over by the Lincoln National Forest's Mayhill Work Center that is clearly marked "No Public Access, Authorized Vehicles Only."

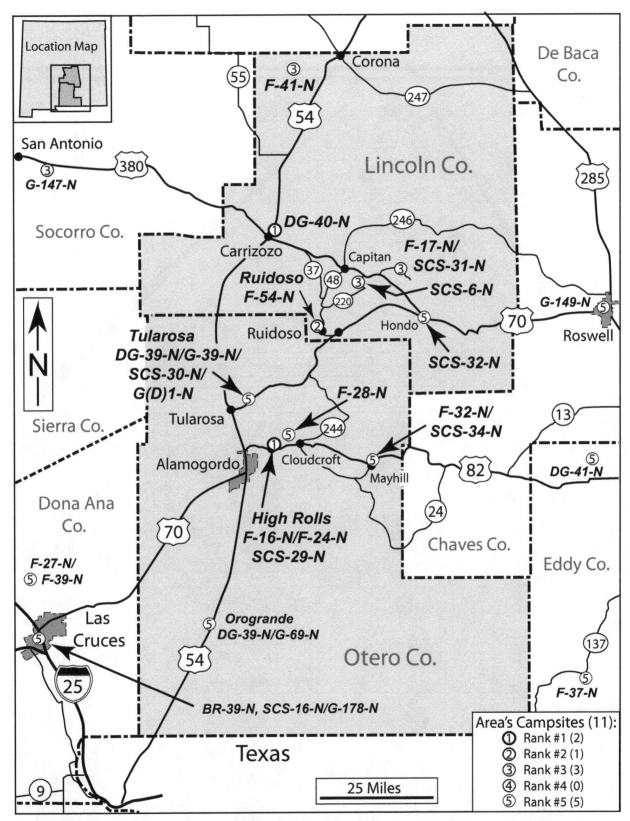

Figure I-1. AREA I / Lincoln and Otero Counties.

Location Map

San Antonio
③
G-147-N

380

Socorro Co.

55

③
F-41-N

54

Corona

247

De Baca Co.

285

Lincoln Co.

DG-40-N
①

Carrizozo

246

Capitan

③

F-17-N/
SCS-31-N

SCS-6-N

G-149-N
⑤
Roswell

37
48
220

Ruidoso
F-54-N

②
Ruidoso

Hondo

⑤

70

SCS-32-N

Tularosa
DG-39-N/G-39-N/
SCS-30-N/
G(D)1-N

⑤
Tularosa

F-28-N

244

13

F-32-N/
SCS-34-N

82

⑤
DG-41-N

Sierra Co.

⑤
①
Alamogordo

Cloudcroft

⑤
Mayhill

24

Chaves Co.

Eddy Co.

Dona Ana Co.

70

High Rolls
F-16-N/F-24-N
SCS-29-N

F-27-N/
⑤ F-39-N

Otero Co.

137

⑤

F-37-N

Las Cruces
⑤

25

54

⑤
Orogrande
DG-39-N/G-69-N

BR-39-N, SCS-16-N/G-178-N

Texas

9

N

25 Miles

Area's Campsites (11):
① Rank #1 (2)
② Rank #2 (1)
③ Rank #3 (3)
④ Rank #4 (0)
⑤ Rank #5 (5)

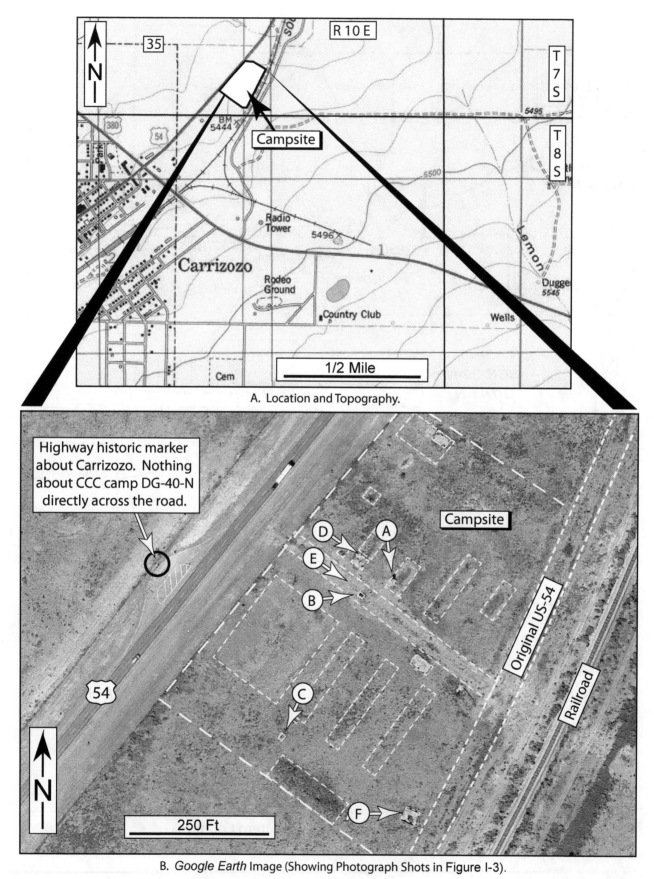

R 10 E

35

T 7 S

T 8 S

N

Campsite

380
54

BM
5444

5495

5500

Radio
Tower

5496

Carrizozo

Lemon

Dugge
5545

Rodeo
Ground

Country Club

Wells

Park

Cem

1/2 Mile

A. Location and Topography.

Highway historic marker
about Carrizozo. Nothing
about CCC camp DG-40-N
directly across the road.

Campsite

D

A

E

B

Original US-54

Railroad

54

C

N

F

250 Ft

B. *Google Earth* Image (Showing Photograph Shots in Figure I-3).

Figure I-2. Camp DG-40-N, Carrizozo I.

A. South View to Recreation Building's Brick Fireplace, 2006 (Photograph by Author).

B. East View to Masonry Bulletin Board, 2018 (with Fireplace in Distance, Photograph by Author).

C. South-Southwest View of Incinerator, 2006 (Photograph by Author).

D. Southeast View of Various Structures, 2018 (Photograph by Author).

E. Southeast View of Perimeter Stones Marking Central Walkway, 2018 (Photograph by Author).

F. East View of Pre-Existing Railroad Coal Bin, 2018 (Later Used by CCC as Swimming Pool, Photograph by Author).

Figure I-3. Camp DG-40-N, Carrizozo II.

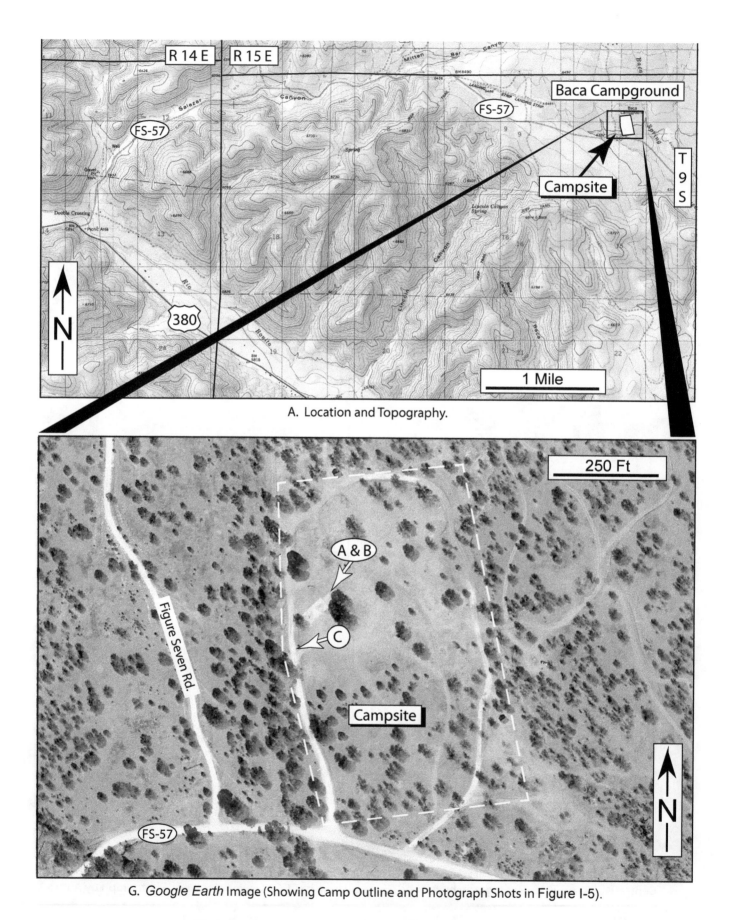

A. Location and Topography.

G. *Google Earth* Image (Showing Camp Outline and Photograph Shots in Figure I-5).

Figure I-4. Camp F-17-N, Capitan/Baca Ranch I.

A. Southwest View of Mess Hall Foundation
and Distant Fire Hearth, 2018 (Photograph by Author).

B. Southwest View of Mess Hall, 1930s
(Sign at Campsite, Photograph by Author).

C. Southwest View of Fire Hearth, 2018
(Photograph by Author).

D. Sketch of Camp by Roy Ebihara, Eight-Year-Old Japanese
Internee, 1942 (Sign at Campsite, Photograph by Author).

E. Camp in 1930s (Photograph from Internet).

Figure I-5. Camp F-17-N/SCS-31-N, Baca Ranch, Capitan II.

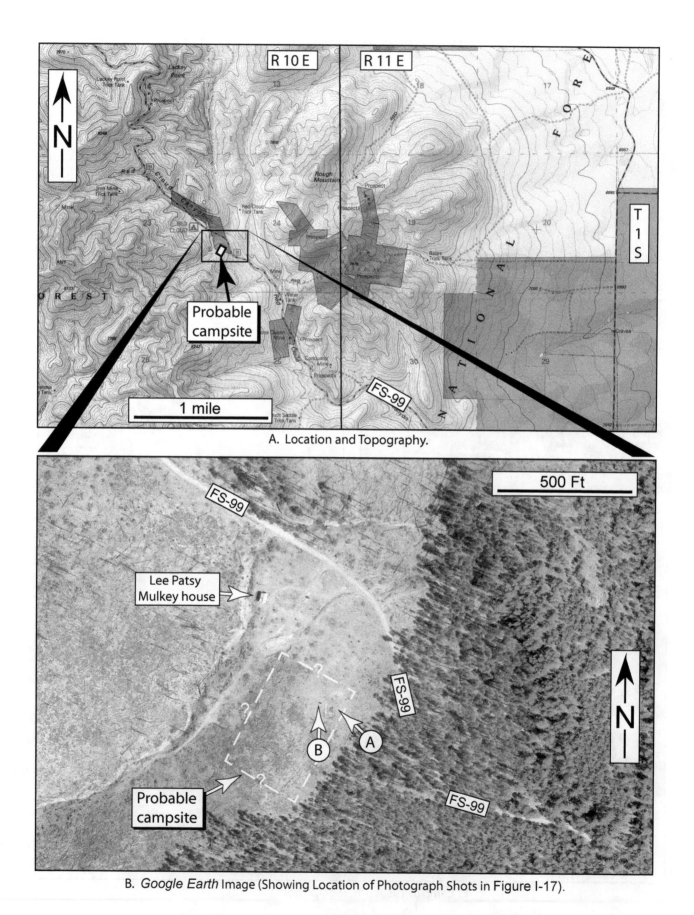

A. Location and Topography.

B. *Google Earth* Image (Showing Location of Photograph Shots in Figure I-17).

Figure I-6. Camp F-41-N, Gallinas Mountains, Corona I.

A. North View of Fireplace Chimney, 2018 (with Mulkey Residence in Distance, Photograph by Author).

B. West-Northwest View of Foundation and Chimney, 2018 (Photograph by Author).

View in D below

C. CCC Company Portrait, Mid-1930s (Photograph from A. Newman).

D. Detail of View in Rectangle in C Above (Showing How Barracks Were Jacked Up and Leveled).

Figure I-7. Camp F-41-N, Gallinas Mountains, Corona II.

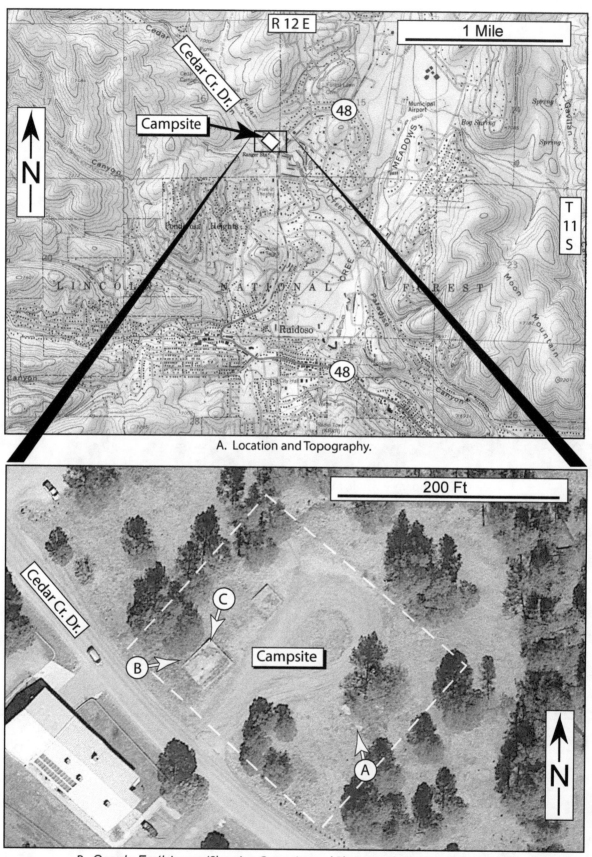

A. Location and Topography.

B. *Google Earth* Image (Showing Campsite and Photograph Shots in Figure I-9).

Figure I-8. Camp F-54-N, Cedar Creek, Ruidoso I.

A. North View of Concrete Slab, 2018
(Photograph by Author).

B. Northeast View of Another Slab, 2018
(Photograph by Author).

C. South View Toward Cedar Creek Road and Smokey Bear Ranger Station, 2018 (Photograph by Author).

Figure I-9. Camp F-54-N, Cedar Creek, Ruidoso II.

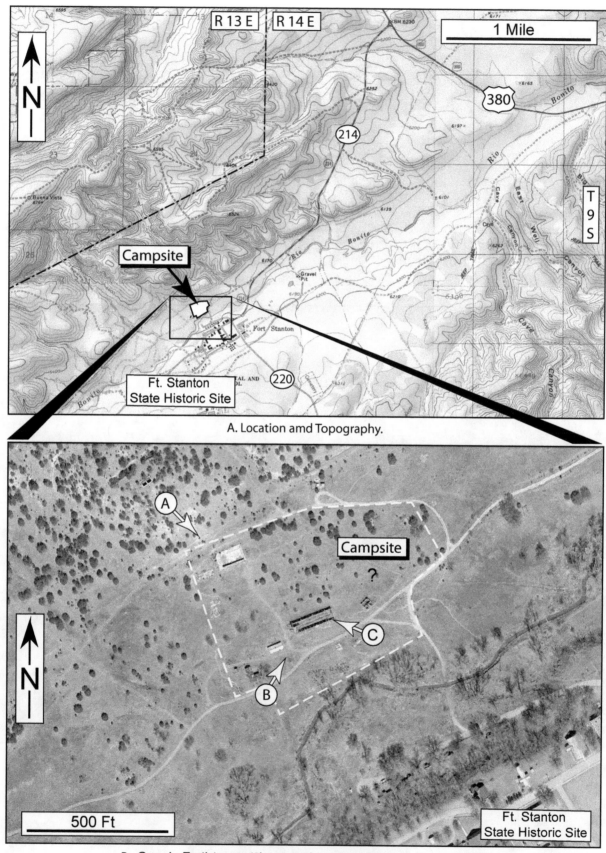

A. Location amd Topography.

B. *Google Earth* Image (Showing Photograph Shots in Figure I-12).

Figure I-10. SCS-6-N, Fort Stanton I.

A. South Aerial Composite View of CCC Camp, ca. 1940
(Showing Fort's Power Plant in Left Distance, Photographs from McBride 2008.)

B. South Aerial View of CCC Camp, ca. 1940
(Photograph from New Mexico Digital Collection).

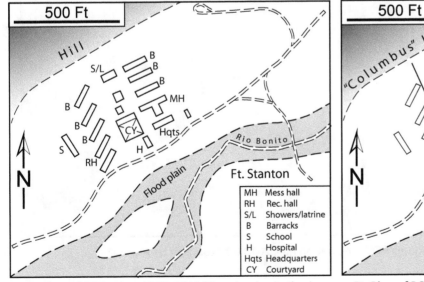

C. Plan of CCC camp, 1935-1940 (Drawing by Author).

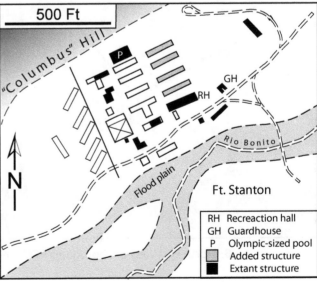

D. Plan of POW camp, 1941-1945 (from McBride 2008).

Figure I-11. Camp SCS-6-N, Fort Stanton II.

A. Northeast View of Camp Headquarters and POW Recreation Hall, 2018 (Photograph by Author).

Erbaut = "built" in German.

B. Northwest View of Photogenic POW Recreation hall, 2018 (Photograph by Author).

Figure I-12. Camp SCS-6-N, Fort Stanton III.

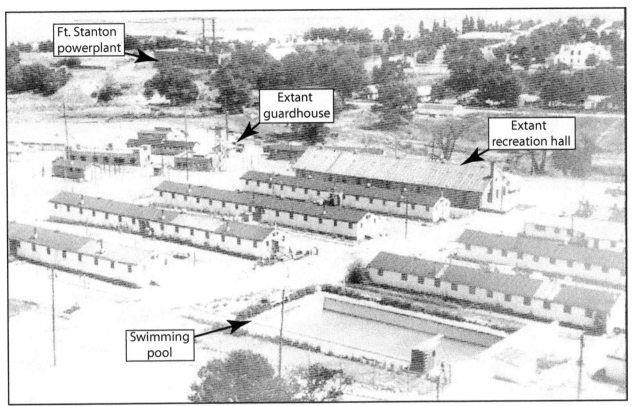

A. Southeast Aerial View of Camp from Columbus Hill, after POWs Left, 1945 (Photograph from McBride, 2008).

B. Southeast View of POW Swimming Pool, with Recreation Hall in Left Distance, 2018
(from Columbus Hill, Photograph by Author).

Figure I-13. Camp SCS-6-N, Fort Stanton IV.

191

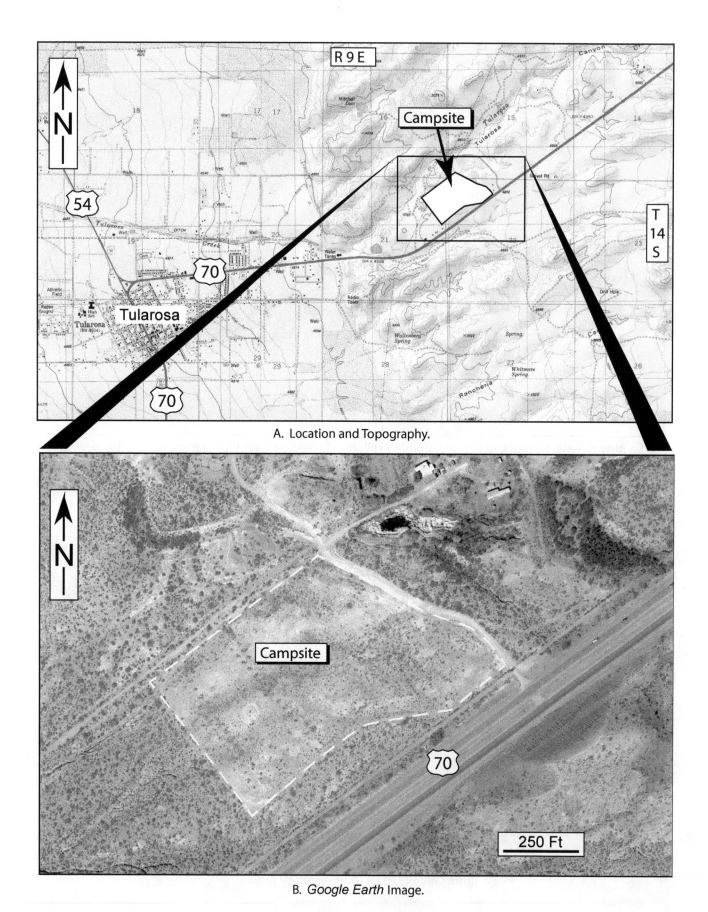

A. Location and Topography.

B. *Google Earth* Image.

Figure I-14. Camp DG-39-N/SCS-30-N/G(D)-1-N, Tularosa I.

A. East View of Camp, 1930s (Photograph from Author's Collection).

A. East Oblique *Google Earth* Image.

Figure I-15. Camp DG-39-N/SCS-30-N/G(D)-1-N, Tularosa II.

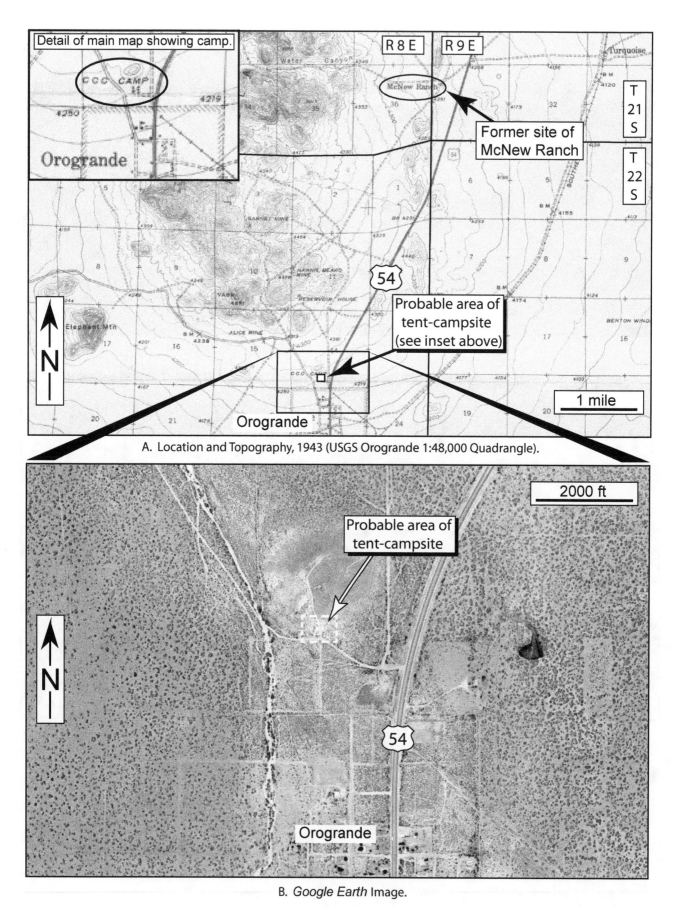

A. Location and Topography, 1943 (USGS Orogrande 1:48,000 Quadrangle).

B. *Google Earth* Image.

Figure I-16. Camp DG-69-N/G-69-N, Little America, Orogrande.

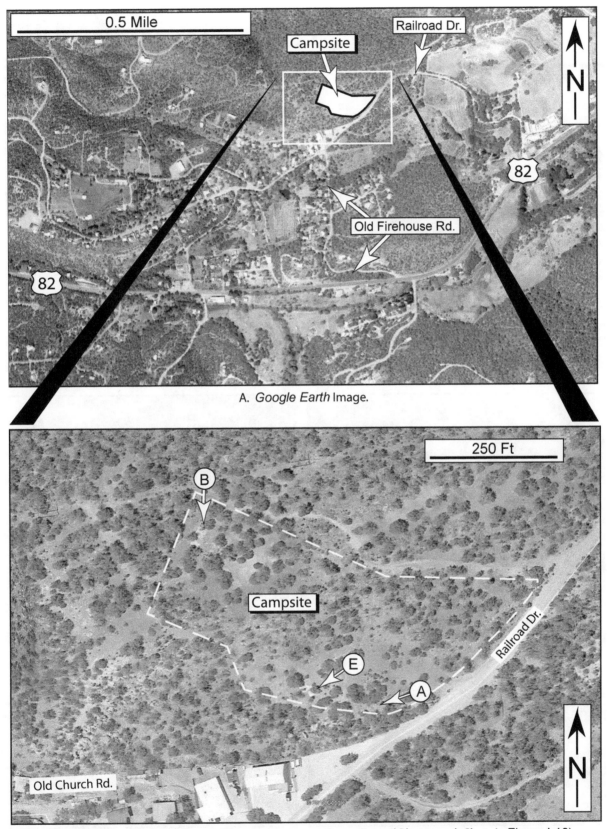

A. *Google Earth* Image.

B. Close-Up *Google Earth* Image (Showing Access to Campsite and Photograph Shots in Figure I-18).

Figure I-17. Camp F-16-N/F-24-N, High Rolls I.

A. Southeast View Down Easily-Overlooked Access Path to Campsite, 2018 (Photograph by Author).

B. South View of Possible Office Complex, 2018. (Photograph by Author).

C. South View of Inside of Large Structure in B, 2018 (Photograph by Author).

D. East View of Room, South of Stairwell in B, 2018 (Photograph by Author).

E. Southwest View of Concrete Slab on Camp's South Side, 2018 (Photograph by Author).

Figure I-18. Camp F-16-N/F-24-N, High Rolls II.

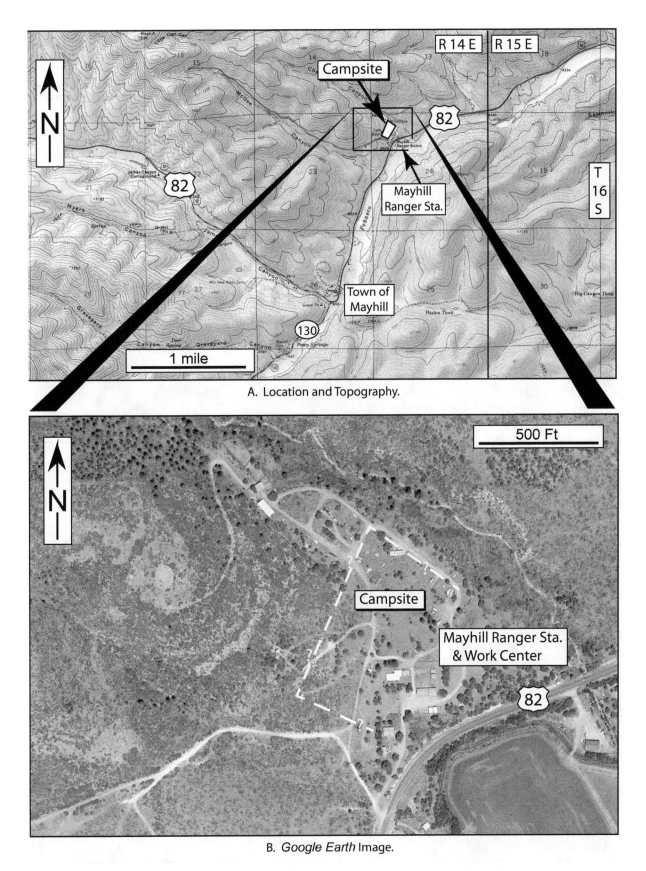

A. Location and Topography.

B. *Google Earth* Image.

Figure I-19. Camp F-32-N-SCS-34-N, Peñasco, Mayhill I.

A. CCC-Boys at Camp, 1940 (Ralph Cericola at Left, Photograph from Lincoln National Forest).

B. East-Southeast Oblique *Google Earth* Image of Campsite Area.

Figure I-20. Camp F-32-N-SCS-34-N, Peñasco, Mayhill II.

A. East-Southeast View of Camp, 1940 (Photograph from Lincoln National Forest).

B. CCC-Boy at Camp Entry Sign, 1940 (Photograph from Lincoln National Forest).

Figure I-21. Camp F-32-N-SCS-34-N, Peñasco, Mayhill III.

AREA J
Southeast New Mexico: Chaves and Eddy Counties
(Figure J-1)

This area contains nine CCC sites.

Chaves County:

1. BS-1-N/FWS-3-N, Bitter Lake National Wildlife Refuge (P.O. Roswell)

2. G-149-N, Roswell (P.O. Roswell)

3. SP-3-N, Bottomless Lakes State Park (P.O. Roswell)

Eddy County:

4. BR-3-N, Carlsbad Medical Center (P.O. Carlsbad)

5. BR-82-N, Carlsbad Medical Center (P.O. Carlsbad)

6. G-148-N, Carlsbad Medical Center (P.O. Carlsbad)

7. DG-41-N, Lake Arthur (P.O. Lake Arthur)

8. F-37-N, "Camp Dark Canyon," Carlsbad (P.O. Carlsbad)

9. NP-1-N, Rattlesnake Spring, Carlsbad (P.O. Carlsbad)

BS-1-N/FWS-3-N, Bitter Lake National Wildlife Refuge (NWR), Chaves County

Rank 5 (III-B-1)

In 1940 the Biological Survey (BS) was combined with the new Fish and Wildlife Service (FWS), thus the camp's name change. NWR manager Steve Alvarez informed me that the campsite is located out on the far west edge of the refuge, and although there is a clear camp outline and a few foundations, it is off limits to the public. (*Figure J-2*)

G-149-N, Roswell, Chaves County

Rank 5 (III-D-1).

The location of this campsite to date remains elusive. The only information I have is from the CCC Legacy's website, which states that the camp was in Roswell, "#1, 1 mi W." This "west" bearing is presumably measured from the city's north-to-south axis, US-285. One mile west of that point is the abandoned airport, built before December 1942 and abandoned before August 1944. No trace of a campsite is evident via *Google Earth* at that location, but I suspect it was there.

SP-3-N, Bottomless Lakes State Park, Chaves County

Rank 4 (I-C-2).

It seemed natural to search for this campsite via *Google Earth* within the Bottomless Lakes State Park limits. Nothing was found. Then I reached out to the park manger, Maxwell Michanczyk, for help. He stated that the campsite was not within the park, but rather on a broad, north-trending ridge called Comanche Ridge, north of the main highway US-380. (*Figures J-3* and *J-4A*) Up there I did find something suspicious, but east of the ridge. When I searched for the site on the ground I found only a derelict shooting range and an west-to-east line of scraggly trees. (*Figure J-4C*) I also found a few chunks of reinforced concrete. The campsite seems to have been thoroughly razed. The trees could use some water.

BR-3-N, BR-82-N, and G-148-N, Carlsbad Medical Center, Eddy County

Rank 5 (I-D-1)

Three individual camps occupied the site of today's Carlsbad Medical Center, but not always at the same time. (*Figure J-5*) The first two camps, BR-3-N and BR-82-N, were tasked to the Carlsbad Project, which focused on area dams for flood control. BR-3-N, was put in place in October 1934 on 10 acres of government land and 30 acres of private land. At first it was a tent camp but was soon replaced by permanent buildings. It had the longest stay, from spring/summer 1935 through the winter of 1940–1941.

BR-82- N came next, and was placed right next to the other camp. BR-82-N operated during winter 1938–1939 through the summer of 1941. G-148-N was the late arrival, and was there during winter 1939–1940 to spring 1942. Following their closure, in September the camps were turned over to the Army Air Base and remained under its jurisdiction at least until the end of March 1944. By that time about 1/3 of the buildings had been removed and the remaining buildings were vacant. (Snyder 2002)

DG-41-N, Lake Arthur, Eddy County

Location unknown; Rank 5 (I-D-2)

Trying to locate this site has been frustrating and unfruitful. One of the descriptions I have is, "33 miles southwest of Roswell, 14 miles west of Lake Arthur, at the Hackberry Wells." Drawing circles with those radii puts it in northwestern Eddy County. (*Figure J-1*) But it's not certain if those distances are crow-miles or road miles. A single suspicious area seen on *Google Earth* in Eddy County reveals no recognizable structures. A second description says, "15 miles *west* [my italics] on highway 285." The problem with this is that US-285 runs north to south, not west to east. The camp was the first "portable" or mobile camp. Mobile camps were cost-effective and easily towed on trailers to location by truck so it's no mystery why little footprint was left behind. The camp was set up in either in spring/summer 1935 (*Number of Camps in each County by Period*) or February 1936. (*The Grazette* 1936) For the time being the location of this campsite must remain uncertain.

F-37-N, "Camp Dark Canyon," Carlsbad, Eddy County

Rank 5 (III-B-3)

I am acquainted with a woman friend here in Albuquerque, Lynn Adkins, whose father, Paul Adkins, was the commanding officer of this camp. F-37-N was located out in the boonies just north of the Carlsbad Caverns National Park boundary, about 35 driving miles west of the city of Carlsbad. Despite its isolation, it was a spic-and-span facility. Today much remains of the old campsite, but it rests on private land and is sadly off limits. (*Figures J-6* and *J-7*)

NP-1-N, Rattlesnake Spring, Carlsbad, Eddy County

Rank 4a (I-C-1)

This is in a detached portion, i.e., a satellite, of Carlsbad Caverns National Park. During WWII the Carlsbad Air Base made use of the CCC buildings. A row of cottonwood trees that line the picnic grounds is about all that remains from the CCC days. (*Figures J-8* and *J-9*)

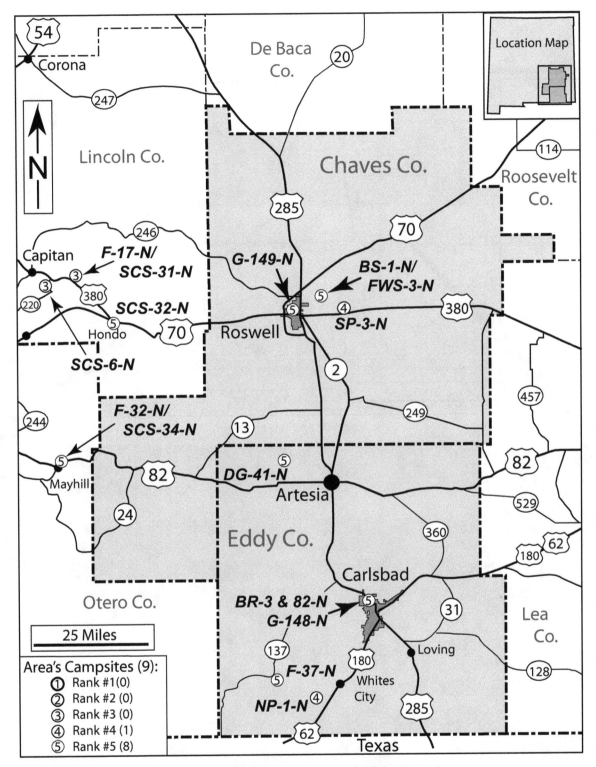

Figure J-1. AREA J / Chaves and Eddy Counties.

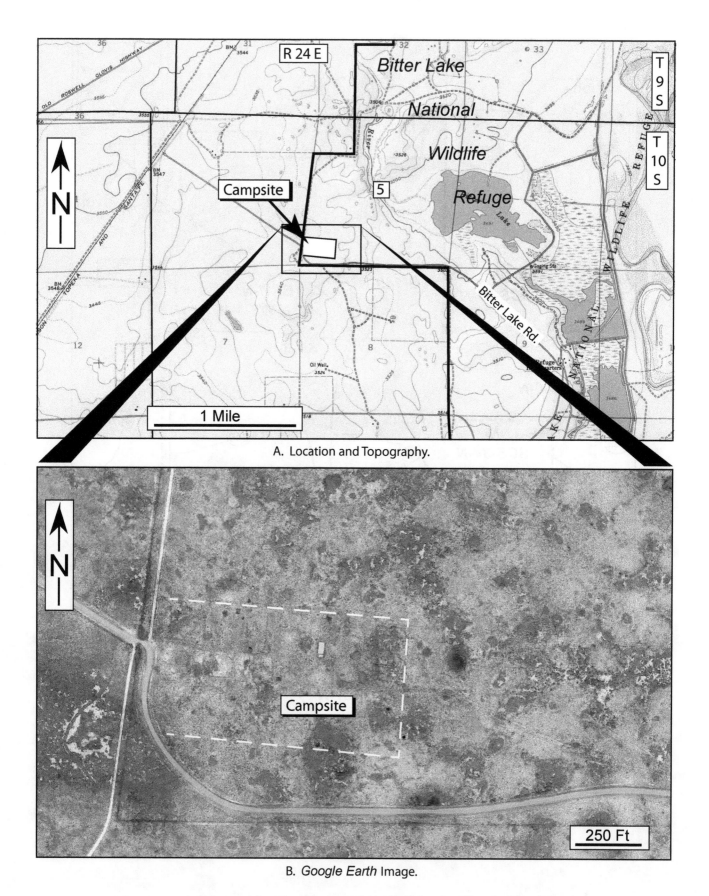

A. Location and Topography.

B. *Google Earth* Image.

Figure J-2. Camp BS-1-N/FWS-3-N, Bitter Lake National Wildlife Refuge.

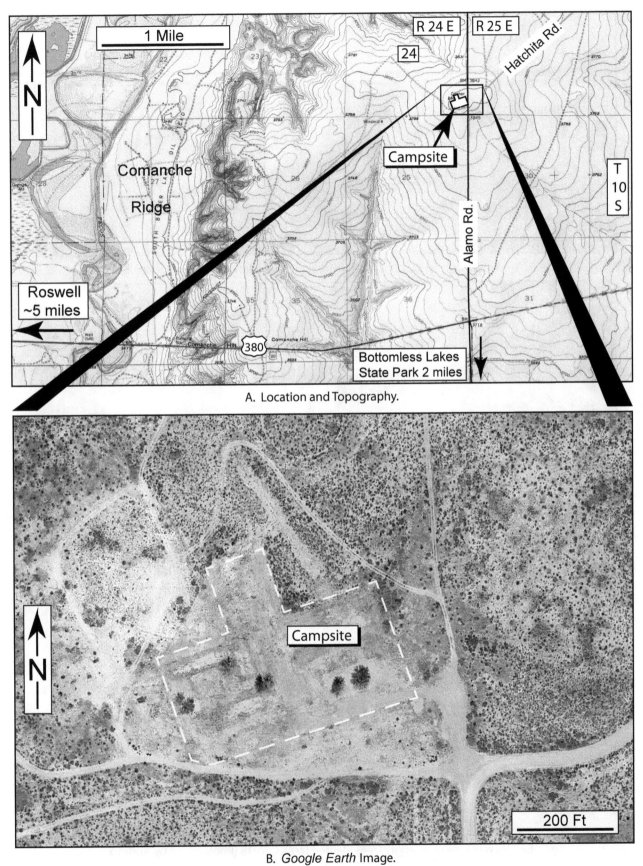

A. Location and Topography.

B. *Google Earth* Image.

Figure J-3. Camp SP-3-N, Bottomless Lakes State Park I.

A. View of Camp, 1937 (Photograph from James F. Justin CCC Museum Website).

B. View of Camp, 1937 (Photograph from Southeast New Mexico Historical Society).

C. East View of Line of Scraggly Trees Planted by CCC, 2018 (Photograph by Author).

Figure J-4. Camp SP-3-N, Bottomless Lakes State Park II.

A. *Google Earth* Image.

B. One of the Three Carlsbad Camps, 1930s (Photograph from *Carlsbad Current-Argus*, Sept. 9, 1990).

Figure J-5. Camps BR-3-N, BR-82-N, and G-148-N, Carlsbad Medical Center.

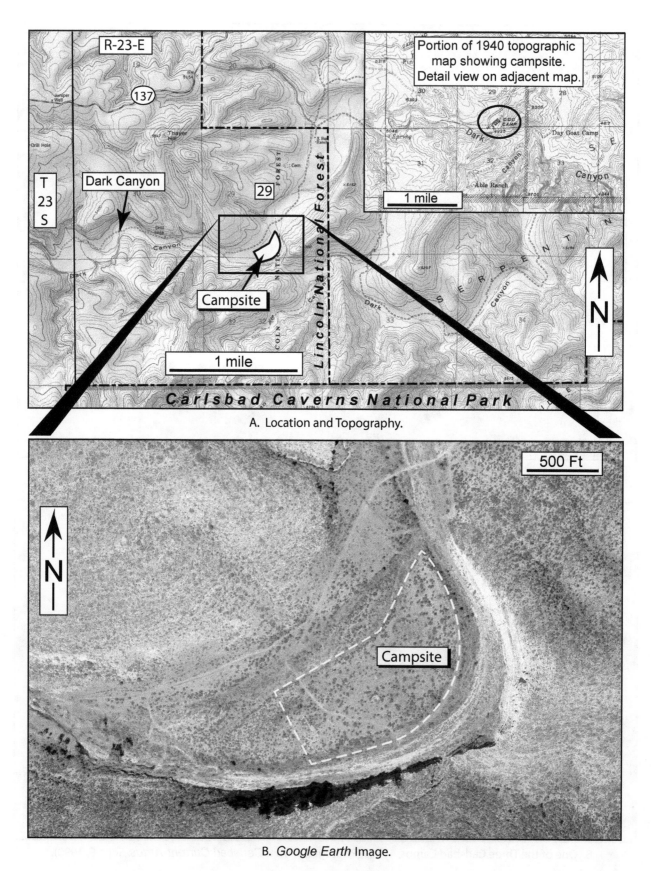

A. Location and Topography.

Portion of 1940 topographic map showing campsite. Detail view on adjacent map.

Dark Canyon

Campsite

B. *Google Earth* Image.

Figure J-6. Camp F-37-N, Dark Canyon, Carlsbad I.

A. North-Northeast View of Camp, 1930s (Photograph from L. Adkins).

B. Camp Was Truly Remote!

C. North View of Camp's North Side, 1930s (Photograph from L. Adkins).

Figure J-7. Camp F-37-N, Dark Canyon, Carlsbad II.

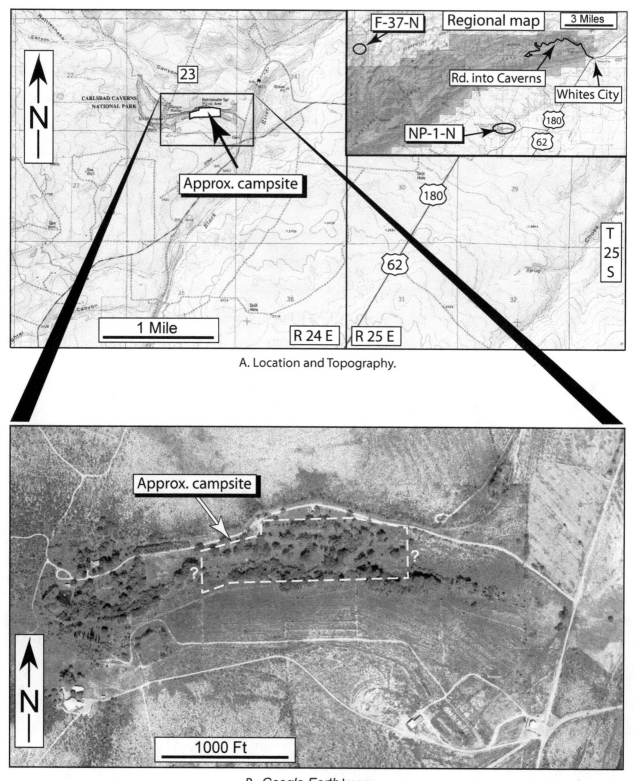

A. Location and Topography.

B. *Google Earth* Image.

Figure J-8. Camp NP-1-N, Rattlesnake Spring, Carlsbad I.

A. Northwest View of Camp, Late 1930s (Photograph by R. Hoff).

B. West-Northwest View of Camp, Late 1930s (Photograph by R. Hoff).

C. West-Northwest Oblique *GoogleEarth* Image of Campsite Area.

Figure J-9. Camp NP-1-N, Rattlesnake Spring, Carlsbad II.

AREA K

EAST-CENTRAL NEW MEXICO: EASTERN SAN MIGUEL COUNTY, QUAY, DE BACA, CURRY, AND ROOSEVELT COUNTIES
(FIGURE K-1)

This huge area contains five campsites, listed below from north to south.

San Miguel County: SP-8-N, Conchas Lake State Park (P.O. Conchas Dam)

De Baca County: SCS-23-N, Fort Sumner (P.O. Fort Sumner)

Quay County: SP-7-N, Municipal Park, Tucumcari (P.O. Tucumcari)

Curry County: SCS-33-N, Field, (P.O. Melrose)

Roosevelt County: SP-5-N, "Camp Roosevelt," Eastern New Mexico State Park (P.O. Portales)

SP-8-N, CONCHAS LAKE STATE PARK, SAN MIGUEL COUNTY

RANK 4 (I-C-1)

The Conchas Lake Dam was built from 1935 to 1939 by the U.S. Corps of Engineers. A construction town for the workers had been constructed in 1935, called Conchas City. After completion in the summer of 1939, the construction camp was used by the CCC to dismantle Conchas City, reuse the adobe bricks, build permanent housing, build a Corps of Engineers administration building, and construct recreation facilities for the new state park. The CCC phase lasted until the spring of 1942. (*Figure K-2*) The few ruined structures that remain of their camp are on the southeast side of Conchas Lake, just east of the state Park and just north of NM-104.

SCS-23-N, Fort Sumner, De Baca County

RANK 5 (III-C-2)

This was one of a group of SCS camps shut down in the spring of 1942 due to the war effort. It only functioned for a short time, from July 1939 into March 1942. The website of the CCC Legacy locates this site as "2 mi NE." That bearing from the town puts it in the Fort Sumner Municipal Airport. (*Figure K-3*) *Google Earth* reveals a rectangular pattern in the northeast corner of the airport, with the "ghosts" of what appear to be building outlines. The site is flanked on the northwest and south by two wartime runways. Today it's off limits.

Back when the CCC was there, the village of Fort Sumner owned the land. In 1942 the Army Air Force took the property and built the air field as a WWII training field, called the Fort Sumner Army Air Field. In March 1946 part of the area was used as a German POW camp. Foundations of barracks used by the POWs are evident.

SP-7-N, Municipal Park, Tucumcari, Quay County

RANK 5 (I-D-I)

The campsite is sandwiched between the railroad tracks to the north and a dirt track to the south that later became 1-40. (*Figures K-4* and *K-5*) Occupation was from summer 1936 through winter 1939–1940. Although nothing remains of the camp itself (hence the low ranking), the CCC's work is evident nearby in the guise of the Municipal Park and its large defunct swimming pool. The pool had been constructed over several years. The land was acquired from local ranchers and the town drilled water wells to supply the pool. The structure was finished in 1940, became wildly popular with the locals, and for a while was the largest outdoor pool in the state. At times as many as 2,000 people gathered at the site. By the 1950s the site became known as Five Mile Park because it was that distance from downtown. However, the roof of the adjoining bathhouse had design defects from the very beginning (the CCC constructed it but did not design it) and the problems accumulated. After construction of a new pool in downtown Tucumcari, this pool was drained in 1977. (Kammer 1995a; Flynn 2012) The pool and bathhouse today sit abandoned and await renovation and financing. Only some of the water wells and their towers remain. (*Figure K-5B*)

SCS-33-N, Field, Melrose, De Baca County

RANK 5 (III-D-3)

SCS-33-N was a difficult place to find. Its post office was listed as Melrose. (*Number of Camps in each County by Period*) It was one of the very last camps to be established, just before Pearl Harbor. It operated only from September 1941 into early 1942, so not much ground trace was expected. In the spring of 2010 I visited Melrose and was determined to locate this site. I barged into a knitting bee at the Senior Center (to the shock of the elderly knitters), into the one-office city hall, into the school, and pestered a number of natives. No one knew a thing about a CCC camp.

A later source I had overlooked had the camp at "Fields, 15 mi N" of Melrose. (*CCC Legacy*) *Google Earth* (not available back in 2010) does reveal a spot called Field (just a ranch house). Julian (1996) describes Field as a tiny community formed by the consolidation of three rural schools, and gives its original site as 1.5 miles north of the one-farm habitation. At that place is a small, lonely graveyard, but just to the southwest of it in the middle of a field is the subtle but telltale footprint of the camp. (*Figure K-6*) What the CCC was working on out here on the plains is not at all obvious. The campsite is now on private land, just west of a section of State land, and is off limits.

SP-5-N, "CAMP ROOSEVELT," EASTERN NEW MEXICO STATE PARK (HISTORICAL), PORTALES, ROOSEVELT COUNTY

RANK 4 (I-C-1)

This was one of New Mexico's first four State Parks, the others being Santa Fe River/Hyde Park Memorial, La Joya, and Bottomless Lakes. Eastern New Mexico was built by the CCC. (*Figure K-7*) The CCC company moved in from the now-defunct La Joya State Park and occupied the site in June 1934. The camp started as a tent facility but later that year was upgraded with permanent–but not prefabricated, structures.

The CCC built a two-lake swimming pool, and an adobe adjacent bathhouse and caretaker's house, all of which still exist in derelict condition. (*Figure K-8*) There are also three concrete slabs. The CCC planted 12,000 trees, most of which died due to lack of water and the chewing by rabbits. The native soil could never retain water, so excessive amounts of gasoline had been required to continually pump water for the lakes and trees. The property of this soil had been known beforehand, but it was ignored by the governor who was from the Clovis area and wanted a state park in his district (i.e., "pork barrel" spending). After the CCC left in 1935, the WPA moved in and built a golf course.

Later, as the place deteriorated, it passed through the hands of the adjacent cities of Clovis and Portales, and in the 1940s the park was held under long-term lease by Eastern New Mexico Junior College in Portales. Today the site is sandwiched between the excellent Blackwater Draw National Landmark and Museum to the southwest and the Eastern New Mexico State University's stadium to the north.

Eastern was a failed park. It was a political stunt, favored by one governor and disdained by his successor. It was not at all suited for the area because it was located on the edge of the Dust Bowl, dependent on hard-to-get (expensive) water, and lack of funding for maintenance. (National Park Service undated report) Despite all this drama, the CCC had dutifully done what it was tasked to do.

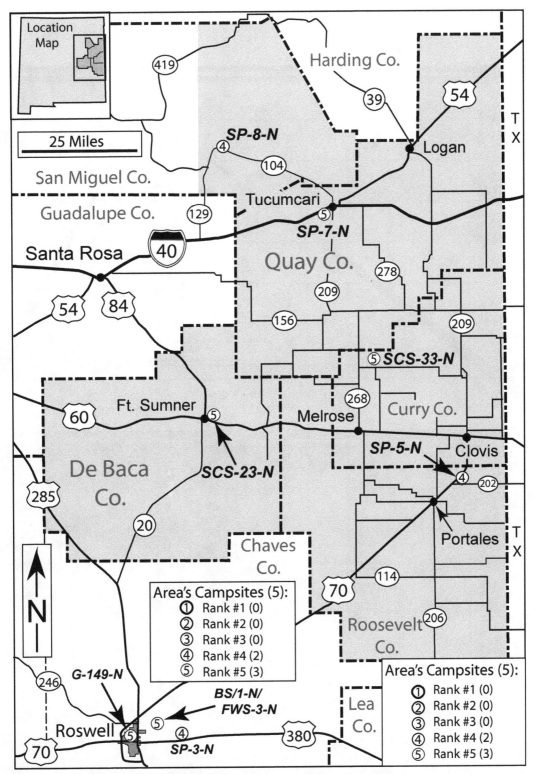

Figure K-1. AREA K / DeBaca, Quay, Roosevelt, Curry, and Eastern San Miguel Counties.

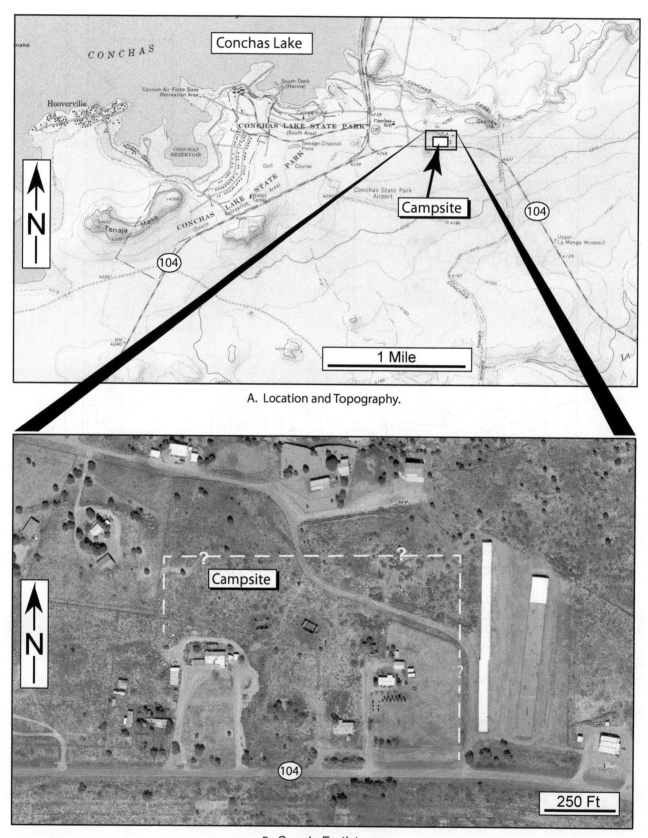

A. Location and Topography.

B. *Google Earth* Image.

Figure K-2. Camp SP-8-N, Conchas Lake.

A. *Google Earth* Image (Probable Campsite at Municipal Airport).

B. South-Southwest View of Camp, 1930s (Photograph from Internet).

Figure K-3. Camp SCS-23-N, Ft. Sumner.

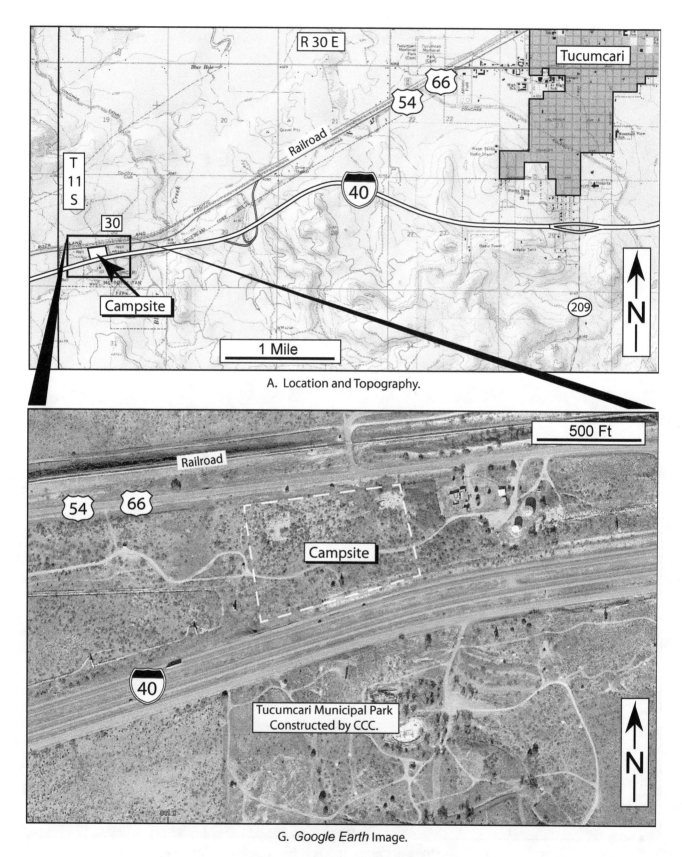

R 30 E

Tucumcari

66

54

Railroad

40

T 11 S

30

Campsite

209

1 Mile

A. Location and Topography.

500 Ft

Railroad

54 66

Campsite

40

Tucumcari Municipal Park Constructed by CCC.

G. *Google Earth* Image.

Figure K-4. Camp SP-7-N, Tucumcari I.

A. North Aerial View of Camp, 1930s (Photograph from James Crocker).

B. Camp-Area Water Well, 2010 (Photograph by Author).

Figure K-5. Camp SP-7-N, Tucumcari II.

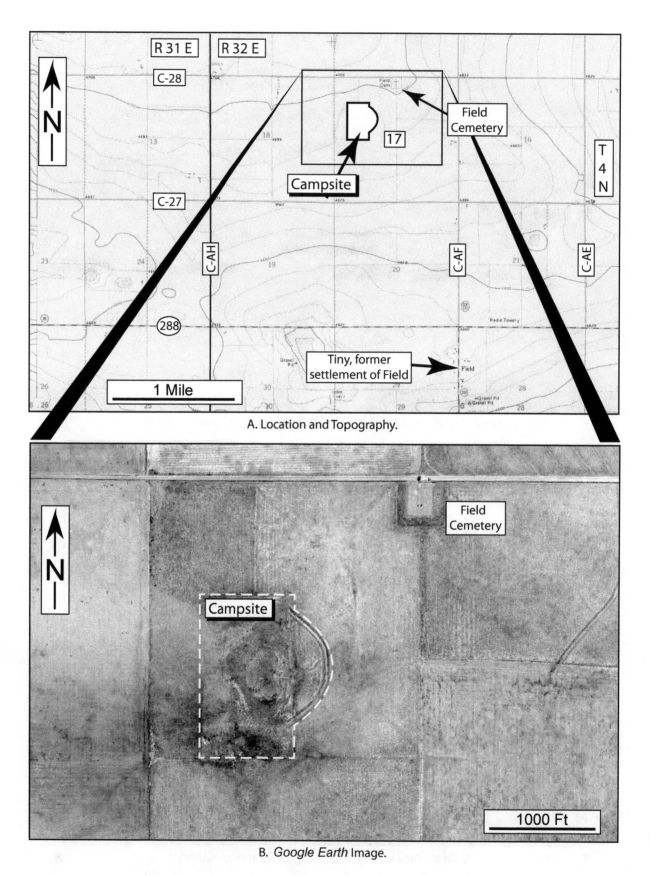

A. Location and Topography.

B. *Google Earth* Image.

Figure K-6. Camp SCS-33-N, Field, Melrose.

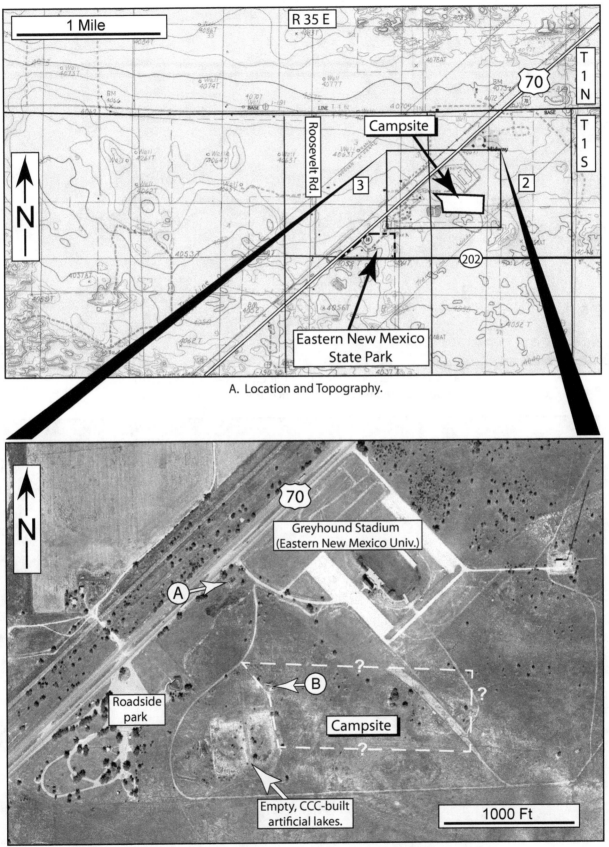

A. Location and Topography.

B. *Google Earth* Image (Showing Photograph Shots in Figure K-8).

Figure K-7. Camp SP-5-N, Camp Roosevelt, Portales I.

221

A. East View of Deteriorating CCC-Built Caretaker's House, 2010
(Greyhound Stadium in Right Distance, Photograph by Author).

B. West View of Deteriorating CCC-Built Bath House, 2010 (Photograph by Author).

Figure K-8. Camp SP-5-N, Camp Roosevelt, Portales II.

We have come to the end of our virtual tour of New Mexico's 90 CCC campsites. It is my hope that you, the reader, now have a better understanding of this "lost" yet fascinating chapter of New Mexico history so that it might be recovered. I hope that these places are now "on your radar screen." I also hope that your curiosity has been tweaked to the point that you may now look for and recognize the remains of these campsites along the road, understand them in context, and be encouraged to check them out. If I have achieved these things I will consider this book a success.

Appendix I
CCC Enrollment Periods

The Civilian Conservation Corps camps were budgeted, staffed, and operated by "periods." Each period (except the program's first and last) were six-months in duration and roughly corresponded to spring/summer and fall/winter seasons, rather than to Federal Fiscal Years, which during the 1930s ran from July 1 through the following June 30 (only in 1976 were the fiscal years changed to October 1 through the following September 30). The seasonal key for understanding the periods is: odd numbers = spring/summers, even numbers = fall/winters.

Inception: March 31, 1933

Period 1 (spring/summer 1933): June 1–September 30, 1933

Period 2 (fall/winter 1933–1934): Oct. 1, 1933–March 31, 1934

Period 3 (spring/summer 1934): April 1–September 30, 1934

Period 4 (fall/winter 1934–1935): October 1, 1934–March 31, 1935

Period 5 (spring/summer 1935): April 1–September 30, 1935

Period 6 (fall/winter 1935–1936): October 1, 1935–March 31, 1936

Period 7 (spring/summer 1936): April 1–September 30, 1936

Period 8 (fall/winter 1936–1937): October 1, 1936–March 31, 1937

Period 9 (spring/summer 1937): April 1–September 30, 1937

Period 10 (fall/winter 1937–1938): October 1, 1937–March 31, 1938

Period 11 (spring/summer 1938): April 1–September 30, 1938

Period 12 (fall/winter 1938–1939): October 1, 1938–March 31, 1939

Period 13 (spring/summer 1939): April 1–September 30, 1939

Period 14 (fall/winter 1939–1940): October 1, 1939–March 31, 1940

Period 15 (spring/summer 1940): April 1–September 30, 1940

Period 16 (fall/winter 1940–1941): October 1, 1940–March 31, 1941

Period 17 (spring/summer 1941): April 1–September 30, 1941

Period 18 (fall/winter 1941–1942): October 1, 1941–March 31, 1942

Period 19 (spring 1942): April 1–June 30, 1942

Termination: June 30, 1942

Appendix II CCC camps by *Periods* and years of operation

Source: "Number of Camps in each County by Period," undated.

New Mexico CCC camps by Period, season & year (S = April thru Sept.; W = Oct. thru March)

Prior name	Next name	Camp name	Location	County	1st S 1933	2nd W 1933-34	3rd S 1934	4th W 1934-35	5th S 1935	6th W 1935-36	7th S 1936	8th W 1936-37	9th S 1937	10th W 1937-38	11th S 1938	12th W 1938-39	13th S 1939	14th W 1939-40	15th S 1940	16th W 1940-41	17th S 1941	18th W 1941-42	19th S 1942
				National Forest Service (1933-1942)																			
		F-1-N	Reserve	Catron	X	X																	
		F-2-N	Apache Creek	Catron	X	X			X														
		F-3-N	Vallecitos	Rio Arriba	X		X																
		F-4-N	Never opened																				
	SCS-4-N	F-5-N	El Rito	Rio Arriba	X		X																
		F-6-N	Vadito	Taos	X																		
		F-7-N	Grants	Cibola	X																		
		F-8-N*	Sulphur Spgs.	Bernalillo	X																		
		F-8-N*	Sandia Park	Bernalillo					X		X		X		X		X		X		X		
		F-9-N	Monica	Socorro	X																		
		F-10-N	Never opened																				
		F-11-N	Mimbres	Grant	X	X																	
		F-12-N	Pinos Altos	Grant	X	X	X																
	PE-202-N	F-15-N	Little Walnut	Grant	X			X						X		X		X		X			
F-16-N	F-24-N?	F-16-N	High Rolls	Otero	X																		
	SCS-31-N	F-17-N	Capitan	Lincoln	X	X																	
		F-19-N	Otowi	Los Alamos	X																		
		F-21-N	Rio Gallinas	San Miguel	X																		
		F-22-N	Jemez Spgs.	Sandoval	X																		
	PE-201-N	F-23-N	Little Tesuque	Santa Fe	X																		
F-16-N		F-24-N	High Rolls	Otero			X	X	X		X	X	X	X	X	X	X	X					
		F-25-N	Glenwood	Catron		X	X	X	X	X	X	X	X	X	X	X	X	X		X		X	
		F-26-N	Juan Tabo	Bernalillo		X																	
	F-38-N?	F-27-N	Jornada Ex. Ra.	Dona Ana		X	X	X															
		F-28-N	La Luz Canyon	Otero		X	X	X	X														
		F-29-N	Alma	Catron		X																	
		F-30-N	Woofter Ranch	Socorro		X																	
		F-31-N	Paliza Canyon	Sandoval		X	X	X	X	?	X	X	X	X	X	?	X						
	SCS-34-N	F-32-N	Mayhill	Otero		X	X	X	X	X	X	X	X	X	X	X	X	X	X				
		F-33-N	Tent Rocks	Sandoval		X	X																
		F-34-N	Beaverhead	Catron			X		X	X					X	X	X		X				
	SCS-21-N	F-35-N	Manzano	Torrance			X			X	X												
		F-36-N	El Rito	Rio Arriba											X	X	X						
SCS-4-N		F-37-N	Guadalupe	Eddy					X	X		X	X	X	X	X	X	X					
		F-38-N	Never opened																				

225

Appendix II CCC camps by *Periods* and years of operation (cont.)

New Mexico CCC camps by Period, season & year (S = April thru Sept.; W = Oct. thru March)

Prior name	Next name	Camp name	Location	County	1st S 1933	2nd W 1933-34	3rd S 1934	4th W 1934-35	5th S 1935	6th W 1935-36	7th S 1936	8th W 1936-37	9th S 1937	10th W 1937-38	11th S 1938	12th W 1938-39	13th S 1939	14th W 1939-40	15th S 1940	16th W 1940-41	17th S 1941	18th W 1941-42	19th S 1942
F-27-N		F-39-N	Jornada del M	Dona Ana							X	?	X										
	SCS-22-N	F-40-N	Kingston	Sierra					X	X	X	?											
		F-41-N	Corona	Lincoln						X	X	X	X										
		F-42-N	Never opened																				
		F-43-N	La Madera	Rio Arriba						X				X		X		X		X			
		F-51-N	Montecello	Sierra						X				X		X		X		X			
		F-52-N	Willow Creek	Grant											X		X		X		X		X
		F-54-N	Ruidoso	Lincoln																			
		F-55-N	El Rito	Rio Arriba																			
SCS-25-N		F-57-N	Augustin	Socorro																			

Park Erosion Service (until 1935)

Prior name	Next name	Camp name	Location	County	1st S 1933	2nd W 1933-34	3rd S 1934	4th W 1934-35	5th S 1935	6th W 1935-36	7th S 1936	8th W 1936-37	9th S 1937	10th W 1937-38	11th S 1938	12th W 1938-39	13th S 1939	14th W 1939-40	15th S 1940	16th W 1940-41	17th S 1941	18th W 1941-42	19th S 1942
F-23-N	SCS-14-N	PE-201-N	Hyde Memorial	Santa Fe		X	X	X															
F-15-N		PE-202-N	Little Walnut	Socorro			X																

National Park Service (Parks & Monuments)

Prior name	Next name	Camp name	Location	County	1st S 1933	2nd W 1933-34	3rd S 1934	4th W 1934-35	5th S 1935	6th W 1935-36	7th S 1936	8th W 1936-37	9th S 1937	10th W 1937-38	11th S 1938	12th W 1938-39	13th S 1939	14th W 1939-40	15th S 1940	16th W 1940-41	17th S 1941	18th W 1941-42	19th S 1942
NP-4-N		NM-1-N	Bandelier	Sandoval	X	X	X	X	X	X	X	X	X	?	X	X	X						
NP-2-N		NM-2-N	Chaco Canyon	San Juan		X		X	X	X	X	X	X	?	X	X	X						
		NP-1-N	Rattlesnake Spgs	Eddy										X	?	X	X					X	
NM-2-N		NP-2-N	Chaco Canyon	San Juan													X	X	X	X	X		
NM-1-N		NP-4-N	Bandelier	Sandoval														X	X	X	X	X	X

State Parks

Prior name	Next name	Camp name	Location	County	1st S 1933	2nd W 1933-34	3rd S 1934	4th W 1934-35	5th S 1935	6th W 1935-36	7th S 1936	8th W 1936-37	9th S 1937	10th W 1937-38	11th S 1938	12th W 1938-39	13th S 1939	14th W 1939-40	15th S 1940	16th W 1940-41	17th S 1941	18th W 1941-42	19th S 1942
		SP-1-N	Santa Fe	Santa Fe		X	X	X	X	X	X	X	X	?	X	X	X	X	X	X	X		
		SP-2-N	La Joya	Socorro		X	X	X	X	X	X	X	X	?	X	X	X	X	X	X			
		SP-3-N	Bottomless L.	Chaves			X	X	X	X	X	X	X	?	X								
		SP-5-N	E. NM S.P.	Roosevelt			X	X	X														
		SP-7-N	Tucumcari	Quay						X								X					
		SP-8-N	Conchas Lake	San Miguel													X	X	X	X	X	X	X

Bureau of Reclamation (from 1935)

Prior name	Next name	Camp name	Location	County	1st S 1933	2nd W 1933-34	3rd S 1934	4th W 1934-35	5th S 1935	6th W 1935-36	7th S 1936	8th W 1936-37	9th S 1937	10th W 1937-38	11th S 1938	12th W 1938-39	13th S 1939	14th W 1939-40	15th S 1940	16th W 1940-41	17th S 1941	18th W 1941-42	19th S 1942
		BR-3-N	Carlsbad/Med.	Eddy					X	X	X	X	X	?	X	X	X	X	X	X	X	X	
		BR-8-N	Elephant Butte	Sierra				X	X	X	?	?	X	?	X	X	X	X	X	X	X	X	
		BR-39-N	Las Cruces	Dona Ana					X	X	X	X	X	?	X	X	X	X	X	X	X	X	
		BR-54-N	Elephant Butte	Sierra					X		X	X	X	?		X	X	X	X	X	X	X	
		BR-82-N	Carlsbad/Med.	Eddy													X	X	X	X	X		X

Appendix II CCC camps by Periods and years of operation (cont.)

New Mexico CCC camps by Period, season & year (S = April thru Sept.; W = Oct. thru March)

Text box: "SCS established in 1935 & took over many FS camp."

Text box: "Taylor Grazing Act of 1934 implemented 1935"

Prior name	Next name	Camp name	Location	County	1st S 1933	2nd W 1933-34	3rd S 1934	4th W 1934-35	5th S 1935	6th W 1935-36	7th S 1936	8th W 1936-37	9th S 1937	10th W 1937-38	11th S 1938	12th W 1938-39	13th S 1939	14th W 1939-40	15th S 1940	16th W 1940-41	17th S 1941	18th W 1941-42	19th S 1942
Soil Erosion Service (SCS after 1935)																						
	SCS-1-N	SES-2-N	Gila	Grant				X															
Soil Conservation Service (from 1935)																						
SES-2-N		SCS-1-N	Gila	Grant					X	X	X	X	X										
		SCS-2-N	Red Rock	Grant					X	X	X	X	X	X		X							
F-5-N		SCS-3-N	Abiquiu	Rio Arriba					X	X	X	?	X										
		SCS-4-N	El Rito	Rio Arriba					X	X	X	X	X	X									
	F-36-N	SCS-5-N	Velarde	Rio Arriba					X	X	X	X	X	?	X						X		
		SCS-6-N	Ft. Stanton	Lincoln					X	X	X	X	X	X	X		X	X	X	X			
		SCS-7-N	Rio Puerco	Sandoval					X	X	X	X	X										
		SCS-8-N	Rio Salado	Sandoval					X	X	X	X	X					X		X			
		SCS-9-N	Rio Puerco	Bernalillo					X	X	X	X	X	X	X	X	X	X					
		SCS-10-N	San Mateo	Cibola					X	X	X	X	X										
		SCS-11-N	Never opened																				
		SCS-12-N	Never opened																				
		SCS-13-N	Never opened																				
PE-202-N		SCS-14-N	Little Walnut	Grant					X	X	X												
	G-178-N?	SCS-15-N	Whitewater	Grant					X	?	?	X	X	X	X	X	X	X	X	X			
		SCS-16-N	Las Cruces	Dona Ana					X	X	X	X	X	X	X	X	X	X	X	X			
		SCS-17-N	Santa Fe	Santa Fe					X	X	?	X	X	X	X	X	X	X	X	X			
		SCS-18-N	Buckhorn	Grant					X	X	X												
		SCS-19-N	Virden	Hidalgo					X	X	X	X	X	X	X	X	X	X					
F-35-N		SCS-20-N	Mangas Canyon	Grant					X	X	X	X	X	X	X	X	X	X	X				
		SCS-21-N	Manzano	Torrance								X	X										
F-40-N		SCS-22-N	Kingston	Sierra								X	X										
		SCS-23-N	Ft. Sumner	De Baca													X	X	X	X			X
DG-42-N	F-57-N	SCS-25-N	Augustin	Socorro														X	X	X	X	X	
		SCS-26-N	Rodeo	Hidalgo													X	X	X	X	X	X	
	A-SCS-1	SCS-27-N	ABQ Mesa	Bernalillo														X	X	X	X	X	
		SCS-28-N	La Cueva	Mora															X	X	X		
F-24-N		SCS-29-N	High Rolls	Otero															X	X			
DG-39-N	G(D)1-N	SCS-30-N	Tularosa	Otero																X			
F-17-N		SCS-31-N	Capitan	Lincoln																X			
		SCS-32-N	Hondo	Lincoln																	X		
		SCS-33-N	Melrose/Field	Curry																	X	X	
F-32-N		SCS-34-N	Mayhill	Otero																	X	X	

227

Appendix II CCC camps by Periods and years of operation (cont.)

New Mexico CCC camps by Period, season & year (S = April thru Sept.; W = Oct. thru March)

Prior name	Next name	Camp name	Location	County	1st S 1933	2nd W 1933-34	3rd S 1934	4th W 1934-35	5th S 1935	6th W 1935-36	7th S 1936	8th W 1936-37	9th S 1937	10th W 1937-38	11th S 1938	12th W 1938-39	13th S 1939	14th W 1939-40	15th S 1940	16th W 1940-41	17th S 1941	18th W 1941-42	19th S 1942
Division of Grazing (through 1938)																							
		DG-36-N	Mirage	Luna					X	X	X	X	X	?	X	X	X	X					
	G-37-N	DG-37-N	Cuchillo	Sierra					X	X	X	X	X	?	X	X	X						
		DG-38-N	Radium Spgs.	Dona Ana					X	X	?	?											
	SCS-30-N	DG-39-N	Tularosa	Otero					X	X	X	X	X	?	X	X	X						
		DG-40-N	Carrizozo	Lincoln					X	X	X	X	X	?	X	X	X						
		DG-41-N	Lake Arthur	Chaves					X	X	X	X	X	?	X	X	X						
	SCS-25-N	DG-42-N	Augustin	Socorro					X	X	X	X	X	?	X	X	X						
		DG-43-N	Animas	Hidalgo					X	X	X	X	X	?	X	X	X						
	G-69-N	DG-69-N	Orogrande	Otero											X	X	X						
	G-101-N	DG-101-N	Bloomfield	San Juan												X	X						
Grazing Service (from 1939)																							
DG-37-N		G-37-N	Cuchillo	Sierra													X	X	X	X			
DG-39-N	SCS-30-N	G-39-N	Tularosa	Otero														X	X				
DG-69-N		G-69-N	Orogrande	Otero														X	X	X	X	X	
DG-101-N		G-101-N	Bloomfield	San Juan														X	X	X	X	X	X
		G-123-N	Quemado	Catron															X	X	X	X	
	G(D)-2-N	G-147-N	Tokay	Socorro														X	X	X	X		
		G-148-N	Carlsbad/Med.	Eddy														X	X	X	X	X	X
		G-149-N	Roswell	Chaves														X	X	X	X		
		G-150-N	Columbus	Luna														X	X	X	X	X	
		G-174-N	Cambray	Luna															X	X	X	X	
SCS-16-N		G-178-N	Las Cruces	Dona Ana														X	X	X	X	X	X
Biological Service (to 1940)																							
FWS-3-N		BS-1-N	Bitter Lake	Chaves												X	X	X	X				
FWS-2-N		BS-2-N	Bosc. del Ap.	Socorro												X	X	X	X				
Fish & Wildlife Service (from 1940)																							
BS-2-N	G(D)-2-N	FWS-2-N	Bosc. del Ap.	Socorro																X	X	X	X
BS-1-N		FWS-3-N	Bitter Lake	Chaves																X	X	X	
Military & National Defence																							
SCS-27-N		A-SCS-1-N	ABQ E. Mesa	Bernalillo																		X	X
SCS-30-N		G(D)-1-N	Tularosa	Otero																		X	X
G-147-N		G(D)-2-N	San Antonio	Socorro																			X

Agency name changed from Division of Grazing to Grazing Service (see below) in 1939

Agency name changed to FWS (see below) in 1940

Appendix III: Occupation History of CCC's 90 Campsites (source: *"Number of Camps in each County by Period,"* undated document)

Note: Pale-gray boxes below = new names applied to earlier campsites.

Period, season, & year (S = summer, April through September; W = winter, October through March)

Camp name	Location	County	1st S 1933	2nd W 1933-34	3rd S 1934	4th W 1934-35	5th S 1935	6th W 1935-36	7th S 1936	8th W 1936-37	9th S 1937	10th W 1937-38	11th S 1938	12th W 1938-39	13th S 1939	14th W 1939-40	15th S 1940	16th W 1940-41	17th S 1941	18th W 1941-42	19th S 1942
F-1-N	Reserve	Catron	F-1-N			F-1-N															
F-2-N	Apache Creek	Catron	F-2-N				F-2-N							F-2-N		F-2-N		F-2-N			
F-3-N	Vallecitos	Rio Arriba			F-3-N																
F-5-N	El Rito	Rio Arriba			F-5-N				SCS-4-N				F-36-N	F-36-N	F-36-N						
F-6-N	Vadito	Taos	F-6-N																		
F-7-N	Grants	Cibola	F-7-N																		
F-8-N	Sulphur Spgs.	Bernalillo	F-8-N																		
F-8-N	Sandia Park	Bernalillo					F-8-N		F-8-N		F-8-N		F-8-N		F-8-N		F-8-N		F-8-N		
F-9-N	Monica	Socorro	F-9-N																		
F-11-N	Mimbres	Grant		F-11-N		F-11-N						F-11-N		F-11-N		F-11-N		F-11-N			
F-12-N	Pinos Altos	Grant	F-12-N		F-12-N																
F-15-N	Little Walnut	Grant		F-15-N	PE-202-N		SCS-14-N														
F-16-N	High Rolls	Otero	F-16-N		F-24-N							F-24-N				F-24-N	SCS-29-N	SCS-31-N			
F-17-N	Capitan	Lincoln	F-17-N																		
F-19-N	Otowi	Los Alamos		F-19-N																	
F-21-N	Rio Gallinas	San Miguel		F-21-N																	
F-22-N	Jemez Spgs.	Sandoval		F-22-N																	
F-23-N	Little Tesuque	Santa Fe	F-23-N		PE-201																
F-25-N	Glenwood	Catron		F-25-N		F-25-N					F-25-N			F-25-N		F-25-N		F-25-N		F-25-N	
F-26-N	Juan Tabo	Bernalillo		F-26-N																	
F-27-N	Jornada Ex. Ra.	Dona Ana		F-27-N		F-27-N			F-39-N												
F-28-N	La Luz Canyon	Otero		F-28-N		F-28-N															
F-29-N	Alma	Catron		F-29-N																	
F-30-N	Woofter Ra.	Socorro		F-30-N						SCS-22-N											
F-31-N	Paliza Canyon	Sandoval							F-31-N		F-32-N										
F-32-N	Mayhill	Otero		F-32-N													F-32-N		SCS-34-N		
F-33-N	Tent Rocks	Sandoval		F-33-N																	
F-34-N	Beaverhead	Catron			F-34-N		F-34-N						F-34-N	F-34-N		F-34-N					
F-35-N	Manzano	Torrance				F-35-N							SCS-21-N								
F-37-N	Guadalupe	Eddy							F-37-N				F-37-N	F-37-N		F-37-N					
F-40-N	Kingston	Sierra					F-40-N														
F-41-N	Corona	Lincoln						F-41-N													
F-43-N	La Madera	Rio Arriba						F-43-N			F-43-N			F-43-N		F-43-N		F-43-N			
F-51-N	Montecello	Sierra						F-51-N			F-51-N			F-51-N		F-51-N		F-51-N			
F-52-N	Willow Creek	Grant											F-52-N		F-52-N		F-52-N		F-52-N		F-52-N
F-54-N	Ruidoso	Lincoln													F-54-N		F-54-N			F-54-N	
F-55-N	Vallecitos	Rio Arriba															F-55-N		F-55-N		F-55-N

229

Appendix III: Occupation History of CCC's 90 Campsites (cont.)

Note: Pale-gray boxes below = new names applied to earlier campsites.

Period, season, & year (S = summer, April through September; W = winter, October through March)

Camps listed by *original* site only

Period/season/year key:

Period	1st	2nd	3rd	4th	5th	6th	7th	8th	9th	10th	11th	12th	13th	14th	15th	16th	17th	18th	19th
Season	S	W	S	W	S	W	S	W	S	W	S	W	S	W	S	W	S	W	S
Year	1933	1933-34	1934	1934-35	1935	1935-36	1936	1936-37	1937	1937-38	1938	1938-39	1939	1939-40	1940	1940-41	1941	1941-42	1942

Camp name	Location	County	1st	2nd	3rd	4th	5th	6th	7th	8th	9th	10th	11th	12th	13th	14th	15th	16th	17th	18th	19th
NM-1-N	Bandelier	Sandoval							NM-1-N												
NM-2-N	Chaco Canyon	San Juan													NM-2-N	NP-4-N					
NP-1-N	Rattlesnake Spgs	Eddy										NP-1-N					NP-1-N	NP-2-N			
SP-1-N	Santa Fe	Santa Fe									SP-1-N										
SP-2-N	La Joya	Socorro		SP-2-N																	
SP-3-N	Bottomless L.	Chaves			SP-3-N						SP-3-N										
SP-5-N	E. NM S.P.	Roosevelt				SP-5-N															
SP-7-N	Tucumcari	Quay										SP-7-N									
SP-8-N	Conchas Lake	San Miguel																SP-8-N			
BR-3-N	Carlsbad/Med.	Eddy											BR-3-N								
BR-8-N	Elephant Butte	Sierra								BR-8-N											
BR-39-N	Las Cruces	Dona Ana											BR-39-N								
BR-54-N	Elephant Butte	Sierra					BR-54-N						BR-54-N								
BR-82-N	Carlsbad/Med.	Eddy														BR-82-N					
SES-2-N	Gila	Grant				SES-2-N															
SCS-2-N	Red Rock	Grant							SCS-1-N					SCS-2-N							
SCS-3-N	Abiquiu	Rio Arriba							SCS-2-N		SCS-3-N										
SCS-5-N	Velarde	Rio Arriba									SCS-5-N									SCS-5-N	
SCS-6-N	Ft. Stanton	Lincoln										SCS-6-N									
SCS-7-N	Rio Puerco	Sandoval							SCS-7-N												
SCS-8-N	Rio Salado	Sandoval									SCS-8-N						?	SCS-8-N			
SCS-9-N	Rio Puerco	Bernalillo								SCS-9-N											
SCS-10-N	San Mateo	Cibola							SCS-10-N		SCS-15-N										
SCS-15-N	Whitewater	Grant									SCS-16-N										
SCS-16-N	Las Cruces	Dona Ana																		G-178-N	
SCS-17-N	Santa Fe	Santa Fe					SCS-17-N								SCS-17-N						
SCS-18-N	Buckhorn	Grant						SCS-18-N					SCS-18-N								
SCS-19-N	Virden	Hidalgo									SCS-19-N										
SCS-20-N	Mangas Cyn.	Grant										SCS-20-N									
SCS-23-N	Ft. Sumner	De Baca																SCS-23-N			
SCS-26-N	Rodeo	Hidalgo																SCS-26-N			
SCS-27-N	ABQ Mesa	Bernalillo																	SCS-27-N		A-SCS-1-N
SCS-28-N	La Cueva	Mora																SCS-28-N			
SCS-32-N	Hondo	Lincoln																	SCS-32-N		
SCS-33-N	Melrose/Field	Curry																	SCS-33-N		

Appendix III: Occupation History of CCC's 90 Campsites (cont.)

Note: Pale-gray boxes below = new names applied to earlier campsites.

Period, season, & year (S = summer, April through September; W = winter, October through March)

Camps listed by *original* site only

Camp name	Location	County	1st	2nd	3rd	4th	5th	6th	7th	8th	9th	10th	11th	12th	13th	14th	15th	16th	17th	18th	19th
Season			S	W	S	W	S	W	S	W	S	W	S	W	S	W	S	W	S	W	S
Years			1933	1933-34	1934	1934-35	1935	1935-36	1936	1936-37	1937	1937-38	1938	1938-39	1939	1939-40	1940	1940-41	1941	1941-42	1942
DG-36-N	Mirage	Luna										DG-36-N									
DG-37-N	Cuchillo	Sierra									DG-37-N						G-37-N				
DG-38-N	Radium Spgs.	Dona Ana						DG-38-N													G(D)-1-N
DG-39-N	Tularosa	Otero									DG-39-N					G-39-N		SCS-30-N			
DG-40-N	Carrizozo	Lincoln									DG-40-N										
DG-41-N	Lake Arthur	Chaves									DG-41-N										
DG-42-N	Augustin	Socorro									DG-42-N					SCS-25-N				F-57-N	
DG-43-N	Animas	Hidalgo									DG-43-N										
DG-69-N	Orogrande	Otero												DG-69-N				G-69-N			
DG-101-N	Bloomfield	San Juan													DG-101-N				G-101-N		
G-123-N	Quemado	Caton															G-123-N				
G-147-N	Tokay	Socorro																G-147-N			G(D)-2-N
G-148-N	Carlsbad/Med.	Eddy																	G-148-N		
G-149-N	Roswell	Chaves																G-149-N			
G-150-N	Columbus	Luna																G-150-N			
G-174-N	Cambray	Luna																G-174-N			
BS-1-N	Bosc. del Ap.	Chaves														BS-1-N			FWS-3-N		
BS-2-N	Bitter Lake	Socorro															BS-2-N		FWS-2-N		

APPENDIX IV: Civilian Conservation Corps (CCC) Campsites in New Mexico -- 1933-1942 (campsites listed & ranked by original name)

AREA	County	Campsite	Location	Acc. Open (I)	Some (II)	None (III)	Camp Much (A)	Mod. (B)	Little (C)	None (D)	Conv. Excellent (1)	Mod. (2)	Remote (3)	RANK	Rank Nos.	#1 I-A-1	#1 I-A-2	#2 I-A-3	#2 I-B-1	#3 I-B-2 to 3	#3 II-A to B	#4 I-C	#4 II-C	#5 I-D, II-D, III
A	Bernalillo	F-26-N	Juan Tabo	X				X			X			2b	I-B-1				X					
A	Bernalillo	SCS-27-N	ABQ Mesa			X				X	X			5	III-D-1									X
A	Bernalillo	F-8-N #1	Sulphur Spgs.		X					X	X			5	II-D-1									X
A	Bernalillo	F-8-N #2	Sandia Park			X	X				X			5	III-A-1									X
A	Bernalillo	SCS-9-N	Rio Puerco			X				X			X	5	III-D-3									X
A	Los Alamos	F-19-N	Water Cyn.			X				X		X		5	III-D-2									X
A	Sandoval	NM-1-N	Bandelier	X						X	X			5	I-D-1									X
A	Sandoval	F-22-N	Battleship Rk.			X				X	X			5	III-D-1									X
A	Sandoval	F-31-N	Paliza Cyn.	X					X			X		4a	I-C-2							X		
A	Sandoval	F-33-N	Tent Rocks			X				X		X		5	III-D-2									X
A	Sandoval	SCS-7-N	Rio Puerco			X	X					X		5	III-A-2									X
A	Sandoval	SCS-8-N	Rio Salado			X			X		X			5	III-C-1									X
A	Torrance	F-35-N	Manzano	X			X					X		1b	I-A-2		X							
B	San Juan	DG-101-N	Bloomfield			X				X	X			5	III-D-1									X
B	San Juan	NM-2-N	Chaco Cyn.	X					X		X			4	I-C-1							X		
B	McKinley	SCS-10-N	San Mateo			X				X		X		5	III-D-2									X
B	Cibola	F-7-N	Grants	X						X		X		5	I-D-2									X
C	Rio Arriba	F-3-N	Vallecitos	X			X					X		5	I-D-2									X
C	Rio Arriba	F-5-N	El Rito	X			X				X			1a	I-A-1	X								
C	Rio Arriba	F-43-N	La Madera	X			X					X		1b	I-A-2		X							
C	Rio Arriba	F-55-N	El Rito	X			X						X	2a	I-A-3			X						
C	Rio Arriba	SCS-3-N	Ghost Ra.			X			X		X			5	III-C-1									X
C	Rio Arriba	SCS-5-N	Velarde	X			X					X		1b	I-A-2		X							
C	Taos	F-6-N	Vadito			X			X		X			5	II-D-1									X
D	Santa Fe	PE-201-N	Little Tesuque	X					X		X			4a	I-C-1							X		
D	Santa Fe	SCS-17-N	Santa Fe			X				X	X			5	III-D-1									X
D	Santa Fe	SP-1-N	Santa Fe			X				X	X			5	III-D-1									X
D	Mora	SCS-28-N	La Cueva		X			X			X			3	II-B-1						X			
D	San Miguel	F-21-N	Las Vegas		X					X	X			5	II-D-1									X

APPENDIX IV: Civilian Conservation Corps (CCC) Campsites in New Mexico -- 1933-1942 (cont.)

County	Campsite	Location	Accessibility Open (I)	Some (II)	None (III)	Camp remains Much (A)	Mod. (B)	Little (C)	None (D)	Convenience Excellent (1)	Mod. (2)	Remote (3)	RANK	Rank Nos.	#1 I-A-1	I-A-2	#2 I-A-3	I-B-1	#3 I-B-2 to 3	II-A to B	#4 I-C	II-C	#5 I-D, II-D, III
Catron	F-1-N	Reserve	X						X	X			5	I-D-1									X
	F-2-N	Apache Cr.	X				X			X			3a	I-B-1					X				
	F-25-N	Glenwood	X					X		X			4a	I-C-1							X		
	F-29-N	Pueblo Park	X						X		X		5	II-D-2									X
	F-34-N	Beaverhead	X						X		X		5	II-D-2									X
	F-52-N	Willow Cr.	X						X			X	5	II-D-3									X
	G-123-N	Quemado	X						X	X			5	II-D-1									X
E (Grant)	F-11-N	Suily			X				X	X			5	III-D-1									X
	F-12-N	Redstone	X				X					X	3a	I-B-3					X				
	F-15-N	Little Walnut	X						X	X			5	I-D-1									X
	SCS-2-N	Redrock			X			X			X		5	III-C-2									X
	SCS-15-N	Whitewater	X			X			X		X		1b	II-A-2		X							
	SCS-18-N	Buckhorn			X			X		X			5	III-C-1									X
	SCS-20-N	Mangas Cyn.	X			X			X		X		1b	I-A-2		X							
	SES-2-N	Gila			X			X		X			5	III-C-1									X
F (Hidalgo)	DG-43-N	Animas	X					X		X			4a	I-C-1							X		
	SCS-19-N	Virden			X			X			X		5	III-C-2									X
	DG-26-N	Rodeo	X			X				X			1a	I-A-1	X								
(Luna)	DG-36-N	Mirage	X			X				X			1b	I-A-2		X							
	G-150-N	Columbus	X						X	X			5	I-D-1									X
	G-174-N	Cambray	X					X			X		4a	I-C-2							X		
G (Socorro)	BS-2-N	B. del Apache			X				X	X			5	III-D-1									X
	DG-42-N	Magdalena	X			X					X		1b	I-A-2		X							
	F-9-N	Monica	X						X			X	5	I-D-3									X
	F-30-N	Woofter Ra.			X				X			X	5	II-D-3									X
	G-147-N	Tokay		X		X					X		3b	II-A-2						X			
	SP-2-N	La Joya			X				X	X			5	III-D-1									X

233

APPENDIX IV: Civilian Conservation Corps (CCC) Campsites in New Mexico -- 1933-1942 (cont.)

AREA	County	Campsite	Location	Acc. Open (I)	Some (II)	None (III)	Remains Much (A)	Mod. (B)	Little (C)	None (D)	Conv. Excellent (1)	Mod. (2)	Remote (3)	RANK	Rank Nos.	I-A-1	I-A-2	I-A-3	I-B-1	I-B-2 to 3	II-A to B	I-C	II-C	I-D, II-D, III
H	Sierra	BR-8-N	Elephant B.	X						X	X			5	I-D-1									X
		BR-54-N	Elephant B.			X			X		X			5	III-C-1									X
		DG-37-N	Cuchillo	X			X						X	2a	I-A-3			X						
		F-40-N	Kingston			X		X			X			5	III-B-1									X
		F-51-N	Montecello			X	X						X	5	III-A-3									X
	Dona Ana	BR-39-N	Las Cruces			X				X	X			5	III-D-1									X
		DG-38-N	J. del Muerto			X				X			X	5	III-D-3									X
		F-27-N	J. del Muerto		X					X		X		5	II-D-2									X
		G-178-N	Las Cruces			X				X	X			5	III-D-1									X
		SCS-16-N	Las Cruces			X				X	X			5	III-D-1									X
I	Lincoln	DG-40-N	Carrizozo	X			X				X			1a	I-A-1	X								
		F-17-N	Capitan	X				X				X		3a	I-B-2					X				
		F-41-N	Corona	X				X					X	3b	I-B-3					X				
		F-54-N	Ruidoso	X				X			X			2b	I-B-1				X					
		SCS-6-N	Ft. Stanton	X				X				X		3a	I-B-2					X				
		SCS-32-N	Hondo	X						?				?										
	Otero	DG-39-N	Tularosa	X						X	X			5	I-D-1									X
		DG-69-N	Orogrande			X				X	X			5	III-D-1									X
		F-16-N	High Rolls	X			X					X		1b	I-A-2		X							
		F-28-N	La Luz Cyn.			X				X			X	5	III-D-3									X
		F-32-N	Mayhill			X			X		X			5	III-C-1									X
J	Chaves	BS-1-N	Bitter Lakes	X				X			X			5	I-B-1				X					X
		G-149-N	Roswell			X				X	X			5	III-D-1									X
		SP-3-N	Bottomless L.	X					X			X		4a	I-C-2							X		
	Eddy	BR-3-N	Carlsbad	X						X	X			5	I-D-1									X
		BR-82-N	Carlsbad	X						X	X			5	I-D-1									X
		G-148-N	Carlsbad	X						X	X			5	I-D-1									X
		DG-41-N	Lake Arthur	?						X		?		5	I-D-2									X
		F-37-N	Dark Cyn.			X		X					X	5	III-B-3									X
		NP-1-N	Rattlesnake S.	X					X		X			4a	I-C-1							X		
K	San Miguel	SP-8-N	Conchas Lake	X					X		X			4a	I-C-1							X		
	De Baca	SCS-23-N	Ft. Sumner			X			X			X		5	III-C-2									X
	Quay	SP-7-N	Tucumcari	X						X	X			5	I-D-1									X
	Curry	SCS-33-N	Field/Melrose			X				X			X	5	III-D-3									X
	Roosevelt	SP-5-N	ENMSP	X					X		X			4a	I-C-1							X		

Appendix V
CCC Camps by Geographic and Land-System Coordinates

Bureau of Reclamation (BR)

Camp #	County	Location	Coordinates, N & W	Land System Loc.	Remarks
BR-3-N	Eddy	Carlsbad Med. Ctr.	32° 26' 29" 104° 15' 23"	NE NE 35-21S 26E	Confirmed
BR-8-N	Sierra	Elephant Butte	33° 08' 52" 107° 11' 10"	Armendaris Grant	Confirmed
BR-39-N	Doña Ana	Las Cruces	32° 18' 14" 106° 47' 00"	535 S. Melendres St.	Confirmed
BR-54-N	Sierra	Elephant Butte	33° 08' 45" 107° 11' 26"	Armendaris Grant	Confirmed
BR-82-N	Eddy	Carlsbad Med. Ctr.	32° 26' 29" 104° 15' 23"	NE NE 35-21S 26E	Confirmed

U.S. Forest Service (F)

Camp #	County	Location	Coordinates, N & W	Land System Loc.	Remarks
F-1-N	Catron	Reserve	33° 43' 01" 108° 46' 39"	SE SW 8-7S 19W	Probable loc.
F-2-N	Catron	Apache Springs	33° 49' 45" 108° 37' 28"	S/2 S/2 33-5S 17W	Confirmed
F-3-N	Rio Arriba	Vallecitos	36° 29' 36" 106° 08' 00"	NW 18-26N 8E	Approximate
F-4-N	Rio Arriba		Camp never opened?	--	--
F-5-N	Rio Arriba	El Rito	36° 16' 11" 106° 10' 32"	NE 34-14N 7E proj	Confirmed
F-6-N	Taos	Tres Ritos, BSA	36° 07' 55" 105° 30' 56"	NW 24-22N 13E	Confirmed
F-7-N	Cibola	Mt. Sedgewick	35° 06' 03" 108° 00' 42"	NE NE 17-10N 11W	Confirmed
F-8-N	Bernalillo	Sulphur Springs	35° 10' 13" 106° 22' 15"	NE NE 23-11N 6E	Confirmed
F-8-N	Bernalillo	Sandia Park	35° 10' 16" 106° 22' 01"	SW San Pedro Grant	Confirmed
F-9-N	Socorro	Bear Trap Canyon	33° 53' 02" 107° 30' 46"	W/2 SE 12-5S 7W	Confirmed
F-10-N	Cibola		Camp never opened?	--	--
F-11-N	Grant	Mimbres	32° 57' 33" 108° 02' 06"	N/2 NE 36-15N 12W	Confirmed
F-12-N	Grant	Redstone	32° 57' 37" 108° 10' 42"	SW 27-15S 13W	Probable loc.
F-13-N	Rio Arriba		Camp never opened?	--	--
F-14-N	Catron		Camp never opened?	--	--
F-15-N	Grant	Little Walnut	32° 51' 13" 108° 16' 27"	C N/2 10-17S 14W	Confirmed
F-16-N	Otero	High Rolls	32° 57' 14" 105° 50' 00"	SE NE 5-16S 11E	Confirmed
F-17-N	Lincoln	Capitán	33° 32' 22" 105° 21' 34"	C 10-9S 15E	Confirmed
F-18-N	Lincoln	Cloudcroft	Side camp	--	
F-19-N	Los Alamos	Otowi	35° 48' 56" 106° 15' 29"	Ramon Vigil Grant	Possible loc.
F-20-N	San Miguel	Rowe	Side camp near Pecos	--	--
F-21-N	San Miguel	Rio Gallinas	35° 41' 57" 105° 25' 20"	Las Vegas Grant	Probable loc.
F-22-N	Sandoval	Battleship Rock	35° 49' 41" 106° 38' 44"	NW NW 5-18N 3E	Confirmed
F-23-N	Santa Fe	Little Tesuque	Previously PE-201-N	--	See PE-201-N
F-24-N	Otero	High Rolls	Previously F-16-N		See F-16-N
F-25-N	Catron	Glenwood	33° 19' 40" 108° 52' 16"	E/2 SE 23-11S 20W	Confirmed
F-26-N	Bernalillo	Juan Tabó	35° 12' 18" 106° 29' 47"	C SW SW 2-11N 4E	Confirmed
F-27-N	Doña Ana	Jornada Ex. Range	32° 37' 00" 106° 44' 34"	N/2 33-19S 2E	Probable loc.
F-28-N	Otero	La Luz Canyon	32° 59' 18" 105° 47' 14"	NW 28-15S 10E	Probable loc.
F-29-N	Catron	Pueblo Park	33° 35' 27" 108° 57' 39"	SE SW 24-8S 21W	Probable loc.
F-30-N	Socorro	Woofter Ranch	33° 45' 49" 107° 18' 17"	NE NE 26-6S 5W	Possible loc.
F-31-N	Sandoval	Paliza Canyon	35° 41' 51" 106° 38' 10"	SE SW 16-17N 3E	Confirmed
F-32-N	Otero	Mayhill	32° 54' 38" 105° 28' 12"	NW NW 24-16S 14E	Confirmed
F-33-N	Sandoval	Tent Rocks	35° 39' 57" 106° 25' 31"	C N/2 33-17S 5E	Probable loc.

Appendix V (cont.)

U.S. Forest Service (F)

Camp #	County	Location	Coordinates, N & W	Land System Loc.	Remarks
F-34-N	Catron	Beaverhead	33° 25' 29" 108° 06' 42"	SE 19-10S 12W	Possible loc.
F-35-N	Torrance	Manzano	34° 36' 58" 106° 23' 07"	NE SW 35-5N 5E	Confirmed
F-36-N	Rio Arriba	El Rito	Previously F-5-N	–	See F-5-N
F-37-N	Eddy	Dark Canyon	32° 10' 53" 104° 37' 17"	C S/2 S/2 29-23S 23E	Confirmed
F-38-N	Rio Arriba		Camp never opened?	--	--
F-39-N	Doña Ana	Jornada Ex. Range	Previously F-27-N	–	See F-27-N
F-40-N	Sierra	Kingston	32° 55' 08" 107° 41' 07"	S/2 NE NE 17-16S 8W	Confirmed
F-41-N	Lincoln	Gallinas	34° 12' 22" 105° 44' 57"	W/2 SW 24-1S 11E	Confirmed
F-42-N			Camp never opened	--	--
F-43-N	Rio Arriba	La Madera	36° 22' 20" 106° 02' 54"	SE SE NW 25-25N 8E	Confirmed
F-51-N	Sierra	Montecello	33° 26' 46" 107° 24' 37"	W/2 NE 13-10S 6W	Confirmed
F-52-N	Grant	Willow Creek	33° 23' 56" 108° 35' 21"	C E/2 33-10S 17W	Probable loc.
F-54-N	Lincoln	Ruidoso	33° 21' 07" 105° 40' 35"	SE SE 16-11S 12E	Confirmed
F-55-N	Rio Arriba	El Rito	36° 29' 53" 106° 16' 15"	SE SW 11-26N 6E	Confirmed
F-56-N	Rio Arriba	Coyote	Side camp	--	--
F-57-N	Socorro	Augustin Plain	Previously DG-42-N	–	See DG-42-N

Biological Survey (BS)

Camp #	County	Location	Coordinates, N & W	Land System Loc.	Remarks
BS-1-N	Chaves	Bitter Lake NWR	33° 28' 11" 104° 26' 01"	SW SW 5-10S 24E	Confirmed
BS-2-N	Socorro	Bosque del Apache	32° 52' 09" 106° 52' 40"	NW NE 19-3S 1E proj.	Confirmed
BS-3-N	Chaves	Roswell	Camp never opened	--	--

Fish and Wildlife Service (FWS)

Camp #	County	Location	Coordinates, N & W	Land System Loc.	Remarks
FWS-2-N	Socorro	Bosque del Apache	Previously BS-2-N	Bosque del Apache NWR	See BS-2-N
FWS-3-N	Chaves	Bitter Lake NWR	Previously BS-1-N	–	See BS-1-N

Division of Grazing, DG (through 1939)

Camp #	County	Location	Coordinates, N & W	Land System Loc.	Remarks
DG-36-N	Luna	Mirage	32° 20' 05" 107° 39' 22"	C W/2 3-23S 8W	Confirmed
DG-37-N	Sierra	Cuchillo	33° 17' 37" 107° 24' 00"	N/2 SW 6-12S 5W	Confirmed
DG-38-N	Doña Ana	Jornada del Muerto	32° 29' 28" 106° 42' 47"	SW NW 14-21S 2	Probable loc.
DG-39-N	Otero	Tularosa	33° 06' 08" 105° 57' 04"	NE NW 14-14S 9E	Confirmed
DG-40-N	Lincoln	Carrizozo	33° 39' 04" 105° 51' 58"	NE NE 2-7S 10E	Confirmed
DG-41-N	Chaves	W. of Lake Arthur	32° 54' 46" 104° 35' 20"	S/2 SW 21-16S 23E	Possible loc.
DG-42-N	Socorro	Augustin Plain	34° 03' 52" 107° 35' 12"	NE NW 10-3S 7W	Confirmed
DG-43-N	Hidalgo	Animas	31° 56' 57" 108° 48' 25"	NE NW 20-27S 19W	Possible loc.
DG-69-N	Otero	Orogrande	32° 23' 06" 106° 05' 36"	SE SW 14-22S 8E	Possible loc.
DG-101-N	San Juan	Bloomfield	36° 41' 38" 107° 59' 20"	SE NE 28-29N 11W	Confirmed

Grazing Service, G (from 1940)

Camp #	County	Location	Coordinates, N & W	Land System Loc.	Remarks
G-69-N	Otero	Orogrande	Previously DG-69-N	–	See DG-69-N
G-101-N	San Juan	Bloomfield	Previously DG-101-N	–	See DG-101-N
G-123-N	Catron	Quemado	34° 20' 26" 108° 29' 48"	–	Possible loc.

Appendix V (cont.)

Grazing Service, G (from 1940)

Camp #	County	Location	Coordinates, N & W	Land System Loc.	Remarks
G-147-N	Socorro	Tokay	33° 52' 16" 106° 44' 40"	C SW 16-5S 2E	Confirmed
G-148-N	Eddy	Carlsbad Med. Ctr.	32° 26' 29" 104° 15' 20"	NE NE 35-21S 26W	Confirmed
G-149-N	Chaves	Roswell airport	32° 24' 19" 104° 32' 40"	Roswell airport area	General Loc.
G-150-N	Luna	Columbus	31° 49' 33" 107° 38' 27"	SE 34-28S 8W	Confirmed
G-174-N	Luna	Cambray	32° 13' 30" 107° 19' 19"	NW NE 14-24S 5W	Confirmed
G-178-N	Doña Ana	Las Cruces	Previously SCS-16-N	--	See SCS-16-N

National Monuments and National Park Service (NM and NP)

Camp #	County	Location	Coordinates, N & W	Land System Loc.	Remarks
NM-1-N	Sandoval	Bandelier	35° 46' 44" 106° 16' 14"	23-18N 6E	Confirmed
NM-2-N	San Juan	Chaco Canyon	36° 01' 43" 107° 55' 26"	E/2 NW 29-21N 11W	Confirmed
NP-1-N	Eddy	Rattlesnake Spgs.	32° 06' 40" 104° 27' 58"	S/2 SE 23-25S 24 E	Confirmed
NP-2-N	San Juan	Chaco Canyon	Previously NM-2-N	–	See NM-2-N
NP-4-N	Sandoval	Bandelier	Previously NM-1-N	–	See NM-1-N

Park Erosion Control (PE)

Camp #	County	Location	Coordinates, N & W	Land System Loc.	Remarks
PE-201-N	Santa Fe	Hyde Mem. Park	35° 44' 07" 105° 50' 09"	N/2 NW 1-17N 10E	Probable loc.
PE-202-N	Grant	Little Walnut	Previously F-15-N	–	See F-15-N

Soil Erosion Service (SES, through 1934)

Camp #	County	Location	Coordinates, N & W	Land System Loc.	Remarks
SES-1-N			Camp never opened		
SES-2-N	Grant	Gila	32° 59' 21" 108° 33' 30"	W/2 W/2 24-15S 17W	Confirmed
SES-21-N	Bernalillo	Moriarty	Side Camp for SCS-27-N	--	--

Soil Conservation Service (SCS, from 1935)

Camp #	County	Location	Coordinates, N & W	Land System Loc.	Remarks
SCS-1-N	Grant	Gila	Previously SES-2-N	–	See SES-2-N
SCS-2-N	Grant	Redrock	32° 40' 39" 108° 46' 04"	S/2 2-19S 19W	Confirmed
SCS-3-N	Rio Arriba	Piedra Lumbre Gt.	36° 17' 40" 106° 26' 37"	19-24N 5E proj.	Confirmed
SCS-4-N	Rio Arriba	El Rito	Previously F-5-N		See F-5-N
SCS-5-N	Rio Arriba	Rio Truchas	36° 08' 18" 105° 58' 09"	Sebastian Martin Grant	Confirmed
SCS-6-N	Lincoln	Ft. Stanton	33° 29' 52" 105° 31' 45"	N/2 S/2 25-9S 14E proj.	Confirmed
SCS-7-N	Sandoval	Espiritu Santo	35° 47' 18" 106° 58' 18"	Ojo del Espiritu Santo	Confirmed
SCS-8-N	Sandoval	Espiritu Santo	35° 42' 00" 106° 56' 00"	Ojo del Espiritu Santo	Confirmed
SCS-9-N	Bernalillo	Rio Puerco	35° 09' 32" 107° 02' 03"	NW NE 27-11N 2W proj.	Confirmed
SCS-10-N	Cibola	San Mateo	35° 19' 40" 107° 40' 45"	SW NW 27-13N 8W proj.	Confirmed
SCS-11-N			Camp never opened	--	--
SCS-12-N			Camp never opened	--	--
SCS-13-N			Camp never opened	--	--
SCS-14-N	Grant	Little Walnut	Previously PE-202-N	–	See PE-202-N
SCS-15-N	Grant	Whitewater	32° 35' 03" 108° 07' 50"	SW NW 7-20S 14W	Confirmed
SCS-16-N	Doña Ana	Las Cruces	E. Lohman Ave., Las Cruces	--	General loc.
SCS-17-N	Santa Fe	Santa Fe	35° 41' 28" 105° 57' 48"	24-17N 9E proj.	Confirmed
SCS-18-N	Grant	Buckhorn	33° 03' 33" 108° 44' 37"	SE NW 30-14S 18W	Confirmed

Appendix V (cont.)

Soil Conservation Service (SCS, from 1935)

Camp #	County	Location	Coordinates, N & W	Land System Loc.	Remarks
SCS-19-N	Hidalgo	Virden	32° 39' 07" 108° 57' 03"	SW 18-19S 20W	Confirmed
SCS-20-N	Grant	Mangas Canyon	33° 11' 11" 108° 47' 41"	N/2 S/2 10-13S 19W	Confirmed
SCS-21-N	Torrance	Manzano	Previously F-35-N	--	See F-35-N
SCS-22-N	Sierra	Kingston	Previously F-40-N	--	See F-40-N
SCS-23-N	De Baca	Ft. Sumner	34° 29' 24" 104° 12' 33"	NW 15-3N 26E	Confirmed
SCS-25-N	Socorro	Augustin Plain	Previously DG-42-N	--	See DG-42-N
SCS-26-N	Hidalgo	Rodeo	31° 55' 19" 109° 00' 51"	SW SW 29-27S 21W	Confirmed
SCS-27-N	Bernalillo	Albuquerque Mesa	35° 04' 52" 106° 32' 51"	SW NW 20-10N 4E	Probable loc.
SCS-28-N	Mora	Mora/La Cueva	35° 57' 00" 105° 14' 50"	Mora Grant	Confirmed
SCS-29-N	Otero	High Rolls	Previously F-28-N	--	See F-28-N
SCS-30-N	Otero	Tularosa	Previously DG-39-N	--	See DG-39-N
SCS-31-N	Lincoln	Capitán	Previously F-17-N	--	See F-17-N
SCS-32-N	Lincoln	Hondo	Unknown location	--	Unknown loc.
SCS-33-N	Curry	Field/Melrose	34° 39' 27" 103° 34' 50"	NW 17-5N 32E	Confirmed
SCS-34-N	Otero	Mayhill	Previously F-32-N	--	See F-32-N

State Parks

Camp #	County	Location	Coordinates, N & W	Land System Loc.	Remarks
SP-1-N	Santa Fe	Santa Fe	35° 41' 28" 105° 57' 48"	24-17N 9E proj.	Confirmed
SP-2-N	Socorro	La Joya S.P.	Unknown location	--	Unknown loc.
SP-3-N	Chaves	Bottomless Lakes	33° 25' 31" 104° 20' 51"	SE SE 24-10S 25E	Confirmed
SP-5-N	Roosevelt	Portales	34° 15' 00" 103° 14' 30"	S/2 S/2 3-1S 35E	Confirmed
SP-6-N	Lea	Carlsbad	Metropolitan "President's" Park, never opened		--
SP-7-N	Quay	Tucumcari	35° 08' 49" 103° 48' 11"	SE SW 30-11N 30E	Confirmed
SP-8-N	San Miguel	Conchas Dam	35° 22' 25" 104° 10' 25"	13N 26E proj.	Confirmed

Military (1942)

Camp #	County	Location	Coordinates, N & W	Land System Loc.	Remarks
A-SCS-1-N	Bernalillo	Albuquerque	Previously SCS-27-N	--	Probable loc.
G(D)-1-N	Otero	Tularosa	Previously DG-39-N	--	See DG-39-N
G(D)-2-N	Socorro	Tokay	Previously G-147-N	--	See G-147-N

Appendix VI

Notes on Government Sponsoring Agencies

U.S. Forest Service (F)

The earliest CCC camps were in the National Forests. Those lands were generally used for livestock grazing, but years of overgrazing led to their severe deterioration. A year after the CCC was formed, in 1934, the *Taylor Grazing Act* was enacted in an attempt to minimize range destruction. The CCC assisted in surveying range allotments, and built fences and cattle guards. Watershed protection involved construction of dams and stock tanks, and fire suppression involved construction of lookout houses and towers. Ranger stations were built in many locations. Because of New Mexico's thinly-spread population, recreation facilities were located near urban centers. The CCC built access roads to these sites and developed campgrounds and picnic areas.

New Mexico had 37 Forest Service ("F") camp *sites*. However, because of subsequent renaming, there were 41 camp *names* in the state, as listed below. **<u>Underlined</u> bold** names indicate a camp's new replacement name.

F-1-N: Reserve

F-2-N: Apache Creek

F-3-N: Vallecitos

F-5-N: El Rito

F-6-N: Vadito

F-7-N: Mt. Sedgewick

F-8-N: Sulphur Springs

F-8-N: Sandia Park

F-9-N: Magdalena

F-11-N: Mimbres

F-12-N: Pinos Altos

F-15-N: Little Walnut

F-16-N: High Rolls

F-17-N: Capitán

F-19-N: Otowi

F-21-N: Las Vegas

F-22-N: Jémez Springs

F-23-N: Little Tesuque

F-24-N: **High Rolls**

F-25-N: Glenwood

F-26-N: Juan Tabó

F-27-N: Jornada Experimental Range

F-28-N: La Luz Canyon

F-29-N: Pueblo Park

F-30-N: Magdalena

F-31-N: Paliza Canyon

F-32-N: Mayhill

F-33-N: Peralta Canyon

F-34-N: Beaverhead

F-35-N: Manzano

F-36-N: **El Rito**

F-37-N: Dark Canyon

F-39-N: **Jornada Experimental Range**

F-40-N: Kingston

F-41-N: Corona

F-43-N: La Madera

F-51-N: Montecello

F-52-N: Willow Creek

F-54-N: Ruidoso

F-55-N: El Rito

F-57-N: **Magdalena**

The U.S. Biological Survey was created in 1934. Some of the first CCC camps were under its supervision. The survey established only two camps in New Mexico: BS-1-N at Bitter Lake Reserve east of Roswell, and BS-2-N at Bosque del Apache along the Rio Grande. In 1940 the agency changed its name to the Fish and Wildlife Service. The two BS camps were renamed: BS-1-N to FWS-3-N, and BS-2-N to FWS-2-N.

Soil Erosion Service (SES) and Soil Conservation Service (SCS)

The Soil Erosion Service (SES) was created in September 1933 within the Department of the Interior. In April 1935 it was transferred to the Department of Agriculture as the Soil Conservation Service (SCS). Upon the implementation of the *Taylor Grazing Act* of 1934, the SCS was tasked in 1935 with controlling erosion, restoring rangeland, controlling pests, and stabilizing stream watersheds. In 1935 and 1936 the agency contracted an extensive aero-photographic survey with Fairchild. In 1935 the SCS took over a number of CCC camps that had previously been supervised by the Forest Service (F). As the Depression ground on, the SCS enlarged its role in the CCC program. At this time local communities were beginning to organize soil conservation districts, and the SCS attempted to provide a CCC camp for every district.

The CCC and the SCS coordinated some very large projects that covered both federal and private lands. The Rio Puerco watershed was a significant SCS project that accounted for roughly 80% of the silt being delivered into Elephant Butte Reservoir. Another example was the Rio Grande watershed, also located above Elephant Butte Reservoir, called the Rio Grande Project. The reservoir, a Bureau of Reclamation project, was completed in 1917. By 1937 inflowing silt had reduced the reservoir's capacity by 20%. By the fall of 1935 the SCS started deploying CCC camps to stem the flow of silt. Seven CCC camps worked above the dam, while three camps below the dam worked mainly on flood control for the nearby towns. The SCS was abolished in 1994 by an act that reorganized the Department of Agriculture. Its functions were taken over by the newly created Natural Resources Conservation Service

New Mexico had 30 SCS numbered camps in 21 physical locations. SCS camps were numbered sequentially within each state. Some numbers were skipped over—probably planned but not implemented. Nine were renamed upon reoccupation of earlier camp sites. The **<u>underlined bold</u>** names below indicate a new name for a pre-existing camp.

SCS-1-N Gila, Grant County

SCS-2-N Red Rock, Grant County

SCS-3-N Piedre Lumbre, Rio Arriba County

<u>SCS-4-N El Rito, Rio Arriba County</u>

SCS-5-N Truchas, Rio Arriba County

SCS-6-N Fort Stanton, Lincoln County

SCS-7-N Rio Puerco, Sandoval County

SCS-8-N Catron Ranch, Sandoval County

SCS-9-N Rio Puerco, Bernalillo County

SCS-10-N San Mateo, Cíbola County

SCS-14-N Little Walnut, Grant County

SCS-15-N Whitewater, Grant County

SCS-16-N Las Cruces, Doña Ana County

SCS-17-N Santa Fe, Santa Fe County

SCS-18-N Buckhorn, Grant County

SCS-19-N Virden, Hidalgo County

SCS-20-N Mangas Canyon, Grant County

SCS-21-N Manzano, Torrance County

SCS-22-N Kingston, Sierra County

SCS-23-N Fort Sumner, De Baca County

SCS-25-N Augustin, Socorro County

SCS-26-N Rodeo, Hidalgo County

SCS-27-N Albuquerque, Bernalillo County

SCS-28-N La Cueva, Mora County

SCS-29-N High Rolls, Otero County

SCS-30-N Tularosa, Otero County

SCS-31-N Capitán, Lincoln County

SCS-32-N Hondo, Lincoln County

SCS-33-N Melrose, Curry County

SCS-34-N Mayhill, Otero County

U.S. Division of Grazing (DG), 1935–1939

This entity was established in 1935 to implement the mandates of the *Taylor Grazing Act* of 1934, which were designed to alleviate range destruction via controlling erosion, restoring rangeland, controlling pests, and stabilizing stream watersheds.

The Division of Grazing ("DG") established 60 camps in ten western states, including Arizona (7), California (3), Colorado (7), Idaho (4), Nevada (10), New Mexico (9), Oregon (6), Texas (1), Utah (10), and Wyoming (3). The Division assigned sequential numbers to the camps collectively for the entire ten-state area, but some numbers were skipped over, explaining why the final camp had the number DG-101. New Mexico had only nine "DG" camps:

DG-36-N: Mirage, Luna County

DG-37-N: Cuchillo, Sierra County

DG-38-N: Radium Springs, Doña Ana County

DG-39-N: Tularosa, Otoro County

DG-40-N: Carrizozo, Lincoln County

DG-41-N: Lake Arthur, Chaves County

DG-42-N: Augustin/Magdalena, Socorro County

DG-43-N: Animas, Hidalgo County

DG-101-N: Bloomfield, San Juan County

U.S. GRAZING SERVICE (G), 1939–1942

In 1939 the Division of Grazing was renamed the Grazing Service ("G"). It, like its predecessor, was tasked to enforce the *Taylor Grazing Act*. In all, some 89 "G" camps were established in those ten western states that had extensive grazing lands, including Arizona (9), California (3), Colorado (7), Idaho (12), Montana (3), Nevada (17), New Mexico (11), Oregon (7), Utah (13), and Wyoming (7). Also, like its predecessor, the Service assigned the camps sequential numbers for the entire ten-state area, and skipped over some numbers. New Mexico had 11 "G" camps:

G-37-N: Cuchillo, Sierra County (renamed from DG-37-N)

G-39-N: Tularosa, Otero County (renamed from DG-39-N)

G-69-N: Orogrande, Otero County

G-123-N: Quemado, Catron County

G-147-N: Tokay, Socorro County

G-148-N: Carlsbad, Eddy County

G-101-N: Bloomfield, San Juan County (renamed from DG-101-N)

G-149-N: Roswell, Chaves County

G-150-N: Columbus, Luna County

G-174-N: Cambray, Luna County

G-178-N: Las Cruces, Doña Ana County

In 1946 the Grazing Service was combined with the General Land Office to form the Bureau of Land Management (BLM).

BUREAU OF RECLAMATION (BR)

The Bureau of Reclamation (BR) is an agency under of the U.S. Department of the Interior. It is tasked with water-resource management that includes diversion, delivery, and storage, as well as the associated hydroelectric-power generation projects. The BR established 82 camps in 15 states in the upper High Plains and the West between 1934 and 1941. These were in Arizona (4), California (4), Colorado (6), Idaho (8), Montana (7), Nebraska (4), Nevada (5), New Mexico (5), North Dakota (1), Oregon (12), South Dakota (2), Texas (1), Utah (6), Washington (7), and Wyoming (10). Like the DG and G, the BR assigned the camps sequential numbers for the entire 15-state area and skipped over some numbers, giving the final camp (in Wyoming) number 102. All were terminated by July 1942. The BR had five camps in New Mexico for two reclamation projects:

BR-3 NM: Carlsbad, Chaves County, Carlsbad Project

BR-8 NM: Elephant Butte Dam, Sierra County, Rio Grande Project

BR-39 NM: Las Cruces, Doña Ana County, Rio Grande Project

BR-54 NM: Elephant Butte Dam, Sierra County, Rio Grande Project

BR-82 NM: Carlsbad, Chaves County, Carlsbad Project

The Rio Grande Project hosted four camps along the Rio Grande, three in New Mexico and one in Texas. The Rio Grande watershed above Elephant Butte Reservoir included both public and private lands. Two camps, BR-8-N and BR-54-N, were constructed on the south side of the reservoir just east of Elephant Butte Dam. The first camp, BR-8, was dated from 1934, and the second camp, BR-54 was built in 1935 about 1/4 mile to the south. A third camp, BR-39-N, was established downstream in the city of Las Cruces. A fourth camp, BR-4-T, was located even farther downstream in Berino, south of Las Cruces, but tasked with work in Fort Bliss, Texas.

The Carlsbad Project focused on the Pecos River watershed. Three camps, were established in the city of Carlsbad. BR-3 was established 1934 and originally called Camp DBR-3 (drought relief). In 1938 a second camp, BR-82-N, was constructed adjacent to BR-3-N. In 1938 the third camp, G-148-N, was constructed next to the other two. (These three campsites are now covered up by the Carlsbad Medical Center.) Upon closure of the camps, they were first turned over to the Advanced Flying School at the Carlsbad Air Force Base, and then, in 1942, to the Army Air Base until 1944.

Appendix VII

"Snapshot" History of two districts

In the southwest U.S., several of the CCC districts issued an "annual" in one year, 1936, containing a wonderful plethora of photos, and company and camp histories. Available are the long-out-of-print annuals from the 1) Albuquerque, New Mexico, 2) Fort Bliss, New Mexico/Texas, 3) Phoenix, Arizona, and 4) Tucson, Arizona Districts. For an unknown reason the Silver City District never issued an annual, so for New Mexico we only have coverage for the Albuquerque and Fort Bliss Districts. The two brief histories below, taken *verbatim* (with only a few omissions about personnel) from these *Annuals* provide a fascinating snapshot of the CCC program in New Mexico as of 1936.

Albuquerque District

(Northern and central New Mexico)

Source: *Official Annual – 1936, Albuquerque District, 8th Corps Area,*

Civilian Conservation Corps

"The Civilian Conservation Corps (CCC), organized under the Director, Emergency Conservation Work, was created by the proclamation of the President of the United States in March 1933, with many of the principal Departments of the Government functioning cooperatively in its administration.

"Immediately following the establishment of the Arizona-New Mexico District in April 1933, the organization of the Santa Fe Area, as a subdivision, was announced to be comprised of the following eight camps: F-3-N, Vallecitos; F-6-B, Tres Ritos; F-7-N Grants; F-8-N, Sulphur Canyon; F-19-N, Otowi; F-21-N, Rio Gallinas; F-22-N, La Cueva; and F-23-N, Little Tesuque. Supervision of these camps was the responsibility of the Area Commander.

"The enrollees who were to man the camps in the Santa Fe Area were enrolled mostly from the states of Texas, New Mexico, and Arizona. Immediately after enrollment the men were sent to conditioning camps, usually located on or near an army Post, to be clothed, vaccinated, and trained for a few of the responsibilities which lay ahead of them.

"Upon completion of this brief training period the enrollees were then assigned to companies and soon transported by rail and motor to the camp locations, which they were to occupy and construct. After the camp was occupied, tents erected, and few minor improvements made toward making the camp livable, the enrollees were turned over to members of the U.S. Forest Service, who exercised technical supervision over the activities in the field on the work projects. Technical work consisted mainly of construction of roads, erecting telephone lines, building fire trails through forest, building drift fences, building check dams, and developing recreational picnic grounds.

"Since October 1933 the scope of the work has been broadened, and other technical agencies have become associated with the organization. The agencies are: Department of Labor and the Veteran's Administration supervising recruitment and selection of enrollees; U.S. Forest Service and the Soil Conservation Service, Department of Agriculture; National Park Service, including the National Monuments; Division of Grazing, Department of Interior; State Park Service, including municipal and metropolitan parks operating in connection with the Park Service.

"In September and October, 1933, officers of the Reserve Corps began to receive orders detailing them to duty with the CCC, and after a short period of training, replaced the officers in the Regular Army. Gradually as qualified enrollees became available and had been given a limited training, the enlisted men were sent back to their posts.

"Early in January 1934 a radiogram from Headquarters, Arizona-New Mexico District, Fort Bliss, Texas, changed the designation of the Santa Fe Area to the Santa Fe Sub-District. Several months after the Santa Fe Sub-District Headquarters Detachment occupied the tourist camp, known as the Sierra Vista Tourist Camp, and located south of town on Cerrillos Road, a miniature Army Post was established. The place took on such a neat appearance that residents of the city often referred to it as "The Headquarters."

"After the passage of a $4.8 million bill on April 5, 1935, the President authorized the increase of the CCC to 600,000 men. As a result of the increase, many new projects and work camps were established within the area that originally comprised the Arizona-New Mexico District. The total number of camps, approximately 115, made it necessary to divide the area into five separate and independent districts due to an impossibility to effectively administer and supply such an organization from a single headquarters. One of the five districts was designated as the Albuquerque District, with headquarters in Albuquerque, New Mexico. The headquarters was established on July 25, 1935, occupying the second floor of the Albuquerque Gas and Electric Building at the corner of Fifth Street and Central Avenue. However, the Albuquerque District did not become an independent organization until September 1, 1935, at which time a district Motor Transportation and Repair Section was opened in the 1200 block on North Fourth Street and the Warehouse located at the intersection of Mountain Road and the railroad tracks was occupied."

FORT BLISS DISTRICT

(SOUTH-CENTRAL NEW MEXICO AND WEST TEXAS)

Source: *Official Annual – 1936, Fort Bliss District, 8th Corps Area,*

Civilian Conservation Corps

"Following the proclamation of the President in March 1933, authorizing and creating the CCC, the Arizona-New Mexico District, comprised of camps in Arizona, New Mexico, and West Texas, was organized in April of that year. Enrollees for this district were drawn from the states of Arizona, New Mexico, and West Texas. Concentration points were established at Fort Bliss, Texas, and Fort Huachuca, Arizona, where conditioning camps were erected and necessary administrative staffs were drawn from the Regular Army. Because Army discipline was not to prevail in the training period, and all discipline was reduced to appealing to the better natures of the enrollees, considerable tact had to be exercised by all Regular Army officers and non-commissioned officers detached for duty with the CCC.

"In the conditioning camps enrollees were thoroughly examined by medical officers and were then passed on to receive adequate training for the responsibilities ahead of their training. Such training consisted of being taught to be entirely self-supporting units capable of requisitioning clothing and food from Army sources by Army methods. Enrollees with an inclination for cooking were instructed in the art of preparing food for large bodies of men. Medical orderlies capable of caring for the sick were given experience in Army Hospitals in order to insure the highest efficiency in this important phase of camp life. Clerks unaccustomed to the paper work of the Army were trained to perform their duties of administrating the needs of the camps to which they were assigned. Inasmuch as the large majority of the camps were to be established in isolated locations, motor transportation was of fundamental importance. To meet this requirement, enrollees were carefully selected and trained in the maintenance and safe operation of motor vehicles, which instruction was imparted through the medium of district motor vehicle schools and safety meetings with qualified officers, state highway officials, and others.

"On completion of training in the conditioning camps, enrollees were turned over to members of the U.S. Forestry Service, who had been selected to supervise the CCC activities on the various work projects. In order that appropriations of public money should be wisely spent, these work projects were selected for their value to the country as a whole and to the various communities in particular. In this district such projects originally comprised the construction of roads through country hitherto impossible, and since telephonic communication between camps, fire-lookout stations, local communities, and the Army posts was highly essential for the expedition of business, telephone poles were cut and erected by the enrollees, under the supervision of U.S. Forestry personnel. In order to provide the means of making all sections of forest accessible, fire lanes and trails were constructed wherever needed.

"Under the direction of the National and State Park organization, recreational areas have been beautified and provided with necessary facilities to afford the American people a place to spend leisure hours.

"Under the direction of the Soil Conservation Service, Bureau of Reclamation and Division of Gazing, erosion control has progressed rapidly. These projects, consisting of flood-control dams, storage dams, irrigation canals, and the planting of vegetation are an effective means of preventing the destruction and disappearance of surface soils, so necessary to growth of agricultural products, and have saved many millions of dollars for the American people.

"Cities and towns in southern New Mexico and West Texas, which hitherto have been threatened from serious damage from flood waters from the Rio Grande, are no longer as vulnerable to the action of flood waters, and will be made secure in the near future.

"In accordance with the President's desire to increase the CCC to 600,000 by October 1935, a number of new projects and work camps were established within the states of Arizona, New Mexico, and West Texas. The total number of camps, approximately 115, made it an impossibility to properly administer and supply such organization from a single district headquarters. As a result, the Arizona-New Mexico District was divided into five separate districts, with headquarters in Phoenix, Arizona; Tucson, Arizona; Albuquerque, New Mexico; Silver City, New Mexico; and Fort Bliss, Texas. The Fort Bliss District Headquarters became independent of the other organizations on September 1, 1935. After May 1, 1936, the staff and District Officer personnel became stabilized as a result of the withdrawal of the policy which limited Reserve Officers to two years of active duty with the CCC.

"In order that the health of enrollees shall be preserved and everything possible to keep them constantly fit, every camp in the District has a medical officer or contract surgeon, assisted by trained medical orderlies, all of whom are available day and night. Minor cases of disease and injury are dealt with in the camp infirmary, but more severe cases, or cases requiring prolonged treatment, are transported by well-designed and comfortable Army ambulances to William Beaumont General Hospital, El Paso, Texas. This hospital is as well-equipped as any hospital in America and the members of its staff are selected for their outstanding abilities as physicians and surgeons.

"Each camp in this district has a camp educational adviser, selected and appointed by the Department of Education and responsible to the company commander for the coordination of educational and recreational facilities. Assisting him is an enrollee adviser chosen from the ranks for his fitness to help in the camp educational program, and in addition, there are usually in each camp two Army Reserve Officers capable of giving instruction in high school and university subjects, and several members of the Technical staff, all of whom are interested in promoting the cause of education and further fitting enrollees to make a successful living upon completion of their service with Civilian Conservation Corps.

"The functions of a camp educational adviser are manifold, for he is called upon to teach, counsel, and advise, not only in the field of education but also in the field of morale. In order to win the confidence of the enrollees he must first prove to them that he is their friend, and, as such, willing to aid them with their problems whether they be spiritual or temporal. It has been the experience of these camp advisers that approximately one-half of the enrollees in their respective camps are farm boys, and the other half either just out of school or with a little experience as common laborers."

Appendix VIII

CCC-Worker Statues in New Mexico

Since 1977 there has been a nationwide CCC alumni organization called the National Association of Civilian Conservation Corps Alumni (NACCCA), later renamed the CCC Legacy. The organization's principal objective was to restore the memory of the CCC because the cataclysm of World War II eclipsed the CCC from nation's collective consciousness. To accomplish this role the organization has been sponsoring the installation of life-sized "CCC Worker" statues in as many states as possible. The first one was in bronze in 1995, and through 2019, 75 statues have been installed in 42 of the 50 states, about half of these in State Parks and the others in other public places. The statues are identified by their sequential numbers. New Mexico has three:

#47. Elephant Butte State Park: dedicated October 18, 2008 (*Figure H-4C*).

South side of lake, in small oval park in marina-area parking lot, east of NM-177.

33° 08' 55.14" N / 107° 11' 05.50" W

#49. New Mexico State Capitol, Santa Fe: dedicated January 16, 2009.

On west side of Capitol building, east side of Don Gaspar Avenue.

35° 40' 59.00" N / 105° 56' 26.10" W

#67. Bandelier National Monument: dedicated October 14, 2016.

Just west of Juniper Family Campground, on foot path to Amphitheater.

35° 47' 45.50" N / 106° 16' 55.60" W

References Cited

Adkins, Lynn. 2008. Camp Capitán: A Depression Era Educational Camp for Unemployed Young Women. *La Crónica de Nuevo México*, Historical Society of New Mexico, Issue 75, April.

Albuquerque Journal. 1933. Frame barracks to be built for 200 CCC men in Sandias.

Albuquerque Journal. 1934. Federal transient shelter in Albuquerque. November 17.

Albuquerque Journal. 1938. Cost of CCC camp construction. February 13.

Albuquerque Journal. 1984. Notes on Orogrande camp DG-69-N, by Norman McNew. July 7.

Albuquerque Journal. 1940. New camp to open June 29, 1 mile east of Fair Grounds. June 13.

Albuquerque Progress. 1935a. New CCC Headquarters, August, pg. 7.

Albuquerque Progress. 1935b. CCC Quartermaster Opens, September, pgs. 2-3.

Albuquerque Progress. 1940. New CCC camp is opened here, September, pg. 2.

Audretsch, Robert W. 2017. *The Civilian Conservation Corps in Colorado, 1933–1942, Vol. 1: U.S. Forest Service and Bureau of Indian Affairs Camps*; Dog Ear Publishing, Indianapolis, Indiana.

Benedict, Cynthia B., 1994. Proposed Graffiti Removal from the Picnic Shelters in Juan Tabó and La Cueva Picnic Areas and the Juan Tabó Cabin. Sandia Ranger District, Cíbola National Forest, Report #1994-03-123.

Bosque del Apache National Wildlife Refuge, 2018. Visitor Center, personal communication.

Bullock, Peter Y, 1998. The testing of LA86739, near Carrizozo, New Mexico. Museum of New Mexico Archaeology Notes, 204, Santa Fe.

Carlsbad Current-Argus. 1990. Photo of a camp at Carlsbad Medical Center. September 9.

CCC, undated. *Number of Camps in each County by Period*; photocopied records from the National Archives, unpublished, author's collection.

CCC, 1936. *Official Annual – 1936, Albuquerque District, 8th Corps Area*; Direct Advertising Co., Baton Rouge, Louisiana.

CCC, 1936. *Official Annual – 1936, Fort Bliss District, 8th Corps Area*; Direct Advertising Co., Baton Rouge, Louisiana.

Churches, John. Undated. *History of the CCC, Cíbola National Forest, New Mexico, 1933–1942*, unpublished.

Cohen, Stan. 1980. *The Tree Army: A Pictorial History of the Civilian Conservation Corps, 1933–1942*; Pictorial Histories Publishing Co., Missoula, Montana.

Crocker, James. Undated. Tucumcari New Mexico photographer, photo of CCC camp SP-7-N, Tucumcari.

Dunnahoo, Janice., 2018. Archivist, Southeastern New Mexico Historical Society, Roswell, personal communication.

Eberhart, Fred G., 1934. The inside story of F-17-C. *Rocky Mountain Region Bulletin* 17, No. 2, February, p. 12.

Flynn, Kathryn A., 2012. *Public Art and Architecture in New Mexico, 1933–1943: A Guide to the New Deal Legacy*. Sunstone Press, Santa Fe, 374 p.

The Grazette. 1936. CCC Company 3829 (Las Cruces) newsletter, February. Division of Grazing, Albuquerque Division.

Guzmán, Alfonso., 2001. Oral history, *New Mexico Farm and Ranch Heritage Museum*, Research and Collections, Las Cruces, New Mexico.

Harrison, Laura.S., Copeland, Randall and Buck, Roger. 1988. *Historic Structure Report: CCC Buildings, Bandelier National Monument, New Mexico*; National Park Service, Denver Service Center, 318 p.

Hendricks, Rick and Stanford, Charles B. 2010. Taking the Wider View: Panoramic Photography in the American Southwest. *Southern New Mexico Historical Review*, v. 16, p. 48-61.

Holland, Thomas. 1991. Draft of speech, unpublished, author's collection.

Hook, Stephen C. 2015. Then and Now, A Brief History of Tokay, New Mexico. *New Mexico Geology*, v. 37/2, p. 47-51.

Hoff, Bob. Bob Hoff's Carksbad Caverns History Blog, *carlsbadcavernshistory.blogspot.com*.

James F. Justin CCC Museum website (see below).

Jémez Thunder. 1996. Monthly Archives: Historical CCC camp was in Paliza. September 15.

Julyan, Robert. 1996. *The Place Names of New Mexico*; University of New Mexico Press, Albuquerque.

Kammer, David. 1994. *The Historic and Architectural Resources of the New Deal in New Mexico*. New Mexico Historic Preservation Division, June.

Kammer, David. 1995a. U.S. Department of Interior National Register of Historic Places Registration Form for Five Mile Park, Tucumcari.

Kammer, David. 1995b. U.S. Department of Interior National Register of Historic Places, Multiple Property Documentation Form, "CCC, CWA, PWA and WPA construction and landscape projects in New Mexico."

Kremeke, M. WWI History of Camp Cody, Deming, New Mexico.
Kremeke Website below.

Krol, Laura V. 2012. *Deming*. Arcadia Publishing, Images of America series.

Lansing State Journal, 1964. Prominent ex-Portland man dies. April 8, p. 45.

Lemons, Roy, undated. Personal communication.

Lincoln National Forest. Undated. *Mayhill CCC Camp, a little of the life and times of the Mayhill CCC camp from 1940*. Ralph Cericola photo collection. Website for Mayhill CCC camp below.

Luna County Museum. Archives.

McBride, James J. 2008. *Interned: Internment of the SS Columbus Crew at Fort Stanton, New Mexico, 1941–1945*. James J. McBride.

McKenna, Peter J. 2006. *Archeological Survey: Civilian Conservation Corps Camp SC S-7-N*; Bureau of Indian Affairs, December 12.

Melzer, Richard. 2000. *Coming of Age in the Great Depression: The Civilian Conservation Corps Experience in New Mexico, 1933–1942*. Yucca Tree Press, Las Cruces.

NACCCA. 1986. National Association of Civilian Conservation Corps Alumni Journal, June.

National Geographic Holdings, Inc., 2001. TOPO! Topographic maps of New Mexico on DVD.

National Park Service. 1988. *Bandelier National Monument, New Mexico, Historic Structure Report, CCC Building*.

National Park Service. Undated. Historical American Landscapes Survey, HALS #NM-9, 39 p.

Organ Echoes. 1938. CCC Company 3829's (camp BR-39-N) newsletter. July.

Pfaff, Christine E. 2010. *The Bureau of Reclamation's CCC Legacy, 1933-1942*. U.S. Dept. Interior, Bureau of Reclamation, Denver.

Reininger, Russell L. Undated. Biography of Russell L. Reininger, Assistant Leader, CCC Man, Co. 831, Camp SP-3-N, Roswell, New Mexico; and CCC photos of SP-3-N, Bottomless Lakes S.P., New Mexico. Website of Justin CCC Museum: justinmuseum/oralbio/reiningerbio.

Richardson, Elmo R. 1966. The Civilian Conservation Corps and the Origins of the New Mexico State Park System. *6 National Resources Journal*, spring.

San Juan County Archaeological Research Center and Library. Bloomfield, New Mexico.

Sherman, James E., and Sherman, Barbara H. 1975. *Ghost Towns and Mining Camps of New Mexico*. University of New Mexico Press, Albuquerque.

Singletary, Charles L. 1997. Time is right for rebirth of the CCC. *Albuquerque Journal*, Letters to the *Journal*, December 22.

Smith, Toby. 2005. Confined to Memories. *Albuquerque Sunday Journal*. May 29, 2005.

Snyder, Jay. 2002. Personal files, San Juan County Archaeological Research Center and Library, Salmon Ruins, Bloomfield New Mexico.

Spidle, Jake W. Jr. 1974. *Axis invasion of the American West: POWs in New Mexico, 1942–1946. New Mexico Historical Review*, April 1974.

Southeast New Mexico Historical Society, Roswell. Photo archives.

True, Robert H., ca. 1992. Personal letter to Vince Wathen.

Van West, Carla, and Sebastian, Lynne. 2010. The legacy of the Civilian Conservation Corps in Chaco Cultural NHP: Stabilized ruins and landscape alterations. Final report to Chaco Culture National Historic Park, August 16.

Van West, Carla and Schelberg, John. 2015. The Civilian Conservation Corps in Chaco Canyon, New Mexico. Paper presented at 80th Annual Meeting of Society for American Archaeology, San Francisco, California.

Warford, Lloyd. Photo collection CCC Company 846, F-15-N. CCC Legacy Digital Archives.

Websites (active at time of publication of this book):

Camp Cody, Deming, New Mexico: demingnewmexico.genealogyvillage.com (M. Kromeke's WWI History of Camp Cody, Deming, New Mexico).

Camp Furlong, Columbus, New Mexico. Same as above.

CCC Legacy: ccclegacy.org

Doña Ana Historical Society, Las Cruces, New Mexico: donaanadcountyhistsoc.org/historicalreview2010/sixhistorical.

James F. Justin CCC Museum: justinmuseum.com/famjustin/cccbio

Kremeke, M., Camp Cody, Deming, New Mexico: demingnewmexico.genealogyvillage.com.

Mayhill CCC camp, New Mexico: flickr.com/photos/lincolnnationalforest/albums

Vintage topographic maps: legacy.lib.utexas.edu/maps/topo/new_mexico

INDEX

Page numbers in bold refer to figures.

Printed in the USA
CPSIA information can be obtained
at www.ICGtesting.com
LVHW010025081123
763339LV00008B/27